The Shopaholic's Guide to Buying Gorgeous Gifts O

Free Subscription Offer

www.thesiteguide.com

www.thesiteguide.com, described by Condé Nast's Glamour.com as 'the web's best shopping directory', is the web version of *The Shopaholic's Guide to Buying Gorgeous Gifts Online*, where you'll find direct links through to all the website reviews, plus regular online shopping features and updates and news of the latest site launches.

We're delighted to offer you a year's free subscription (normally £9.99) to www.thesiteguide.com to thank you for purchasing this book. To take up this offer you need to click on to the site and subscribe. When you're prompted for a media code just use the password you'll find at the end of the introduction to Chapter 9: Jewellery, and you'll be able to use the guide online.

If you would like to receive up-to-date information on other Shopaholics Guides to buying online, just sign up on the website to receive regular newsletters.

'Thesiteguide.com is the most comprehensive shopping directory I've found on the web, and is also the first to report on fabulous new sites.'
Condé Nast

'A comprehensive guide to all the best shopping destinations on the web.'
Vogue mail

'This is a good shortcut to smart shopping'
The *Evening Standard*

'thesiteguide.com ... provides a discerning and easy-to-use guide to the best retail sites on the web.'
The Times

The Shopaholic's Guide to

Buying Gorgeous Gifts Online

Patricia Davidson

CAPSTONE

BICENTENNIAL
1807
WILEY
2007
BICENTENNIAL

First published 2007 by
Capstone Publishing Ltd. (a Wiley Company)
The Atrium, Southern Gate, Chichester, PO19 8SQ, UK.
www.wileyeurope.com
Email (for orders and customer service enquires): cs-books@wiley.co.uk

Other Wiley Editorial Offices: Hoboken, San Fransisco, Weinheim, Australia, Singapore and
Canada
Wiley also publishes its books in a variety of electronic formats. Some content that
appears in print may not be available in electronic books.

Library of Congress Cataloging-in-Publication Data
Davidson, Patricia.
  The shopaholic's guide to buying gorgeous gifts online / Patricia Davidson.
      p. cm.
  Includes index.
  ISBN 978-1-84112-784-2 (pbk. : alk. paper)
1. Shopping--Computer network resources. 2. Gifts--Computer network resources. I.
Title.
  381'.10285467--dc22
  381'.142--dc22

                                                                    2007019145

ISBN   978-184112-784-2

Anniversary Logo Design: Richard J. Pacifico

Set in Lucida Bright by Sparks (www.sparks.co.uk)
Printed and bound in Great Britain by TJ International Ltd, Padstow, Cornwall

Contents

Dedication and Acknowledgements   vii
About the Author   viii
Introduction   ix

Section 1	**The Essentials**	**1**
Chapter 1	Cards and Balloons	3
Chapter 2	Ribbon and Wrap	6
Chapter 3	Chocolates for Chocoholics	9
Chapter 4	Flowers	13
Chapter 5	Champagne and Wine	18
Chapter 6	Hampers and Food Gifts	25
Section 2	**Just for Her**	**35**
Chapter 7	Pampering Presents	41
Chapter 8	Spa and Experience Days	46
Chapter 9	Jewellery	49
Chapter 10	Cashmere	55
Chapter 11	Fashion Accessories	58
Chapter 12	Lingerie	64
Chapter 13	Home Accessories	71
Section 3	**Strictly for Him?**	**81**
Chapter 14	Gadgets, Games and Experience Days	83
Chapter 15	Cigars, Pens and Small Leathers	89
Chapter 16	Shirts and Accessories	94

Chapter 17	Men's Toiletries	99
Chapter 18	For That Really Special Gift	103
Chapter 19	Gift Stores for Men	109
Section 4	**For VSPs (Very Special People)**	**113**
Chapter 20	Precious Gifts for New Babies	115
Chapter 21	For New Mums	124
Chapter 22	For Toddlers up to 4	129
Chapter 23	Children from 4 to 11	134
Section 5	**For the Enthusiast**	**143**
Chapter 24	Cook	145
Chapter 25	Gardener	150
Chapter 26	Sport Mad	156
Chapter 27	Bookworm	167
Chapter 28	Music, Movies and Games	173
Chapter 29	Photographer	178
Chapter 30	Artist and Musician	183
Chapter 31	Traveller	187
Section 6	**Gifts by Occasion**	**193**
Chapter 32	Christening Gifts	195
Chapter 33	Valentine's Day	200
Chapter 34	Mother's Day	206
Chapter 35	Easter	211
Chapter 36	Weddings	216
Chapter 37	Silver Weddings	222
Chapter 38	A Word About Christmas	226
Chapter 39	General Gift Stores	228
Chapter 40	Luxury Gifts	233
Section 7	**Useful Information**	**241**
Chapter 41	Top Tips for Safe Shopping Online	243
Chapter 42	Deliveries and Returns –	
	What to Look For and How to Make Them Easier	246
Chapter 43	Price Comparison Websites	249
Chapter 44	Help If Something Goes Wrong	251
Chapter 45	UK, European and US Clothing Size Conversions	253
Chapter 46	Top 20 Emergency Gift Retailers	256
Index		265

Dedication

This book is dedicated to Sally and Charles, two AIDS orphans from the Ringili Arms of Jesus Orphanage in Arua, northern Uganda, whose education has been sponsored by my husband, Andrew.

The orphanage is run by Reverend Erifasi Dradria, who started it in response to the desperate need of children orphaned often because of AIDS. He receives no funding from the Ugandan government or any of the major charities.

As the children usually receive basic food and shelter from relatives, Reverend Erifasi raises funds for their education to give them skills that will enable them to earn a living - secondary education and occupational training which will make a lifetime's difference.

All money received goes directly to supporting the children: there are no administration or staff charges. If you would like to help this orphanage, please contact me at phd@thesiteguide.com and I'll be delighted to give you further details.

Acknowledgements

My thanks to everyone at John Wiley - to Sally Smith, Emma Swaisland, Iain Campbell, Julia Lampan, Kate Stanley and Grace O'Byrne - and my apologies if I've left anyone out. To Kate Hordern, my agent, not just for doing such a great job but also for picking up the pieces along the way. And as ever to my family - Andrew, Sholto, Calum and Kirstie - and to my new and excellent helpers, Sarah and Sue, your work is absolutely essential and much appreciated. Also to Lee, Richard, Chris and Simon at e2e.co.uk for their help and design for my website.

About the Author

*A*fter twelve years in international designer fashion mail order, Patricia Davidson started www.thesiteguide.com, an online upmarket fashion, beauty and lifestyle website directory. Her first book, *The Shopaholic's Guide to Buying Online*, was published by Capstone in October 2006, followed by *The Shopaholic's Guide to Buying Fashion and Beauty Online* in May 2007. Patricia is a regular contributor to Condé Nast's easylivingmagazine.com and has also been published on online shopping in other women's titles and national press. She lives in Buckinghamshire with her husband, three children and two dogs.

Introduction

I am, as I think everyone knows by now, a self-confessed online shopping addict. I also like to buy certain things in the shops (just in case you were wondering), but for some items, such as my favourite cosmetics and fragrances, essential food and drink, books, CDs and DVDs, and most particularly gifts, I generally shop online only.

Why? Because it's easier, because there's so much more to choose from, because I know exactly where to shop and it saves me loads of time. And, when the shops are really busy, I can sit at home and order everything I need without having to do battle with the crowds and queues, let alone having to find somewhere to park.

This was really brought home to me last December, when my younger son, having played just one too many games of rugby at his school, fell foul of an unintentionally violent tackle (no, I don't like rugby) and had to have a major operation on his knee.

So there I was, sitting in the hospital room (with no computer access), wondering what to do, when it came to me in a flash – I was within a short bus ride of Sloane Square, where I could surely do a great deal of my Christmas shopping. Off I went, list in hand, to do the thing I had promised myself I would never do again. Yes, I managed to buy quite a lot of the gifts I needed, and yes, they were lovely, but I battled through the masses, I queued at the tills, I carried heavy carrier bags and no, there weren't any buses, there weren't any taxis and yes, to crown it all, it rained the whole time. I proved it once and for all – Christmas shopping on the high street is for masochists only.

Here then is this book of gorgeous gifts. Not just for Christmas but for birthdays, anniversaries, Easter, Valentine's Day, Mother's Day, weddings and any other occasion you can think of when you might need to find that perfect present. You don't have to make that mad, stressful dash to the shops to search for that special gift. You just have to sit down at your computer, coffee or wine at your side, and choose that gift from the online retailers here. Then you can relax in the knowledge that your gift will arrive at your chosen destination, beautifully wrapped and accompanied by your personal message. In a lot of cases this can be the day after you place your order. What more could you possibly ask for?

Website information

The best websites will take you speedily and clearly to the products you're looking for, without long, flash intros which you don't need or want and which usually have very little to do with what the retailer is selling. They are much more about the retailer's image and profile and I think they get right in the way.

Really well-designed websites will also give you clear and easy access to their shopping categories, plus all the essential customer information – delivery, returns and contact details – right there on the Home Page, so you don't have to waste time looking for them. The worst hide this information within their Terms and Conditions, or make you wait until you've almost placed your order and registered all your details before telling you that actually they don't deliver to your country after all. You can do them a great favour by finding their contact details and letting them know that they should have given you that information from the start, otherwise they won't change.

Just take a look, for example, at www.eluxury.com and www.neiman-marcus.com, two top US websites offering every designer from Marc Jacobs to Manolo Blahnik, with Louis Vuitton and Christian Dior in between. There they are on the front page, ready and waiting for you to browse and buy, with clear information about delivery, returns and every other question you can think of just one click away. No 'clever' flash intros, no extra Home Page; no nonsense, just straight to what you want to buy.

Using this Book

All the websites included in the guide have been looked at carefully not only for the service and products they offer but also for how easy the retailers make it for you to shop.

For almost every website you'll find something like the following:

Site Usability:	★★★★★	Based:	UK
Product Range:	★★★★★	Express Delivery Option? (UK)	Yes
Price Range:	Medium	Gift Wrapping Option?	Yes
Delivery Area:	Worldwide	Returns Procedure:	Down to you

In all cases the stars range from ★★★★★ to ★★★ – I'll explain as follows.

Site Usability
How quick and easy is it for you to click round the website and get to the products you're looking for? How quickly can you get to information on delivery, returns, whether or not gift wrapping is offered and how to contact the retailer? Are the pictures clear and attractive? Is there adequate information about every product offered?

Product Range
How much choice is there on the website? Fewer stars here do not mean a lower-quality product, just a smaller range.

Price Range
This is just a guide so you know what to expect.

Delivery Area
Does the retailer deliver to the UK, EU countries or worldwide?

Based

This tells you where the retailer is based, so you'll know straight away if you're going to be in for duty or extra shipping costs.

Express Delivery Option

Can you have your order tomorrow? Some websites are very quick anyway, but this is specifically for where next-day or express service is offered, usually within the country where the retailer is based.

Gift Wrapping Option

Do they or don't they?

Returns Procedure

'Down to you' means you pack it up and pay to send it back (unless your goods are faulty, in which case the retailer should pay for postage both ways). 'Free' means just that and they may even collect it from you. 'Complicated' means that they want you to call them and tell them you're sending your order back. This normally applies only where the product you've ordered is particularly valuable. 'In agreement with them' means that you've ordered something which in some way is difficult to return and so you need to talk to them about sending it back.

Section 1
The Essentials

This is the place where you'll find all those gift essentials that cover a number of celebrations and occasions, starting with your cards and wrap and taking in chocolates, flowers and gifts of food and wine. When you're really in doubt as to what to give, this is a good section to begin with as you're unlikely to go completely wrong. Many of these websites offer express delivery (or even same day, for flowers) and will send whatever you order wherever you need it to arrive, even in some cases halfway across the world.

As these online retailers offer gift ideas that are suitable for so many events, don't forget to keep checking back. They're not duplicated within this book, so, for example, all the websites in the flower chapter will have special ideas for Mother's Day plus the particular sites mentioned in that section and most of the chocolate retailers have suggestions for Valentine's Day and Christmas. You'll probably use this section more than most.

Chapter 1

Cards and Balloons

My kids have now almost universally decided that a birthday away from home without the delivery of an almost embarrassingly large (probably singing) box of balloons is not a proper birthday. No, a card is not enough. Well that one was definitely my fault and if you have more than one child I suggest you take care, as they end up competing for who got the largest box and the most balloons.

There are lots of places on the web where you can order cards and most of them are very good indeed, offering you not just a good range but also your own online address book in which to store all your birthdays and special dates, for which they'll send you reminders well ahead of time. These are excellent services and well worth taking advantage of.

Just one word of advice: you can order e-cards to be sent out as well, but if you're going to go down that route, make absolutely sure that the recipient opens his or her email every day. It's a completely worthless exercise if they don't.

Sites to Visit

www.charitycards.co.uk

On this site there are some lovely cards for every type of occasion, plus thank-you cards and luxury Christmas cards, Advent calendars and stocking fillers (for girls). You can also order your printed Christmas cards here and if you buy ten or more cards, shipping is free. When you're ordering Christmas cards you can buy books of Christmas stamps at the checkout.

Site Usability:	★★★★★	Delivery Area:	Worldwide
Product Range:	★★★★★	Based:;	UK
Price Range:	Medium	Express Delivery Option? (UK)	Yes

www.clintoncards.co.uk

Here you can order a card to be sent to you to send to someone or for Clinton to personalise on your behalf. You can also use their reminder service for future birthdays and anniversaries. It's quite an attractive and unusual website, with links to other gift websites on the home page plus information about who did what on the day you've chosen to visit the site.

Site Usability:	★★★★★	Delivery Area:	Worldwide
Product Range:	★★★★	Based:	UK
Price Range:	Medium	Express Delivery Option? (UK)	Yes

www.moonpig.com

This is definitely one of my favourites – there are more than enough different types of cards here for whenever you might need them and they'll personalise them for you and send them out within 24 hours. It's a good site, quick and easy to navigate, with some excellent cards for birthdays in which you can change the name and date to those of the recipient. The cards really are funny (provided you want funny) and there's everything else from traditional to modern art cards as well. Expect a good and reliable service.

Site Usability:	★★★★★	Delivery Area:	Worldwide
Product Range:	★★★★★	Based:	UK
Price Range:	Medium	Express Delivery Option? (UK)	Yes

www.royalmail.com

Go to the 'Buy Online' section and order your books of stamps here (or your special editions or ready-stamped envelopes). You do have to order quite a number of stamps, but it's the easiest way if you're going to be posting a lot of mail in the near future. Alternatively, download 'SmartStamp', which allows you to print your postage directly onto your envelopes from your own printer.

Site Usability: ★★★★★	Based:	UK
Product Range: ★★★★★	Express Delivery Option? (UK)	Yes
Delivery Area: UK		

www.sharpcards.com

Cards for anniversaries, weddings, Easter, Valentine's Day, birthdays or Christmas, with handwritten greetings and sent out for you, are all waiting for you here. They also have an address book and reminder service so you won't ever forget that birthday or anniversary again. The site is clear and easy to use, but the range of cards is not as large as on some other sites, so have a look round on some other card websites before choosing.

Site Usability: ★★★★★	Delivery Area:	Worldwide
Product Range: ★★★★	Based:	UK
Price Range: Medium	Express Delivery Option? (UK)	Yes

www.skyhi.co.uk

Sky Hi balloons will deliver anything from a single balloon in a box with your message to a huge bouquet of balloons. They also offer a same-day delivery service which, although expensive, can be a lifesaver if you've forgotten an important event and want to make a statement. They're very reliable too, which is essential if you're going for the last-minute panic send. You'll find balloons here for just about every type of occasion.

Site Usability: ★★★★	Delivery Area:	UK
Product Range: ★★★★	Based:	UK
Price Range: Medium/Very Good Value	Express Delivery Option? (UK)	Yes

Chapter 2

Ribbon and Wrap

I'm always searching for new places to tell you about where you can buy a really good selection of wrapping paper – and always surprised that (at time of writing) there really is very little apart from at Christmas. I hope this will improve soon.

Where ribbon is concerned there *is* a good choice, particularly if you send a lot of gifts, as you can buy large reels of lovely ribbons at very good prices, much better than those little rolls of ribbon that you buy at the last minute and that (in my opinion) do little to add to the presentation of your gift and, even worse, can detract from your gorgeous expensive wrap. So think ahead and order from the websites here – you'll find it well worth the effort.

Sites to Visit

www.carnmeal.co.uk

This site is a must for anyone who has more than a few presents to wrap up. They specialise in a wide choice of beautiful ribbons and craft accessories for all occasions (and particularly weddings). Rather than buying those small, irritating balls of gold and silver ribbon, here you can choose from wired and unwired ribbons, organzas and tartans in lots of different widths and a great selection of colours. Most ribbons are available in 25 metre lengths.

Site Usability: ★★★		Based:	UK
Product Range: ★★★★★		Express Delivery Option? (UK)	No
Price Range: Medium/Very Good Value		Gift Wrapping Option?	No
Delivery Area: Worldwide		Returns Procedure:	Down to you

www.jaycotts.co.uk

Online haberdashers and sewing machine retailers Jaycotts offer a great deal more than ribbons as you can buy all your sewing essentials and accessories here. However, click through to Haberdashery and then Ribbons and choose from double-faced satin, taffeta, tartan, gold-edged satin and gold and silver lamé, all sold by the metre. Orders over £25 have free delivery.

Site Usability: ★★★★★		Based:	UK
Product Range: ★★★		Express Delivery Option? (UK)	No
Price Range: Medium/Very Good Value		Gift Wrapping Option?	No
Delivery Area: Worldwide		Returns Procedure:	Down to you

www.millcrofttextiles.co.uk

Millcroft supply general haberdashery items and textiles worldwide, specialising in the bridal industry. They also have a small but lovely selection of ribbons, including taffeta, tartan and metallic lamé, in lots of different colours, all of which they show very clearly. You can choose from various widths and lengths, although the reels usually start at 20 metres. When you're buying these quantities, prices are inevitably much better than you'll find in the shops, so buy to use throughout the year.

Site Usability: ★★★★		Based:	UK
Product Range: ★★★★		Express Delivery Option? (UK)	No
Price Range: Medium/Very Good Value		Gift Wrapping Option?	No
Delivery Area: Worldwide		Returns Procedure:	Down to you

www.nationaltrust-shop.co.uk

The National Trust shop online always has one of the best selections of high-quality wrapping paper and gift tags. When you click through to their online shop you'll find not just a wide choice of designs but you can also buy your wrap in different lengths right up to 20 metres - ideal

7

if you've lots of gifts to organise. You'll also find crackers at a range of prices, Christmas cards and gift ideas and ordering is quick and easy.

Site Usability: ★★★★★	Based:	UK
Product Range: ★★★★	Express Delivery Option? (UK)	No
Price Range: Medium/Very Good Value	Gift Wrapping Option?	No
Delivery Area: UK	Returns Procedure:	Down to you

www.nspccshop.co.uk

You often find some attractive ornaments, crackers, decorations and well-priced gift suggestions in the NSPCC Christmas catalogue and when you know that you're giving for such a good cause, it makes sense to buy here. There's also usually a wide selection of Christmas cards, excellent gift wrap, ribbons and calendars.

Site Usability: ★★★★★	Based:	UK
Product Range: ★★★★★	Express Delivery Option? (UK)	No
Price Range: Medium/Very Good Value	Gift Wrapping Option?	No
Delivery Area: UK	Returns Procedure:	Down to you

www.thewrappingco.com

Here's a small collection of beautiful but quite expensive wrap, ribbon and cards which would be suitable if you have just a few presents you want to wrap superbly. The site gives suggestions on which ribbon to use with which paper. It doesn't keep its Christmas selection up all the year round, so you need to visit in October for the full range, although you can of course use them at any time of year for other occasions.

Site Usability: ★★★★	Based:	UK
Product Range: ★★★	Express Delivery Option? (UK)	No
Price Range: Luxury/Medium	Gift Wrapping Option?	No
Delivery Area: UK	Returns Procedure:	Down to you

Also take a look at the following for Christmas ribbon and wrap:

Website address	You'll find it in
www.johnlewis.com	Chapter 24: Cook
www.lakelandlimited.co.uk	Chapter 6: Hampers and Food Gifts

Chapter 3

Chocolates for Chocoholics

This is a dangerous area for chocoholics to browse around, mainly because the photography on most of these websites is really lovely. I dare you to look and not be tempted.

There are chocolates at a wide range of prices here, from children's chocolate coins to beautifully boxed handmade truffles, and most make very good presents. For real chocolate addicts there are chocolate hampers and enormous boxes which might, in some households, last a while. On the other hand, if given to some of the people I know they'd disappear in a flash, never to be seen again. How can anyone eat that much chocolate?

Sites to Visit

www.brownes.co.uk

Brownes offer luxurious handmade chocolates in four sizes of boxes, from a small selection to their 1kg presentation box, plus after-dinner 'mint chasers', buttered brazils, party crackers, dusted almonds and chocolate-covered raisins. They all look totally delicious and once you reach this website you'll almost certainly want to give them a try.

Site Usability:	★★★★★	Based:	UK
Product Range:	★★★	Express Delivery Option? (UK)	No
Price Range:	Medium	Gift Wrapping Option?	No
Delivery Area:	Worldwide	Returns Procedure:	Down to you

www.chocolatebuttons.co.uk

Let your children on this website at your peril! From old-fashioned sherbert to Toblerone, chocolate coins, novelties and gifts, jelly beans and natural candy canes, this site is a cornucopia of irresistible sweets. Not only that, but you can buy in quantity. They won't stop you from buying one bag of chocolate Victorian coins, but why not buy 30 – surely you'll find a use for them?

Site Usability:	★★★★	Based:	UK
Product Range:	★★★★	Express Delivery Option? (UK)	Yes
Price Range:	Medium/Very Good Value	Gift Wrapping Option?	Yes, for their gift packs
Delivery Area:	Worldwide	Returns Procedure:	Down to you

www.chocolatetradingco.com

Here's a mouthwatering selection of chocolates, from Charbonel et Walker serious chocolate indulgences and chocoholics' hampers to funky and fun chocolates such as chocolate sardines and Jungle Crunch. They'll send your chocolates out for you with a personalised gift card and also offer you lots of information on how to tell when you're tasting the highest quality chocolate.

Site Usability:	★★★★★	Based:	UK
Product Range:	★★★★	Express Delivery Option? (UK)	Yes
Price Range:	Medium	Gift Wrapping Option?	Yes
Delivery Area:	UK	Returns Procedure:	Down to you

www.cocoaloco.co.uk

Started in 2005, Cocoa Loco is a small, family business based in Partridge Green, West Sussex, dedicated to producing handmade organic chocolates from high-quality ingredients. Try treats such as Organic Dark Chocolate Covered Ginger and Mango, Orange and Hazelnut Milk Chocolate Truffles, the Hot and Spicy Special (with Chocolate Chilli Brownies) or jumbo chocolate buttons. Everything can be sent out in a (recyclable) box with the message of your choice.

Site Usability:	★★★★	Based:	UK
Product Range:	★★★	Express Delivery Option? (UK)	Yes
Price Range:	Medium	Gift Wrapping Option?	No
Delivery Area:	Worldwide	Returns Procedure:	Down to you

www.darksugars.co.uk

Dark Sugars handmake rich chocolate truffles with flavours such as apricot and brandy, cardamom and orange, dry apple cider and cinnamon. Then there are the chocolate-dipped, liqueur-soaked dried fruits, prunes in Armagnac, cherries in cherry brandy and peaches in schnapps. And for each there is a choice of box or packet size. You can also buy the highest quality cooking chocolate and cocoa here – the essential ingredients which they use themselves.

Site Usability:	★★★★★	Based:	UK
Product Range:	★★★	Express Delivery Option? (UK)	No
Price Range:	Medium	Gift Wrapping Option?	No
Delivery Area:	Worldwide	Returns Procedure:	Down to you

www.hotelchocolat.co.uk

This is a lovely and well designed website with a large selection of beautifully packaged chocolates. Send someone a Chocogram Delux, Champagne Truffles, the Seasonal Selection, or let them choose for themselves. The site also has some unusual goodies such as strawberries in white chocolate, Christmas hampers, chocolate logs, goody bags and rocky road slabs. Resist if you can.

Site Usability:	★★★★★	Based:	UK
Product Range:	★★★★★	Express Delivery Option? (UK)	Yes
Price Range:	Luxury/Medium	Gift Wrapping Option?	No
Delivery Area:	Worldwide	Returns Procedure:	Down to you

www.montezumas.co.uk

Montezumas produce a range of around 40 handmade truffles, with names such as Caribbean Rhythm, Irish Tipple and Lost in Space. You can order by selecting one of the ready-made collections or choose your own from the complete list. Buy organic cocoa drinking chocolate, fantastic fudge and chocolate hampers here too.

Site Usability:	★★★★	Based:	UK
Product Range:	★★★	Express Delivery Option? (UK)	Yes
Price Range:	Luxury	Gift Wrapping Option?	No
Delivery Area:	Worldwide	Returns Procedure:	Down to you

www.thankheavenforchocolate.co.uk

In the Chocolate Shop at thankheavenforchocolate.co.uk there are decorative chocolate hampers, selections of Belgian chocolates, gorgeous special chocs for Valentine's Day, handmade boxes of chocolate truffles and cute chocolate novelties such as Saddleback Piglets and Happy Ducks. This isn't a huge selection but a very well thought out range and prices include free postage plus gift presentation and a card so that you can have your choice sent on your behalf to anywhere in the UK.

Site Usability:	★★★★★	Based:	UK
Product Range:	★★★★	Express Delivery Option? (UK)	Yes
Price Range:	Luxury/Medium	Gift Wrapping Option?	Yes
Delivery Area:	UK	Returns Procedure:	Down to you

Also take a look at these websites for chocolates:

Website Address	You'll find it in
www.chococo.co.uk	Chapter 35: Easter
www.theobroma-cacao.co.uk	Chapter 35: Easter
www.thorntons.co.uk	Chapter 35: Easter
www.groovychocolate.co.uk	Chapter 35: Easter

Chapter 4

Flowers

o you know anyone (female, I mean) who doesn't love to receive a gorgeous bunch of flowers? I certainly don't. In my opinion everyone, from girls to grannies, loves the ring at the door that means someone has thought of them, to say 'thank you', 'Happy Birthday' or just 'we're thinking of you'.

It is possible to spend a horrendous amount on a bunch of flowers, but it's not necessary. With designers such as Jane Packer offering bouquets at really reasonable prices, you don't have far to look to find something pretty and unusual that won't break the bank. There are a lot of flower websites that are not included here as I've tried to pick just those which offer flowers that are, in my opinion, special and different. I'd be happy to receive flowers from all and any of them. (Are you listening, Andrew?)

Sites to Visit

www.bloom.uk.com

If you're fed up of throwing out dead flowers and having to spend real money to replace them, take a look at this website offering the new generation of silk flowers online. They are incredibly real looking in most cases – you may well have admired some in a friend's house without realising they were silk, I certainly have. The site offers all types of

13

arrangements, from Dorset cream roses and cabbages to orchids and seasonal designs.

Site Usability: ★★★★★	Delivery Area:	UK
Product Range: ★★★★	Based:	UK
Price Range: Medium	Express Delivery Option? (UK)	Yes

www.bunches.co.uk

What you'll find here is excellent value for money. There are very few florists who will offer to send out flowers by post for under £20 (including delivery) and although these may not be the most sophisticated of flowers, if you don't want to spend too much you certainly should have a look. They also have a luxury bouquet selection, plus rose bouquets, and nothing is unreasonably priced. You can include chocolates, teddies and mini birthday cakes to send with your flowers.

Site Usability: ★★★★	Delivery Area:	UK
Product Range: ★★★	Based:	UK
Price Range: Medium/Very Good Value	Express Delivery Option? (UK)	Yes

www.designerflowers.org.uk

At Designer Flowers all the arrangements are created by their own florists and delivered direct by courier in secure boxes to London and around the UK. You can also include champagne, Belgian chocolates and soft toys and choose from the selection of special occasion bouquets. Prices are not inexpensive and delivery is extra at £4.50. You can order from them for next-day delivery or, if your order is urgent, they'll use their network of florists (rather than their own) to provide a same-day delivery service.

Site Usability: ★★★★★	Delivery Area:	UK
Product Range: ★★★★	Based:	UK
Price Range: Luxury/Medium	Express Delivery Option? (UK)	Yes

www.flowergram.co.uk

On this website you can buy reasonably priced and attractive hand-tied flowers. You also have the opportunity of choosing between small, medium and large-size bouquets, depending on how much you want to spend. All prices include delivery and if you order before midday, your choice can be delivered the same day. If you want to send flowers to someone overseas, you can do this here as well.

Site Usability:	★★★★★	Delivery Area:	Worldwide
Product Range:	★★★★	Based:	UK
Price Range:	Medium	Express Delivery Option? (UK)	Yes

www.flowersdirect.co.uk

You'll find a good collection of hand-tied and traditional bouquets here (and you can select the size you want to send), with a same-day delivery option if you order before 2pm, Monday to Saturday. Choose one of the exotic arrangements if you want to give something a bit different, with names such as Oriental Orchids and Exotic Paradise. You can include extras such as wine and champagne, spirits, chocolates, balloons and cuddly toys.

Site Usability:	★★★★	Delivery Area:	UK
Product Range:	★★★★	Based:	UK
Price Range:	Medium	Express Delivery Option? (UK)	Yes

www.flowerworksoxford.co.uk

Flowerworks offer a nationwide delivery service and the facility to select from their favourite seasonal bouquets or to design your own. To do this you just have to answer their questions: How would you like your flowers to be arranged – flamboyantly or compactly? In what style would you like them to be – vibrant, classic or exotic? Then you provide information on colour choice, price and the recipient and leave the rest to them.

Site Usability:	★★★★	Delivery Area:	UK
Product Range:	★★★	Based:	UK
Price Range:	Luxury/Medium	Express Delivery Option? (UK)	Yes

www.hayesflorist.co.uk

Well-priced and attractive planters and hand-tied bunches, international and same-day delivery are just some of the services offered here. The designs are essentially modern and beautifully photographed, so you can see exactly what you're ordering, from the Heavenly Rose hand-tied bouquet to the Autumn Planter or Conservatory Basket. You can include

THE SHOPAHOLIC'S GUIDE TO BUYING GORGEOUS GIFTS ONLINE

chocolates, balloons, champagne and candles or select from one of the ready-designed gift sets.

Site Usability:	★★★★	Delivery Area:	Worldwide
Product Range:	★★★★	Based:	UK
Price Range:	Medium	Express Delivery Option? (UK)	Yes

www.jwflowers.com

Visit this website if you want to buy something really special and not if you want 'flowers for less', as you should expect to pay upwards of £60 for an arrangement or bouquet. Having said that, the flowers here are exquisite, with unusual combinations (such as pale pink hyacinths, white ranunculuses and Candy Bianca roses, or burnt orange Adrema tulips with china grass loops and Guelda roses) used to create designs you won't find anywhere else.

Site Usability:	★★★★	Delivery Area:	UK
Product Range:	★★★	Based:	UK
Price Range:	Luxury	Express Delivery Option? (UK)	Yes

www.moysesstevens.co.uk

Since 1876, when Miss Moyses and Mr Stevens started their business, Moyses Stevens have been known for the artistry and quality of their floristry. They choose their in-house florists specifically for their originality and capacity to inspire and to create designs that are innovative, stylish and fun. Expect to find inspirational flowers, fresh, full of life and wonderful to receive. You can order orchids and small plants here too and set up an address book to make your life easy the next time you want to order.

Site Usability:	★★★★★	Based:	UK
Product Range:	★★★★	Express Delivery Option? (UK)	Yes for some bouquets provided you
Price Range:	Luxury/Medium		order early enough
Delivery Area:	UK		

www.vivelarose.com

Using mainly hybrid tea roses for their beautiful full blooms and long stems, Vive la Rose adapt their unique bouquets to the latest trends

16

in interiors. The roses travel in special hydrating travel packs and are delivered by courier, enabling the site to offer a next-day delivery service within the UK. Don't expect a vast selection here, just beautiful bouquets in a variety of colours that you won't find anywhere else. They offer a wedding flower service as well.

Site Usability:	★★★★★	Based:	UK
Product Range:	★★★	Express Delivery Option? (UK)	Yes
Price Range:	Medium	Gift Wrapping	No
Delivery Area:	UK		

www.worldofroses.com

Yes, this is the place to find the most outstanding roses of all varieties, from climbing and floribundas to ground cover and hybrid tea varieties. However, don't expect to find your standard hand-tied bunches here as these are gorgeous roses for planting in your garden. You can order them in pots, bare root or gift wrapped, and select the date that you want them delivered. If you want something unique, you can name your own rose here as well.

Site Usability:	★★★★★	Delivery Area:	UK
Product Range:	★★★★★	Based:	UK
Price Range:	Medium	Express Delivery Option? (UK)	No

Also take a look at these websites for flowers:

Website Address	You'll find it in
www.imogenstone.co.uk	Chapter 33: Valentine's Day
www.janepackerdelivered.com	Chapter 21: For New Mums
www.lambertsflowercompany.co.uk	Chapter 21: For New Mums

Chapter 5

Champagne and Wine

You may think that giving wine and champagne as a gift is just that little bit too easy, but turn it on its head and think of yourself: when have you ever been disappointed to receive a bottle of bubbly? I certainly haven't.

Some of the websites here offer you the facility to personalise the bottle label or to order Jeroboams, Methuselahs and Nebuchadnezzars of champagne (and no, I'm not going to tell you, you'll find out below). These would make wonderful gifts for special occasions such as silver weddings and special birthdays. On other sites you'll find high-quality selections of wines where you can just choose yourself or take their advice. If you know that someone likes a particular wine you could use www.wine-searcher.com to track it down. Just bear in mind that the prices you'll find there do not include VAT before you shell out for that bottle of Pomerol.

Sites to Visit

www.ballsbrothers.co.uk

Balls Brothers is a well-established business, having shipped and traded wines for more than 150 years. You'll discover a handpicked selection of over 400 wines and you can be sure that everything has been carefully chosen, from the least expensive (reds starting at around £4.50 a bottle) right up to Chateau Palmer Margaux at over £100. The search facility is quite difficult to use as you can't see the complete list, so just input the type or colour of wine you're looking for and you'll get a selection.

Site Usability:	★★★	Based:	UK
Product Range:	★★★★	Express Delivery Option? (UK)	No
Price Range:	Luxury/Medium	Gift Wrapping Option?	No
Delivery Area:	Worldwide	Returns Procedure:	Down to you

www.butlerswines.co.uk

Butlers specialise in high-quality wine and champagne gifts and offer more reasonable prices than most, in that you can see the price of each individual bottle, add the gift packaging and then the handmade truffles. Personally, I think this is better than putting everything together and hoping that you won't notice the price, but obviously it takes a few more clicks. There's a good choice of hampers as well and express delivery.

Site Usability:	★★★★★	Based:	UK
Product Range:	★★★★	Express Delivery Option? (UK)	Yes
Price Range:	Medium	Gift Wrapping Option?	No
Delivery Area:	UK	Returns Procedure:	Down to you

www.cambridgewine.com

This is a beautifully designed website from a Cambridge-based independent wine merchant and one that's a pleasure to browse through. You can choose by category and by country, select from the mixed cases and promotional offers and take advantage of the gift and En Primeur services. It's the perfect website if you prefer one that isn't too busy and where it's easy to place your order.

Site Usability:	★★★★★	Based:	UK
Product Range:	★★★★★	Express Delivery Option? (UK)	No
Price Range:	Luxury/Medium	Gift Wrapping Option?	Yes
Delivery Area:	UK	Returns Procedure:	Down to you

www.champagnewarehouse.co.uk

Here is an attractive website from a retailer established just a few years ago to offer personally selected, top-quality champagnes throughout the UK. You can buy your champagne by the bottle or in cases of six or twelve and prices start at around £14 a bottle. The site also offers tasting cases containing two different champagnes. The selection of champagnes changes from month to month as new deliveries arrive.

Site Usability:	★★★★	Based:	UK
Product Range:	★★★	Express Delivery Option? (UK)	No
Price Range:	Medium/Very Good Value	Gift Wrapping Option?	No
Delivery Area:	UK	Returns Procedure:	Down to you

www.everywine.co.uk

Everywine is a wine retailer combining an excellent search facility, wines from the reasonably priced to the extremely expensive and some very good deals. You do need to buy by the case here and if you want a mixed case then you just click through to the sister site at www.booths-wine. co.uk. This is another award-winning wine merchant, having won the International Wine Challenge Regional Wine Merchant of the Year 2005.

Site Usability:	★★★★	Based:	UK
Product Range:	★★★★★	Express Delivery Option? (UK)	No
Price Range:	Medium	Gift Wrapping Option?	No
Delivery Area:	UK	Returns Procedure:	Down to you

www.jeroboams.co.uk

This is a seriously beautifully photographed website from a luxury cheese specialist, deli and fine wine importer, based in South Kensington. On this site you can order from the cheese selections or gifts of food and wine, which include port with stilton, vodka and caviar or whisky and cheddar, choose from one of the luxury hampers or from the list of wines, champagnes and spirits. This would be an excellent place to find a gift for a real food or wine lover, although it's definitely at the luxury end.

Site Usability:	★★★★	Based:	UK
Product Range:	★★★	Express Delivery Option? (UK)	No
Price Range:	Luxury	Gift Wrapping Option?	No
Delivery Area:	UK	Returns Procedure:	Down to you

www.justchampagne.co.uk

So you're not going to be surprised to find champagne here, I suspect. You may be surprised that you'll find not 'just' champagne (could it ever be 'just'?) but champagne gifts too, with chocolate truffles, picnic bags, teddies and sterling silver cufflinks, plus wonderful large bottles such as the Jeroboam (3 litres), Methuselahs (6 litres) and Nebuchadnezzar (15 litres). That one's definitely mine – anyone want to share?

Site Usability:	★★★	Based:	UK
Product Range:	★★★★★	Express Delivery Option? (UK)	Yes
Price Range:	Luxury/Medium	Gift Wrapping Option?	No
Delivery Area:	Most EU and US	Returns Procedure:	Down to you

www.laithwaites.co.uk

Laithwaites is an excellent, family-run online (and offline) wine merchant, with a personal and efficient service and a good choice across all price ranges. They offer wines and champagnes, mixed cases and a wide range of fortified wines and spirits. There's also a clever food-matching service, plus all the other options you would expect, including bin ends, mixed case offers and wine plans.

Site Usability:	★★★★★	Based:	UK
Product Range:	★★★★	Express Delivery Option? (UK)	No
Price Range:	Luxury/Medium/Very Good Value	Gift Wrapping Option?	No
Delivery Area:	UK	Returns Procedure:	Down to you

www.laywheeler.co.uk

Based in Colchester and specialising in Bordeaux and Burgundy, Lay and Wheeler are also agents for wine producers in Australia, California, South Africa and other areas. There's a wide range of wine on offer on this busy website, plus assistance if you need it. You can choose from the current offers or the full wine list, use the gift service, view the tasting programme and find out about the Bin Club and Wine Discovery Club as well.

Site Usability: ★★★★	Based:	UK
Product Range: ★★★★	Express Delivery Option? (UK)	No
Price Range: Luxury/Medium	Gift Wrapping Option?	No
Delivery Area: UK	Returns Procedure:	Down to you

www.lordswines.co.uk

There's a good selection of food and wine gifts here, from beautifully packaged bottles of wine and champagne to more traditional ideas such as port and stilton and champagne and chocolates, plus excellent hampers, particularly at Christmas. Most gifts can be personalised – not just the card but the box as well – and they'll even produce a special wine or champagne bottle label for you.

Site Usability: ★★★★★	Based:	UK
Product Range: ★★★★	Express Delivery Option? (UK)	Yes
Price Range: Luxury/Medium	Gift Wrapping Option?	Yes
Delivery Area: UK	Returns Procedure:	Down to you

www.nextday-champagne.co.uk

There are lots of places you can buy champagne online, so these days a retailer has to offer something a little bit different to catch your attention. Here at nextday-champagne.co.uk you can order from their standard range of champagnes which they'll send out with your message, together with everything from a teddy bear to a Christmas pudding. You can also choose from their Lanson vintage selection and design a personalised label. Prices are steep, but if you're looking for a luxury gift take a look round.

Site Usability: ★★★★★	Express Delivery Option? (UK)	Next working day if you order before
Product Range: ★★★★		3pm
Price Range: Luxury/Medium	Gift Wrapping Option?	No
Delivery Area: UK	Returns Procedure:	Down to you
Based: UK		

www.tanners-wines.co.uk

You'll find a comprehensive range of wine, champagne, liqueurs and spirits on this clear and well laid out site. Tanners are a traditional wine merchant with a calm style (very different from the 'full on' style of Majestic and Oddbins), offering an excellent service and reasonable prices, plus lots of advice and information about everything on offer. So you may not always find the cheapest deals here, but you'll certainly enjoy buying from them.

Site Usability:	★★★★★	Based:	UK
Product Range:	★★★★	Express Delivery Option? (UK)	No
Price Range:	Luxury/Medium	Gift Wrapping Option?	No
Delivery Area:	UK	Returns Procedure:	Down to you

www.thewhiskyexchange.com

Although you can buy blended and some single malt whiskies from just about every supermarket and wine merchant, if you want a really good selection of specialist whisky you need to have a look here. The site offers a good range, from the reasonably priced to the not so reasonably priced, and includes help and advice for the drinker, collector and investor. The list of single malts is amazing and prices go up to (don't faint) over £2,000, but of course there are plenty between £20 and £25.

Site Usability:	★★★★★	Based:	UK
Product Range:	★★★★★	Express Delivery Option? (UK)	No
Price Range:	Luxury/Medium	Gift Wrapping Option?	No
Delivery Area:	Worldwide	Returns Procedure:	Down to you

www.winedancer.com

You can, of course, just walk into your local wine merchant and buy your bottle of bubbly then and there. Or you could do something a bit different and send a bottle of Veuve Clicquot in its very own ice bucket with your personalised card, or a boxed mini bottle of Laurent Perrier with a candle and bath essence. If you want to be really popular send a Methuselah of champagne in a wooden crate (the equivalent of eight bottles) and cross your fingers you'll be invited to share it. This is a really good selection of unusual gift ideas.

Site Usability:	★★★★	Based:	UK
Product Range:	★★★★	Express Delivery Option? (UK)	Yes
Price Range:	Luxury/Medium	Gift Wrapping Option?	No
Delivery Area:	Worldwide	Returns Procedure:	Down to you

www.wine-searcher.com

Looking for a particular vintage of Pomerol, or just Oyster Bay Chardonnay? With prices differing by as much as 40% you need this fantastic worldwide wine-comparison website if you're considering buying more than a single bottle of wine. Do register for the pro-version to get all the benefits. There are literally hundreds of wine merchants online all over the world and it's simply not possible to list all the good ones. Wine-searcher will take you to many you've never heard of, so take a good look at the sites you visit, make sure they're secure, compare the prices and enjoy.

Site Usability:	★★★★★	Price Range:	Luxury/Medium
Product Range:	★★★★★	Based:	New Zealand

www.woodenwinebox.co.uk

Provided you place your order before 2.30pm, The Wooden Wine Box Company will ensure that it arrives the next working day. Take a look through this well-photographed and easy-to-navigate website for wine and champagne gifts which, for a change, do not include teddies, chocolates and flowers but just high-quality, hand-picked wines and champagnes. All the gifts are packed into pine gift boxes and can be sent out with your personal message. Delivery is to the UK and business addresses in the EU.

Site Usability:	★★★★★	Based: UK	
Product Range:	★★★★	Express Delivery Option? (UK)	Yes
Price Range:	Luxury/Medium	Gift Wrapping Option?	No
Delivery Area:	UK and EU business addresses	Returns Procedure:	Down to you

Also take a look at the following for wine and champagne:

Website Address	You'll find it in
www.bbr.com	Chapter 32: Christening Gifts

Chapter 6

Hampers and Food Gifts

I always used to think that giving someone a hamper was a bit of a cop-out, but that was well before the days of the online retailers you'll find here, who all offer a fantastic selection of goodies. In most cases you can choose from their ready-prepared hampers and boxes or, better still, put the selection together yourself. They make it so easy you'll be hard put not to order some of the delicious treats for yourself. Go on – I'm sure you deserve it.

Sites to Visit

www.agold.co.uk

Here you can order the Brushfield Basket, containing hand-baked lemon biscuits, plum bread, Spyder Cream Soda and Darlington's lemon curd; the Hawksmoore Hamper with Fentiman's hot ginger beer, poacher's relish and a selection of cheeses; or the Regency Hamper containing cheese, pork pies, sloe gin and lots of other delicious-sounding goodies. Alternatively you can select from the excellent online deli and choose exactly what you want to send (which I always prefer). Allow at least five days for delivery.

Site Usability:	★★★★	Based:	UK
Product Range:	★★★★	Express Delivery Option? (UK)	No
Price Range:	Medium	Gift Wrapping Option?	No
Delivery Area:	UK	Returns Procedure:	Down to you

www.bayley-sage.co.uk

Bayley and Sage is a top-quality delicatessen based in Wimbledon. On the website you can't actually visit the deli, but you can buy one of their well put together gift selections, with names like Sweet Sensation (jelly beans, chocolate brownies, mini cakes and marshmallows, etc.) or Gentlemen's Selection (wine, coffee, marmalade, nuts and Gentleman's Relish). Everything is clearly photographed and the prices are reasonable.

Site Usability:	★★★★	Based:	UK
Product Range:	★★★★	Express Delivery Option? (UK)	No
Price Range:	Medium	Gift Wrapping Option?	No
Delivery Area:	UK	Returns Procedure:	Down to you

www.beverlyhillsbakery.com

If you live outside London don't even think of looking at the full range here, as you'll probably be disappointed when you realise that they can't deliver to you. Do, however, click through to the selection that they will send to you anywhere in the UK (and overseas, in some cases), which includes carrot cake, apple and cinnamon cake and pear and ginger cake, or one of the attractive gift tins containing delicious mini muffins, cookies and brownies.

Site Usability:	★★★★	Based:	UK
Product Range:	★★★	Express Delivery Option? (UK)	No
Price Range:	Medium	Gift Wrapping Option?	No
Delivery Area:	Worldwide for some items	Returns Procedure:	Down to you

www.claire-macdonald.com

There are so many online retailers offering you (frequently very good) selections of food and drink put together by totally anonymous people that I always find it a joy to discover a real name, someone who has taken the trouble to create their own range and isn't afraid to announce themselves. Claire Macdonald is one who offers her gifts of food and wine such as The Chocolate Pudding Collection, Savoury Sauces and Chocolate Fudge, all beautifully packaged in signature dark-green gift boxes. Buy from her.

Site Usability:	★★★★	Based:	UK
Product Range:	★★★	Express Delivery Option? (UK)	No
Price Range:	Medium	Gift Wrapping Option?	No
Delivery Area:	Worldwide	Returns Procedure:	Down to you

www.collinstreet.com

This is a really, really bad website to visit if you're on a diet. The Collins Street Bakery is based in Texas and sells the most delicious, fruit- and nut-filled, luxury fruit cakes, pecan cakes (think Apple Cinnamon and Pineapple Pecan) you've ever tasted. Don't get too excited about the toffee, cookies and cheesecake here as those items they'll ship only to the US. The cakes, however, they'll ship to anywhere in the world, so take care if you have a really sweet tooth.

Site Usability:	★★★★★	Based:	US
Product Range:	★★★	Express Delivery Option? (UK)	No
Price Range:	Medium	Gift Wrapping Option?	No
Delivery Area:	Worldwide	Returns Procedure:	Down to you

www.efoodies.co.uk

This is an extremely tempting website, where you can order the highest quality olive oil and balsamic vinegar, British and French cheese, caviar, foie gras, black and white truffles and truffle oil, spices, mushrooms and champagne. Everything is beautifully photographed, with lots of information about every product – where it comes from and what makes it special. The prices here are good, particularly when you consider the quality of what you're buying. They offer gift vouchers as well.

Site Usability:	★★★★★	Based:	UK
Product Range:	★★★	Express Delivery Option? (UK)	Yes
Price Range:	Luxury/Medium	Gift Wrapping Option?	No
Delivery Area:	UK	Returns Procedure:	Down to you

www.fruit-4u.com

This company will put together the most mouthwatering mix of fresh fruit and present it beautifully in a basket so that you can send it as a gift, with names such as the Exotic Fruit Basket and the Supreme Fruit Basket, both packed with perfect Class 1 seasonal fruits. You can also add cheese, wine, teddies and champagne to your selected basket.

Site Usability:	★★★★	Based:	UK
Product Range:	★★★	Express Delivery Option? (UK)	Yes
Price Range:	Medium	Gift Wrapping Option?	No
Delivery Area:	UK	Returns Procedure:	Down to you

www.gogofruitbasket.com

Gogofruitbasket offers free delivery in mainland UK and you can buy, alongside the fruits, all sorts of 'hampers', including 'Pink Fizz, Strawberries and Chocs', 'Cheese and Wine' (plus grapes and clementines), 'Mighty Fruit n Muffin' (fruit with The Fabulous Bakin' Boys muffins and shortcake) and 'Big Fat Thank You' (forget the fruit here, this is muffins, caramel slices, macaroons, flapjack bars, caramelts and cup cakes). It's a very easy website to navigate and as they say, 'with the freshest fruit – there can only be next-day delivery'.

Site Usability:	★★★★	Based:	UK
Product Range:	★★★	Express Delivery Option? (UK)	Yes
Price Range:	Medium	Gift Wrapping Option?	No
Delivery Area:	UK	Returns Procedure:	Down to you

www.gorgeous-food.co.uk

Here's a really attractive website, using traditional script and clear pictures to make you want to stay and browse. The site offers a selection of hampers, from Decadence, Luxury and Indulgence to themed selections such as Afternoon Tea, Chocoholic, Spanish and Chilli Lover. For each one you see not only the filled hamper but also each individual ingredient as well as the list of what's included. In the 'Other Goodies' section you'll find Booja Booja truffles (!), Catalan Mountain Honey and lots more.

Site Usability:	★★★★★	Based:	UK
Product Range:	★★★★	Express Delivery Option? (UK)	Yes
Price Range:	Luxury/Medium	Gift Wrapping Option?	No
Delivery Area:	UK	Returns Procedure:	Down to you

www.hamper.com

Winner of the Queen's Award for Enterprise for International Trade in 2003, Clearwater Hampers can deliver your choice of hamper to just about anywhere in the world. You can create your own from their range of wines and food goodies and they give lots of tips to help you create the perfect gift depending on the recipient. Alternatively choose from their Classic Collection, where you can spend between £30 and £300. It really is a well-designed website and you should certainly find something here.

Site Usability:	★★★★★	Based:	UK
Product Range:	★★★★	Express Delivery Option? (UK)	No
Price Range:	Luxury/Medium	Gift Wrapping Option?	No
Delivery Area:	Worldwide	Returns Procedure:	Down to you

www.lakelandlimited.co.uk

If you thought (as I always have) that Lakeland was about gifts and gizmos for the kitchen and home and clever picnic and tableware, then think again. A selection of chocolates, Bay Tree Turkish delight, apricots in Moscato, candied fruits, marrons glacés, olive oils, jalapeño spiced nuts, plus the famous Australian Celebration Cake, are just some of the goodies this site offers at different times of the year. Couple this with Lakeland's emphasis on quality and service and you certainly won't go wrong when you place an order here.

Site Usability:	★★★★★	Based:	UK
Product Range:	★★★★★	Express Delivery Option? (UK)	Yes
Price Range:	Medium/Very Good Value	Gift Wrapping Option?	No
Delivery Area:	Worldwide	Returns Procedure:	Down to you

www.lewisandcooper.com

Lewis and Cooper is a family-run business offering a marvellous selection of hampers for all tastes and price levels. You can choose one of their ready-selected hampers or pick the items that you want included. Some of the items on offer include Cropwell Bishops Stilton, Inverawe Smoked Salmon and pears in caramel sauce, alongside the finest York ham, hand-made plum puddings and Yorkshire Moors honey on the comb.

Site Usability:	★★★★★	Based:	UK
Product Range:	★★★★	Express Delivery Option? (UK)	Yes
Price Range:	Luxury/Medium	Gift Wrapping Option?	No
Delivery Area:	UK	Returns Procedure:	Down to you

www.mortimerandbennett.co.uk

This online deli is crammed full of speciality foods from around the world, many of which are exclusive to this site. You'll find an extensive range of cheeses, breads, oil and charcuterie, as well as a selection of fun foodie gifts such as the La Maison du Miel honey, Italian flower jellies and gold and silver buttons. There's also panettone from Turin, extra virgin olive oil from New Zealand and biscuits from Sardinia – lots to choose from and all easy to see.

Site Usability:	★★★★★	Based:	UK
Product Range:	★★★★	Express Delivery Option? (UK)	Yes
Price Range:	Luxury/Medium	Gift Wrapping Option?	No
Delivery Area:	UK	Returns Procedure:	Down to you

www.optimacompany.com

Optima specialises in making traditional willow picnic baskets and accessories, including picnic bags, rugs and furniture. There is also a chic, colourful 'Carnival' picnic range, including a fun, shocking-pink polka-dot basket. They combine picnic baskets with gourmet food and wines, creating luxury gift hampers. UK mainland delivery is free.

Site Usability:	★★★★★	Based:	UK
Product Range:	★★★★	Express Delivery Option? (UK)	No
Price Range:	Luxury/Medium	Gift Wrapping Option?	No
Delivery Area:	UK	Returns Procedure:	Down to you

www.saralouisekakes.co.uk

If you know someone who has a sweet tooth and needs cheering up, you could consider sending them a Hansel and Gretel House cake, decorated in white and pink buttercream and handmade sugared hearts and flowers. Alternatively, how about a box of boozy triple chocolate and cherry brownies covered in chocolate fudge icing and decorated with milk chocolate curls? Have I got your attention yet? Thought so. You'll probably want to order some for yourself as well.

Site Usability:	★★★★	Based:	UK
Product Range:	★★★	Express Delivery Option? (UK)	No
Price Range:	Medium	Gift Wrapping Option?	No
Delivery Area:	UK	Returns Procedure:	Down to you

www.thedrinkshop.com

Here's a selection of unusual luxury chocolate boxes from Belgian retailers Gudrun and Lassiter, plus a wide choice of champagnes, wines and spirits. They also have cocktail kits for different types of drinks, gift hampers and presentation boxes, so there are some good gift ideas here (which you know will almost certainly be used). A full range of reasonably priced glassware is available by US company Anchor Hocking.

Site Usability:	★★★★	Based:	UK
Product Range:	★★★	Express Delivery Option? (UK)	Yes
Price Range:	Luxury/Medium	Gift Wrapping Option?	No
Delivery Area:	Europe	Returns Procedure:	Down to you

www.thegiftgourmet.co.uk

The Gift Gourmet has an easy-to-navigate website which offers a broad and innovative range of affordable food gift sets containing the highest quality ingredients, all presented within 'gift-ready' packaging so that you don't have to do any more work. There's a wide range of prices, from expensive hampers at around £100 to suggestions at under £20.

Site Usability:	★★★★	Based:	UK
Product Range:	★★★	Express Delivery Option? (UK)	Yes
Price Range:	Medium/Very Good Value	Gift Wrapping Option?	Yes
Delivery Area:	UK	Returns Procedure:	Down to you

www.theheavenlyhampercompany.co.uk

The aim of Heavenly Hampers is to offer food and wine gifts that you won't find anywhere else. The collection isn't huge; however, they've definitely found some interesting products to include, such as red chilli jelly, aubergines stuffed with anchovies and onions marinated in balsamic vinegar. Combine these with excellent presentation and speedy service and you may well find the answer to your next gift-giving problem here.

Site Usability:	★★★★	Based:	UK
Product Range:	★★★	Express Delivery Option? (UK)	Yes
Price Range:	Luxury/Medium	Gift Wrapping Option?	No
Delivery Area:	UK	Returns Procedure:	Down to you

www.valvonacrolla-online.co.uk

Valvona & Crolla is an independent family business based in Edinburgh, specialising in gourmet Italian products, plus their handpicked range of good-value, quality Italian wines from artisan producers and progressive co-operatives. In 2005 they won the *Which?* award for the Italian Specialist Wine Merchant, so if you're fond of Italian wines take a good look at their collection. They also offer an excellent selection of reasonably priced food and wine gift ideas.

Site Usability:	★★★★★	Based:	UK
Product Range:	★★★★	Express Delivery Option? (UK)	Yes
Price Range:	Luxury/Medium	Gift Wrapping Option?	No
Delivery Area:	UK	Returns Procedure:	Down to you

www.virginiahayward.com

Established in 1984, Virginia Hayward offers a beautifully presented traditional range of gifts and hampers. They offer gifts for all seasons and events and can fulfil large corporate orders as well individual purchases. They have a wide choice of other food- and wine-related gifts and a range of romantic and pampering gifts. You can choose from a named or standard delivery and they'll deliver to BFPO addresses.

Site Usability: ★★★★★	Based:	UK
Product Range: ★★★★	Express Delivery Option? (UK)	Yes
Price Range: Luxury/Medium	Gift Wrapping Option?	No
Delivery Area: UK	Returns Procedure:	Down to you

www.whiskhampers.co.uk

Whisk Hampers has drawn on over 15 years' experience in the restaurant and fine food retail business to bring you a range of stylish, modern food gifts. All of these are 'natural', avoiding artificial additives and preservatives, and are carefully packaged on striking black shred with a quotation postcard based on the contents and with your personalised message included. Choose from excellent champagnes and wines, plus hampers with names such as Kitchen Confidential, Dressing to Impress and Instant Karma.

Site Usability: ★★★★	Based:	UK
Product Range: ★★★	Express Delivery Option? (UK)	Yes
Price Range: Luxury/Medium	Gift Wrapping Option?	No
Delivery Area: UK	Returns Procedure:	Down to you

www.whittard.co.uk

Famous for fine tea and coffee since 1886, Whittard of Chelsea has a wide range of teas and coffees (choose from Monsoon Malabar, Old Brown Java and Very Very Berry Fruit Infusion) and also offers instant flavoured cappuccinos, plus coffee and tea gifts. They have a very high-quality hot chocolate to order here and you'll also find machines, grinders, roasters and cafetières, accessories and equipment spares as well as very attractive ceramics, fine bone china and seasonal hampers.

Site Usability: ★★★★★	Based:	UK
Product Range: ★★★★	Express Delivery Option? (UK)	Yes
Price Range: Medium	Gift Wrapping Option?	No
Delivery Area: Worldwide	Returns Procedure:	Down to you

Section 2
Just for Her

This, of course, is the most important section of the book (just kidding). It is a really important place if you're looking for a special girly gift, as included below there are fragrant candles, fragrance and bath and body products; places to find spa days out; jewellery and accessory gifts such as handbags, belts and glittering costume jewels (as well as the real thing); plus exquisite lingerie to buy for yourself, for someone you know well, or for him to give to her.

There are also lovely objects (as in the French pronunciation) for the home – cushions and throws, unusual candle holders and book stands, lighting and other accessories, nearly all of which would make excellent gifts for the home interiors lover. In many cases they're presented as gifts on the websites to make your life even easier, together with the essential services of gift wrapping, speedy delivery and worldwide shipping.

Chapter 7

Pampering Presents

This is another of those areas I'm immediately drawn to as I think there's little nicer than being given a prettily tied box with beautifully fragranced products inside. My specific problem is that my family think that it's too easy to give me something that they already know I like and go rushing around to try to find things that are different and new.

My advice is, if you know someone loves a particular fragrance, lotion or shower gel – go for it. It's almost impossible to go wrong and you can spend just that little bit more on the candle, luxury travel set or cologne. They'll be delighted, I promise you.

Sites to Visit

www.austique.co.uk

Here's an attractive and well-designed website offering a bit of everything: accessories, lingerie, Rococo chocolates, modern jewellery and unusual bathroom treats such as Limoncello Body Butter and Arnaud Chamomile and Lavender Bubble Bath. The range changes frequently depending on the season. Services include gift wrapping, express delivery and international orders by special request.

Site Usability: ★★★★	Based:	UK
Product Range: ★★★	Express Delivery Option? (UK)	Yes
Price Range: Medium	Gift Wrapping Option?	Yes
Delivery Area: Worldwide	Returns Procedure:	Down to you

www.bootik.co.uk

On this well laid out website you'll find lots of gift ideas, from pretty, well-priced jewellery set with semi-precious stones to beaded bags and attractive cosmetic bags, bath and body products, unusual cushions and tableware and a small and very different (but not so inexpensive) collection of clothes. Most of the items here can't be found elsewhere, so it could be well worth having a look round.

Site Usability: ★★★	Based:	UK
Product Range: ★★★	Express Delivery Option? (UK)	Yes
Price Range: Medium	Gift Wrapping Option?	Yes
Delivery Area: Worldwide	Returns Procedure:	Down to you

www.boutiquetoyou.co.uk

Boutique to You specialises in personalised gifts, gadgets and jewellery perfect for lots of different occasions. They've also been responsible for introducing some cult jewellery brands from the US, including Mummy & Daddy Tags, Lisa Goodwin New York and Fairy Tale Jewels. On the website there's a wish list facility, so you can send ' wish mails' to your nearest and dearest with hints of what you'd like to receive. The site is also introducing a loyalty scheme.

Site Usability: ★★★	Based:	UK
Product Range: ★★★★	Express Delivery Option? (UK)	No
Price Range: Medium	Gift Wrapping Option	Yes
Delivery Area: Worldwide	Returns Procedure:	Down to you

www.cocoribbon.com

Calling itself London's lifestyle boutique, Coco Ribbon offers a selection of contemporary clothing by designers such as Collette Dinnigan, Rebecca Taylor and Cynthia Vincent. There is pretty, modern lingerie and swimwear, a small but beautiful range of handbags and jewellery, plus gorgeous and unusual girly gifts and candles. There's a lot to choose from here and the range is constantly updated, so you need to return regularly for another browse.

Site Usability:	★★★★	Based:	UK
Product Range:	★★★★	Express Delivery Option? (UK)	Yes
Price Range:	Luxury/Medium	Gift Wrapping Option	Yes
Delivery Area:	Worldwide	Returns Procedure:	Down to you

www.crabtree-evelyn.co.uk

Well known and sold throughout the world, Crabtree & Evelyn offers a wide range of bath, body and spa products from classic fragrances such as Lily of the Valley to the ultra modern La Source and the new India Hicks Island Living collection. Everything is cleverly and attractively packaged and offered here on this well-designed and easy-to-navigate website. Particularly good as gifts are the pretty boxes containing miniatures of the most popular products.

Site Usability:	★★★★★	Based:	UK
Product Range:	★★★★★	Express Delivery Option? (UK)	No
Price Range:	Medium	Gift Wrapping Option?	No
Delivery Area:	Worldwide	Returns Procedure:	Down to you

www.escentual.co.uk

Escentual carries what is probably the widest range of fragrance for men and women in the UK. Choose a fragrance or fragrance-linked bath and body product and then search for it on this site – you're almost certain to find it. Bath and body products include Burberry, Bvlgari, Calvin Klein, Gucci, Guerlain, Rochas and Versace, plus Crabtree & Evelyn, Tisserand and I Coloniali. Delivery is free on orders over £30 and they also offer free gift wrapping.

Site Usability:	★★★★★	Based:	UK
Product Range:	★★★★★	Express Delivery Option? (UK)	Yes
Price Range:	Luxury/Medium/Very Good Value	Gift Wrapping Option?	Yes
Delivery Area:	Worldwide	Returns Procedure:	Down to you

www.florislondon.com

Floris is one of the oldest and most traditional perfumers, having been established in 1730. You'll find favourites Lavender, China Rose, Gardenia and Stephanotis and more modern fragrances Night Scented Jasmin, Bouquet de la Reine and No 89. The updated packaging is lovely and for each fragrance there's a full range of bath and body products, plus special wrapped sets for Christmas.

Site Usability:	★★★★★	Based:	UK
Product Range:	★★★★★	Express Delivery Option? (UK)	Yes
Price Range:	Luxury/Medium	Gift Wrapping Option?	Yes
Delivery Area:	Worldwide	Returns Procedure:	Down to you

www.garden.co.uk

The Garden Pharmacy's list of top brands seems to be growing by the day. Here you'll find Chanel, Elizabeth Arden, Lancome, Revlon, Clinique and Clarins online, together with Vichy, Avene, Caudalie and Roc and spa products by I Coloniali, L'Occitane, Roger et Gallet and Segreti Mediterranei (and no doubt a few more will have appeared by the time you read this). The range of fragrances is huge as well. They also offer free gift wrapping and 24-hour delivery.

Site Usability:	★★★★	Based:	UK
Product Range:	★★★★★	Express Delivery Option? (UK)	Yes
Price Range:	Luxury/Medium/Very Good Value	Gift Wrapping Option?	Yes
Delivery Area:	Worldwide	Returns Procedure:	Down to you

www.hqhair.com

If you haven't used it already, you should try this fun and incredibly useful website. Along with funky beauty products and jewellery (and absolutely everything you could need for your hair including Blax, Nexxus and Paul Mitchell products), you'll discover Anya Hindmarch, Kate Spade and Lulu Guinness exquisite cosmetic bags (perfect for presents and also for treats) and lots of beauty accessories, including high-quality make-up and hair brushes.

Site Usability:	★★★★★	Based: UK	
Product Range:	★★★★	Express Delivery Option? (UK)	No
Price Range:	Luxury/Medium	Gift Wrapping Option?	No
Delivery Area:	Worldwide	Returns Procedure:	Down to you

www.jomalone.co.uk

This has to be one of my favourites, where you can buy Jo Malone's beautifully packaged range of luxurious fragrances, plus bath and body products with names like Pomegranate Noir and Blue Agava & Cacao. You'll also find her cleansers, serums and moisturisers, facial finishers such as mascara and lip gloss, and irresistible travel sets. New products are being developed all the time, which makes this a great place for feel-good treats and gifts you won't want to part with. The service is excellent and if you need a last-minute gift, this is definitely the place to come.

Site Usability:	★★★★★	Based:	UK
Product Range:	★★★★★	Express Delivery Option? (UK)	Yes
Price Range:	Luxury	Gift Wrapping Option?	Yes
Delivery Area:	Worldwide	Returns Procedure:	Down to you

www.kiarie.co.uk

Kiarie has one of the best ranges of scented candles, by brands such as Geodosis, Kenneth Turner, Manuel Canovas, Creation Mathias, Rigaud and Millefiori. There are literally hundreds to choose from at all price levels (this site is very fast, so don't panic) and you can also make your selection by brand, fragrance, colour and season. Once you've made your choice you can ask them to gift wrap it for you and include a handwritten message.

Site Usability:	★★★★★	Based:	UK
Product Range:	★★★★★	Express Delivery Option? (UK)	Yes
Price Range:	Medium	Gift Wrapping Option?	Yes
Delivery Area:	Worldwide	Returns Procedure:	Down to you

www.laboutiquedelartisanparfumeur.com

If you're not already aware of this gorgeous collection of French fragrance and bath and body products by L'Artisan Parfumeur, with names such as

Mure et Musc, Figuier and Orchidée Blanche, then now's the time to discover what is a beautifully presented range and order it online. You'll also find unusual ideas such as the blackberry-shaped glass bottle, scented silk peonies and terracotta amber balls, all of which make exceptional gifts.

Site Usability:	★★★★	Based:	UK
Product Range:	★★★	Express Delivery Option? (UK)	Yes
Price Range:	Luxury	Gift Wrapping Option?	Automatic
Delivery Area:	Worldwide	Returns Procedure:	Down to you

www.loccitane.com

L'Occitane is another brand you're sure to have heard of, offering products ranging from personal care to home fragrance, all manufactured in traditional ways using natural ingredients, mainly from Provence. The range includes fragrance, body and hand care, bath and shower products, skin care, hair care and home fragrance with Verbena Harvest, Eau d'Ambre, Lavender, Orange and Green Tea forming the bases for eau de toilette, soaps, hand creams, shower gels and shampoos.

Site Usability:	★★★★★	Based:	UK
Product Range:	★★★★★	Express Delivery Option? (UK)	No
Price Range:	Medium	Gift Wrapping Option?	Yes
Delivery Area:	Worldwide	Returns Procedure:	Down to you

www.naturalmagicuk.com

Unlike almost all conventional candles (which contain paraffin wax and synthetic oils), Natural Magic candles are made from clean, pure vegetable wax, scented with the best-quality organic aromatherapy oils. They're also twice the size of the average candle (1 kg) with three wicks and up to 75 hours of burn time. Each candle has a specific therapeutic task, such as uplifting, inspiring, soothing and de-stressing, and all are beautifully packaged and perfect for treats and gifts.

Site Usability:	★★★★★	Based:	UK
Product Range:	★★★	Express Delivery Option? (UK)	Yes
Price Range:	Medium	Gift Wrapping Option?	No
Delivery Area:	Worldwide	Returns Procedure:	Down to you

www.ormondejayne.co.uk

Sometimes you feel that you'd really like to find a new range of fragrance and candles, one that most people haven't heard of but one that's totally luxurious and beautifully presented. That's exactly what you'll find here, with a unique range of fragrances such as the citrussy Osmanthus and floral Champaca. There are bath and body products to complement the fragrances, plus the most beautiful candles, and everything is gorgeously packaged.

Site Usability:	★★★★	Based:	UK
Product Range:	★★★	Express Delivery Option? (UK)	No
Price Range:	Luxury	Gift Wrapping Option?	Yes
Delivery Area:	Worldwide	Returns Procedure:	Down to you

www.penhaligons.co.uk

Penhaligons offers fragrance, candles and bath and body products for perfect and luxurious gifts for men and women. Choose from classics Lily of the Valley, Elizabethan Rose or Bluebell or the more modern and spicy Malabah, Artemesia or LP No 9. Each fragrance is matched up to its own shower gel, soap, body lotion and candle. Gift wrapping is gorgeous and free and they deliver worldwide.

Site Usability:	★★★★★	Based:	UK
Product Range:	★★★★★	Express Delivery Option? (UK)	Yes
Price Range:	Luxury	Gift Wrapping Option?	Automatic
Delivery Area:	Worldwide	Returns Procedure:	Down to you

www.rose-apothecary.co.uk

Here's a natural beauty website with a difference, as it offers lots of its own different, prettily packaged products such as rose petal bath and shower creme, lavender shampoo and luxurious gift boxes, plus J & E Atkinson fragrances, I Coloniali, Rice and Segreti Mediterranei, Yardley English Lavender, 4711 Cologne and Soir de Paris. The aromatherapy products, remedy oils and creams and massage oils are all blended in-house.

Site Usability:	★★★★	Based:	UK
Product Range:	★★★★	Express Delivery Option? (UK)	No
Price Range:	Medium	Gift Wrapping Option?	No
Delivery Area:	Worldwide	Returns Procedure:	Down to you

www.savonneriesoap.com

This is a beautiful website with an extremely luxurious feel where you can buy exquisitely packaged handmade soaps (think Flower Garden and Honey Cake), bath and body products such as Geranium and Bergamot Oil, perfect gift boxes and The Naughty Weekend Kit – take a look and you'll find out. Be warned, the photography alone makes you want to buy something immediately.

Site Usability:	★★★★★	Based:	UK
Product Range:	★★★	Express Delivery Option? (UK)	No
Price Range:	Luxury/Medium	Gift Wrapping Option?	No
Delivery Area:	Worldwide	Returns Procedure:	Down to You

www.spacenk.co.uk

Nars, Stila, Darphin, Laura Mercier, Eve Lom, Diptyque, Frederic Fekkai and Dr Sebagh are just some of the 60-plus brands offered here by this retailer, famous for bringing unusual and hard-to-find products to the UK. (So you don't have to go to New York any more to buy your Frederic Fekkai shampoo: shame.) This is also an excellent place for gifts as they offer a personalised message and gift wrapping service and next-day delivery if you need it. It's a well-designed and easy-to-navigate website with very clear pictures.

Site Usability:	★★★★★	Based:	UK
Product Range:	★★★★	Express Delivery Option? (UK)	Yes
Price Range:	Luxury/Medium	Gift Wrapping Option?	Yes
Delivery Area:	Worldwide	Returns Procedure:	Down to you

www.timothyhan.com

If you haven't already come across these luxurious candles, take a look now. Timothy Han has a small but gorgeous range, including aromatherapy candles with names such as Orange Grapefruit and Clove, Lavender and Scent of Fig, and his non-fragranced candles which are perfect for entertaining. You can also buy his candles in Bill Amberg's specially created leather travel case. Call for urgent deliveries.

Site Usability:	★★★★★	Based:	UK
Product Range:	★★★	Express Delivery Option? (UK)	Yes, but call them
Price Range:	Luxury/Medium	Gift Wrapping Option?	Yes
Delivery Area:	Worldwide	Returns Procedure:	Down to you

www.truegrace.co.uk

If you want to pamper someone with something small and beautiful and you don't want to spend a fortune, you should choose from the gorgeous candles here. All beautifully wrapped and in glass containers, you'll find the Never a Dull Day range in pretty printed boxes, with fragrances such as Vine Tomato, Stem Ginger and Hyacinth, and As It Should Be, the slightly more simply (but equally attractively) boxed candle in 37 fragrances, including Citrus, Cappuccino and Raspberry. Try them.

Site Usability:	★★★★	Based: UK	
Product Range:	★★★★	Express Delivery Option? (UK)	No
Price Range:	Medium	Gift Wrapping Option?	No
Delivery Area:	Worldwide	Returns Procedure:	Down to you

Also take a look at the websites below for pampering presents:

Website address	You'll find it in
www.zpm.com	Chapter 31: Traveller
www.cologneandcotton.com	Chapter 21: For New Mums
www.gorgeousthingsonline.com	Chapter 21: For New Mums
www.kennethturner.co.uk	Chapter 21: For New Mums
www.laline.co.uk	Chapter 21: For New Mums

Chapter 8

Spa and Experience Days

Gift vouchers for spas and spa days out are probably the kinds of gifts you'll give to someone you know very well and for special types of occasions. Most of them are quite expensive and you need to be certain that they'll be used, otherwise they're a complete waste of your money.

An excellent way of dealing with this is to organise a treat or trip that you'll go on too. That way not only can you be certain that your money is well spent but you get to go with. I really like the idea of that – don't you?

Sites to Visit

www.leadingspasoftheworld.com

All you need to know here is when you want to go (did I say this was for a gift? I must have been mad), roughly where you want to go, i.e. which country, and you're away. Use the excellent search facility to find the most luxurious spas throughout the world, where you can choose from spas with hydrotherapy, Ayurvedic spas, spas with Yoga, Pilates and Tai Chi, or somewhere gorgeous to just relax and be pampered.

Site Usability:	★★★★★	Delivery Area:	Worldwide
Product Range:	★★★★★	Based:	US
Price Range:	Luxury		

www.spabreak.co.uk

Spa Break offers comprehensive information on luxury spas all over the UK, with plenty of advice and pictures to help you make up your mind. You can purchase gift vouchers for a specific monetary value or type of break and these can be sent to you or to whomever you want, together with the relevant colour brochure. You can see exactly where each of the spas is in the UK and call for advice if you need to.

Site Usability:	★★★★★	Delivery Area:	UK
Product Range:	★★★★	Based:	UK
Price Range:	Luxury/Medium		

www.spafinder.com

You can find a spa anywhere in the world through the links on Spa Finder's website, although this particular resource is for the UK only. It's easy to use: you just click on Spa Search to find the types of services you want or use the Spa Guide first to narrow down your choice. You can order the worldwide Spa Directory here, check out day spa deals and group specials and buy gift vouchers to spas throughout Europe. Next time you need a bit of pampering, definitely take a look here.

Site Usability:	★★★★★	Delivery Area:	Worldwide
Product Range:	★★★★★	Based:	US
Price Range:	Luxury/Medium		

www.thanksdarling.com

Yes, thanks indeed, here are some wonderful pampering spa breaks and days out, mainly in the south of England. On ordering, you (or your recipient) are sent an open-dated voucher pack for the break you've chosen, whether it's a 'Special Chill Out Spa Break for Two' or just a 'Luxury Pamper Day'. You'll no doubt be extremely popular if you give one of these as a gift to someone – and hopefully you'll be invited along.

Site Usability:	★★★★	Delivery Area:	UK
Product Range:	★★★★	Based:	UK
Price Range:	Luxury/Medium	Express Delivery Option? (UK)	No

www.thespasdirectory.com

Whatever you're looking for, whether it's a relaxing and pampering day out, a Pilates class or fitness advice, you'll find it here using The Spa Directory's advanced search facility. There's almost too much to choose from as the site covers the whole world. Does it make you feel better or worse to discover that the spa of your dreams is in Baja, Mexico? However, you'll surely find one nearer to home while you wait for your chance to leap on a plane. The site is very clear and there are full profiles with pictures on every spa listed, plus a direct link to each spa's website.

Site Usability:	★★★★	Delivery Area:	Worldwide
Product Range:	★★★★	Based:	UK
Price Range:	Luxury/Medium		

Chapter 9

Jewellery

I always think of jewellery in three categories: The Real Thing – where you can spend as much as you want and the sky really is the limit; Accessible Jewels – where you buy real silver and gold, probably set with semi-precious stones; and Costume Pieces – big, bold and often sparkling pieces that make a statement but won't set you back as much as the rest.

Be careful when considering buying jewellery as a gift that you're certain it's something the recipient will like – fake thanks you do not want. Take a reading of what they wear usually and base your choice on that, coupled with the amount you have to spend. You're most likely to be successful with earrings (provided you know whether or not they have their ears pierced) or a pendant. Never buy what *you* would like, always choose for them. If you're unsure, buy something else.

** Your siteguide.com password is SG014. Please use this as the media code when subscribing for your free year's login.

Sites to Visit

www.bobijou.com

BoBijou is a reasonably priced, European designer jewellery brand offering a collection of chic, colourful pieces designed in-house and handmade combining natural cultured pearls and gemstones with silver and gold. Many designs carry the signature design feature, MLMF (Multi Look Multi Function), so a long design can be a belt, a lariat-style necklace, a chunky choker or a bracelet, making them very flexible and giving you more value for money. New styles are added each season.

Site Usability:	★★★★★	Based:	UK
Product Range:	★★★★	Express Delivery Option? (UK)	Yes
Price Range:	Luxury/Medium	Gift Wrapping Option?	No
Delivery Area:	EU	Returns Procedure:	Down to you

www.butlerandwilson.co.uk

Butler and Wilson is famous for its signature whimsical fashion jewellery and you can now choose from a glamorous and well-priced online range of necklaces, bracelets, earrings and brooches. Both costume jewellery and jewellery using semi-precious stones, such as rose quartz, agate, amber and jade, are available. You can also see (and order from) the collection of pretty printed and beaded handbags, plus bridal jewellery and accessories.

Site Usability:	★★★★	Based:	UK
Product Range:	★★★★	Express Delivery Option? (UK)	No
Price Range:	Medium	Gift Wrapping Option?	No, but everything is beautifully packaged
Delivery Area:	Worldwide	Returns Procedure:	Down to you

www.chapmansjewellery.co.uk

Dower and Hall, Vivienne Westwood, Shaun Leans, Colman Douglas Pearls and Mounir are just some of the designers you'll find here alongside their own range (although the collection changes regularly). While you can order everything online, if you should have a query they have staff you can call for advice. Some of the pieces are stunningly pretty (as is the website) and there are several clear views of each.

Site Usability:	★★★★★	Based:	UK
Product Range:	★★★★	Express Delivery Option? (UK)	No
Price Range:	Medium	Gift Wrapping Option?	Yes
Delivery Area:	UK	Returns Procedure:	Down to you

www.chezbec.com

For a pretty and well-priced jewellery fix from an attractive and helpful website, you need look no further. Chez Bec has an unusual selection sourced from designers around the world, incorporating shells, semi-precious stones, pearls, silver and glass beads. Most pieces retail for under £100 and everything is beautifully presented in Chez Bec's fuchsia pink gift boxes.

Site Usability:	★★★★★	Based:	UK
Product Range:	★★★★	Express Delivery Option? (UK)	Yes
Price Range:	Medium	Gift Wrapping Option?	Yes
Delivery Area:	Worldwide	Returns Procedure:	Down to you

www.emmachapmanjewels.com

Emma Chapman is a new jewellery designer, based in London, who creates beautiful and glamorous designer gemstone jewellery which is exotic with a contemporary edge. It's a covetable collection grouped by descriptions such as Beach Babe, Baroque Goddess and Indian Princess. Everything is individually made and reasonably priced, so if you see something you like you need to contact them immediately.

Site Usability:	★★★★	Based:	UK
Product Range:	★★★	Express Delivery Option? (UK)	No
Price Range:	Medium	Gift Wrapping Option?	No
Delivery Area:	Worldwide	Returns Procedure:	Down to you

www.icecool.co.uk

At Ice Cool you can select from a range of modern and classic well-priced jewels, including diamond studs, tennis bracelets, pendants and rings, mostly set in 18ct gold and with sparkling diamonds. Prices start at around £100. One of the best things here is the Trend section, where you can find out what you should be wearing jewellery-wise this year. There is also Discover Diamonds, where you can read all you could possibly want to know (and more) about what are definitely my favourite stones.

Site Usability:	★★★★★	Based:	UK
Product Range:	★★★★	Express Delivery Option? (UK)	No
Price Range:	Medium	Gift Wrapping Option?	No
Delivery Area:	Worldwide	Returns Procedure:	Down to you

www.jewel-garden.co.uk

New online jewellery company Jewel Garden offers an attractive range of well-priced jewellery by modern designers that you won't find in the stores. They concentrate on silver and semi-precious stones, such as smoky quartz, agate, turquoise and citrine, plus pearl, crystal and coloured glass. Combine this with clear layout, fast worldwide delivery and gift wrapping services and this becomes a very attractive place to shop for gifts or treats.

Site Usability:	★★★★★	Based:	UK
Product Range:	★★★	Express Delivery Option? (UK)	Yes
Price Range:	Medium/Very Good Value	Gift Wrapping Option?	Yes
Delivery Area:	Worldwide	Returns Procedure:	Down to you

www.kabiri.co.uk

Kabiri is a jewellery shop on London's Marylebone High Street, carrying an eclectic range of modern, international designers such as Wendy Nichol, Adina, Carolina Bucci, Pippa Small and Tracy Matthews. The website's search facility is excellent – you can look by designer, type of jewellery and price – and as there's so much to see I suggest you use it. Be prepared to spend some time here – with this amount of choice you're bound to find something you like. For express delivery, call them.

Site Usability:	★★★★★	Based:	UK
Product Range:	★★★★★	Express Delivery Option? (UK)	Yes
Price Range:	Luxury/Medium	Gift Wrapping Option?	No
Delivery Area:	Worldwide	Returns Procedure:	Down to you

www.linksoflondon.com

Links of London is well known for an eclectic mix of jewellery in sterling silver and 18ct gold, charms and charm bracelets, cufflinks, gorgeous gifts and leather and silver accessories for your home. Inevitably each season they design a new collection of totally desirable pieces (in other words, I want them), such as the 'Sweetie Rolled Gold Bracelet', or 'Annoushka' gold and ruby charm. This website is perfect for gifts and if you need something sent in a hurry they offer an express service worldwide.

Site Usability: ★★★★★		Based:	UK
Product Range: ★★★★★		Express Delivery Option? (UK)	Yes
Price Range:	Luxury/Medium	Gift Wrapping Option?	Yes
Delivery Area:	Worldwide	Returns Procedure:	Down to you

www.manjoh.com

On Manjoh's attractively designed contemporary jewellery website, you'll find designers such as Izabel Camille, Benedicte Mouret, Vinnie Day and Scott Wilson and the list is regularly being updated. Most recent additions include DAY Jewels, a luxury jewellery line from Day Birger et Mikkelsen, which they sell exclusively online, and ultra fashionable R jewellery. The site also includes monthly features on the latest trends and interviews with designers.

Site Usability: ★★★★★		Based:	UK
Product Range: ★★★		Express Delivery Option? (UK)	Yes
Price Range:	Medium	Gift Wrapping Option?	Yes
Delivery Area:	Worldwide	Returns Procedure:	Down to you

www.pascal-jewellery.com

Here's a collection of timeless stylish jewellery from a retailer that was established in Liberty of London about 25 years ago and which you can now find in stores such as Harvey Nichols and Harrods. As a member of the National Association of Goldsmiths, you can be sure that you're buying real quality. The collection is updated at least four times a year, so you can be tempted regularly. Prices start at around £50 (and average about £300).

Site Usability: ★★★★★		Based:	UK
Product Range: ★★★★		Express Delivery Option? (UK)	No
Price Range:	Luxury/Medium	Gift Wrapping Option?	Yes
Delivery Area:	UK	Returns Procedure:	Down to you

www.piajewellery.com

Pia has a quick and clever website where you can choose from the creative jewellery by type or browse page by page through the catalogue. The pictures of this modern, well-priced jewellery range are extremely clear and definitely make you want to buy. There are natural stones such as carnelian, agate, labradorite and coral mixed with silver, all turned into very wearable necklaces, earrings and bracelets. They also offer soft leather handbags, a small selection of leather and cashmere clothing and pretty scarves and shawls.

Site Usability:	★★★★★	Based:	UK
Product Range:	★★★★	Express Delivery Option? (UK)	Yes
Price Range:	Medium	Gift Wrapping Option?	Yes
Delivery Area:	Worldwide	Returns Procedure:	Down to you

www.reglisse.co.uk

For those of you who are looking for something different and unusual, take a look round here. This collection of accessories and jewellery, created by an eclectic group of modern luxury designers, includes some beautiful pieces, such as the lizard-embossed calfskin passport cover, asymmetric glass wine carafe and crystal and hammered gold necklace. There's a good choice at a wide range of prices and a speedy delivery service within the UK.

Site Usability:	★★★★★	Based:	UK
Product Range:	★★★★	Express Delivery Option? (UK)	Yes
Price Range:	Luxury/Medium	Gift Wrapping Option?	Yes
Delivery Area:	Worldwide	Returns Procedure:	Down to you

www.swarovski.com

Most people have almost certainly heard of Swarovski (and seen those sparkling faceted crystal collectibles and objects). You may also have passed their glorious shops with glittering and stylish jewellery and accessories inside (and I mean really glittering – I always find them far too tempting). You'll no doubt be delighted to know that you can buy a wide selection online, all set with the signature crystals and extremely hard to resist.

Site Usability:	★★★★★	Based:	Germany
Product Range:	★★★★★	Express Delivery Option? (UK)	No
Price Range:	Medium	Gift Wrapping Option?	Yes
Delivery Area:	Worldwide	Returns Procedure:	Down to you

Chapter 10

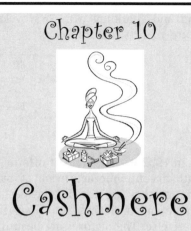

Cashmere

I'm not suggesting that you should go out and buy a cashmere sweater as a gift unless you know the person it's intended for very well and want to spend quite a lot, in which case make sure that you're buying the colour and style (and size, of course) for them rather than for you.

These online retailers also offer some very special pieces, plus gorgeous pashminas, scarves and other small accessories, and these all make lovely presents. If you're buying a pashmina or scarf, don't try to be clever with the colour unless you know that it will suit the recipient. Green may be the 'of the moment' colour but black (boring, I know, but so wearable) or a great neutral are far, far safer and will be worn for years.

Sites to Visit

www.belindarobertson.com

Award-winning Belinda Dickson, CEO of Belinda Robertson, is a knit-wear designer whose international reputation for quality, colour and modern eclectic style has earned her the affectionate title of 'Queen of Cashmere'. On her website you'll find her two different labels, the White Label collection, offering affordable but beautifully designed cashmere, and her signature Cashmere Couture range of the finest cashmere made exclusively in Scotland and sparkling with Swarovski crystals and satin trims, all available in up to 120 colours.

Site Usability:	★★★★	Based:	UK
Product Range:	★★★★	Express Delivery Option? (UK)	Yes
Price Range:	Luxury/Medium	Gift Wrapping Option?	Yes
Delivery Area:	Worldwide	Returns Procedure:	Down to you

www.brora.co.uk

Brora was established in 1992 with the aim of offering classic, fine-quality Scottish cashmere with a contemporary twist, at prices that offer real value for money. Although they are not the cheapest, they offer some of the best quality available and in designs and a selection of colours that you won't find anywhere else. The pictures are beautifully clear and you'll almost certainly find them hard to resist. The collection extends to men, children and babies.

Site Usability:	★★★★★	Based:	UK
Product Range:	★★★★	Express Delivery Option? (UK)	Yes
Price Range:	Luxury/Medium	Gift Wrapping Option?	Yes
Delivery Area:	Worldwide	Returns Procedure:	Down to you

www.isla.uk.com

Isla was set up to provide high-quality cashmere accessories primarily in vibrant colours, using Scottish yarn and production techniques. This is not a big collection, but a lovely choice of scarves and knitted pashminas, mittens (for girls) and beanies (for guys) available in colours such as viola, midnight blue, shocking pink and turquoise, plus naturals black, white, grey and oatmeal.

Site Usability:	★★★★	Based:	UK
Product Range:	★★★	Express Delivery Option? (UK)	No
Price Range:	Medium	Gift Wrapping Option?	No
Delivery Area:	UK and US	Returns Procedure:	Down to you

www.purecollection.com

This is chic, high-quality cashmere in a wide range of styles, with the emphasis on modern shapes and the new season's colours. Alongside the less expensive range they also offer 'Superfine' cashmere at a higher price which is perfect for layering or wearing on its own. Delivery and service are excellent and the prices are very good too. If you want something particular in a hurry, call to make sure it's in stock and you can have it the next day.

Site Usability:	★★★★★	Based:	UK
Product Range:	★★★★	Express Delivery Option? (UK)	Yes
Price Range:	Luxury/Medium	Gift Wrapping Option?	Yes
Delivery Area:	Worldwide	Returns Procedure:	Free

Chapter 11

Fashion Accessories

These are the places where you can find some wonderful girly gifts and they often cover a surprisingly wide range, from prettily packaged toiletries to sparkly earrings and necklaces, plus gorgeous handbags and clothing from silk camis to full outfits.

These sites specialise in an eclectic mix – some are small, boutique-style online stores, while others are full-on designer fashion retailers, but at all of them you can find totally 'of the moment' pieces that any fashionista would be truly delighted to receive. Not only that – most of them offer lovely gift wrapping as well, so your presents can be sent straight out for you.

Sites to Visit

www.anusha.co.uk

This is a boudoir-style online boutique where you can buy pretty and indulgent designer pieces, from clothes, luxurious loungewear, vintage-inspired jewellery and unique accessories to pampering gifts. When your order arrives it will be beautifully wrapped in layers of fuchsia tissue paper and finished off with a feather butterfly and chocolate-brown Anusha label. So come here for a treat for yourself or for perfect presents. They deliver worldwide and in the UK you need to allow 5–7 days.

Site Usability:	★★★★	Based:	UK
Product Range:	★★★	Express Delivery Option? (UK)	No
Price Range:	Medium	Gift Wrapping Option?	Yes
Delivery Area:	Worldwide	Returns Procedure:	Down to you

www.belenechandia.com

Here are soft leather handbags in a choice of colours, with names such as Rock Me, Hold Me and Take Me Away by accessory label Belen Echandia. Choose your style of handbag, check out the measurements and detailing and then use the semi-bespoke service to select your particular leather, from croc finish to metallics and brights to neutrals. These are definitely at the luxury end of the market, with prices starting at about £400, but they're unique and different and investments that'll last you for years.

Site Usability:	★★★★	Based:	UK
Product Range:	★★★	Express Delivery Option? (UK)	Yes
Price Range:	Luxury	Gift Wrapping Option?	Yes
Delivery Area:	Worldwide	Returns Procedure:	Down to you

www.black.co.uk

If you're not a black and neutral person, you won't like this website. However, if, like me, you're known for being a black addict, you should have a browse through this website offering beautiful – and beautifully photographed – accessories, such as shawls and scarves, gloves, bags, jewellery and belts in (you guessed it) black, grey, cream and beige. Look out for the new swimwear and homeware ranges.

Site Usability:	★★★★	Based:	UK
Product Range:	★★★	Express Delivery Option? (UK)	Yes
Price Range:	Luxury/Medium	Gift Wrapping Option?	Yes
Delivery Area:	Worldwide	Returns Procedure:	Down to you

www.brittique.com

Brittique is a beautifully designed new online boutique featuring designers such as Amanda Wakeley, Maria Grachvogel and Louise Amstrap and the list is sure to grow. You'll also find accessories and jewellery by Vinnie Day, Lucy J, Deal and Wire and more, some of which would make perfect gifts, particularly with their speedy delivery services and high-quality packaging. The express service covers the UK and Europe. Keep an eye on this website – it's excellent.

Site Usability: ★★★★★	Based:	UK
Product Range: ★★★★★	Express Delivery Option? (UK)	Yes
Price Range: Luxury/Medium	Gift Wrapping Option?	Yes
Delivery Area: Worldwide	Returns Procedure:	Down to you

www.caxtonlondon.com

Browse round here for a wide choice of high-quality gifts, including leather travel accessories, photograph albums, address books and organisers in colours such as cerise, white, sky blue, lilac and lime. You'll also find games such as backgammon and solitaire, silver pens by Lalex, the Mont Blanc Meisterstuck range and delightful baby and christening gifts. Postage within the UK is free and they offer a free gift wrapping service as well.

Site Usability: ★★★★	Based:	UK
Product Range: ★★★★	Express Delivery Option? (UK)	No
Price Range: Medium/Very Good Value	Gift Wrapping Option?	Yes
Delivery Area: Worldwide	Returns Procedure:	Down to you

www.celtic-sheepskin.co.uk

There are some excellent clothes and accessories here, particularly for the winter months, including chic Toscana shearling jackets and coats, gloves, scarves, sheepskin-lined boots and slippers, waistcoats and gilets and cute shearling duffles and boots for children. Prices are reasonable and everything's clearly pictured. If you want to order a coat or jacket, you'll probably have to wait a couple of weeks, so take a look now.

Site Usability: ★★★★★	Based:	UK
Product Range: ★★★	Express Delivery Option? (UK)	No
Price Range: Luxury/Medium	Gift Wrapping Option?	No
Delivery Area: UK	Returns Procedure:	Down to you

www.cityorg.co.uk

You may well not have heard of this excellent website, offering Filofax organisers and accessories, Cocinelle handbags, wallets and keyrings, Lo

Scritto leather-bound notebooks in lots of colours, Quo Vadis diaries, Paul Smith handbags and accessories, pens by Cross, Azuni jewellery, Paul Smith and Mont Blanc cufflinks, Leatherman tools and gadgets by Oregon Scientific. The website is easy to navigate and the pictures are large and clear. This is an excellent place for accessories.

Site Usability:	★★★★	Based:	UK
Product Range:	★★★★	Express Delivery Option? (UK)	No
Price Range:	Luxury/Medium	Gift Wrapping Option?	Yes
Delivery Area:	Worldwide	Returns Procedure:	Down to you

www.forzieri.com

Italian company Forzieri offers handbags and wallets by Dolce & Gabbanna, Prada, Tods, Gucci and Burberry, plus superb leather and shearling jackets, an excellent, stylish shoe collection, gloves, leather travel bags and other accessories. There's also a wide choice of reasonably priced, high-quality Italian brands. Very good descriptions are given about all the products, plus lots of different views, so you know exactly what you're buying. They offer gift wrapping and an express delivery worldwide.

Site Usability:	★★★★★	Based:	Italy
Product Range:	★★★★★	Express Delivery Option? (UK)	Yes
Price Range:	Luxury/Medium	Gift Wrapping Option?	Yes
Delivery Area:	Worldwide	Returns Procedure:	Down to you

www.heroshop.co.uk

There are lots of places you can buy leather goods online, but very few that offer the quality and service you'll find here. It's not a huge range but a selection of classic luggage and weekenders, photo albums, home accessories, document wallets, jewellery boxes and cosmetic bags for her, wet packs for him, plus shooting accessories and luxury dog leads, collars and baskets.

Site Usability:	★★★★	Based:	UK
Product Range:	★★★	Express Delivery Option? (UK)	No
Price Range:	Medium	Gift Wrapping Option?	No
Delivery Area:	Worldwide	Returns Procedure:	Down to you

www.julieslaterandson.co.uk

Everything on this website is beautifully pictured, so you'll know exactly what you're ordering. There's a wonderful selection of leather purses, gifts and travel accessories here and you'd have to search long and hard elsewhere to find the colour range offered, which includes pistachio, pale blue, meadow green, hot pink, carnation and royal blue. Delivery is worldwide, with an express delivery option for the UK, and they'll gift wrap for you as well.

Site Usability:	★★★★	Based:	UK
Product Range:	★★★	Express Delivery Option? (UK)	Yes
Price Range:	Medium	Gift Wrapping Option	Yes
Delivery Area:	Worldwide	Returns Procedure:	Down to you

www.notonthehighstreet.com

Notonthehighstreet.com has established itself as the home of some gorgeous small gift websites and the list of retailers and products is growing all the time. You'll find jewellery, scarves and shawls, pretty evening and day handbags, Cote Bastide and Willow bath and body products, unusual camisoles and t-shirts, albums and keepsake boxes, plus a selection of home accessories. Note that delivery will come from their partners and not from them so may take a few days.

Site Usability:	★★★★★	Based:	UK
Product Range:	★★★★★	Express Delivery Option? (UK)	No
Price Range:	Medium	Gift Wrapping Option	No
Delivery Area:	Worldwide	Returns Procedure:	Down to you

www.ollieandnic.com

Ollie & Nic offers a stylish and chic range of accessories at excellent prices, including pretty bags for day, evening and holiday, umbrellas, sunglasses, scarves, brooches and other accessories. The collection is very seasonal, with new products being introduced all the time, and each season will have a specific theme so you can visit this website regularly and you'll never be bored. There are good gift ideas here for anyone who collects accessories, particularly in the winter season.

Site Usability:	★★★★	Based:	UK
Product Range:	★★★	Express Delivery Option? (UK)	No
Price Range:	Medium	Gift Wrapping Option?	No
Delivery Area:	Worldwide	Returns Procedure:	Down to you

www.plumo.co.uk

At Plumo you'll always find something different and interesting, from a gold-trimmed basket to a floral print tote. They also offer homewares, clothes and accessories, including shoes and jewellery. It's not a huge collection but beautifully edited to be feminine and chic at the same time. There are some lovely ideas here for presents at any time of the year and express delivery and gift wrapping are just two of the services offered to make your life easy.

Site Usability:	★★★★	Based:	UK
Product Range:	★★★	Express Delivery Option? (UK)	Yes
Price Range:	Medium	Gift Wrapping Option?	Yes
Delivery Area:	Worldwide	Returns Procedure:	Down to you

www.valentineandfrench.co.uk

At the Valentine and French boutique there's a treasure trove full of accessories, home treats and gift ideas, such as glamorous clutch bags, unusual and beautifully fragranced body products, cashmere separates and pretty jewellery. This is an attractively designed website and you'll discover all the products under headings such as 'Stepping Out', 'Staying In', 'Little Pleasures' and 'Jewellery Box'.

Site Usability:	★★★★	Based:	UK
Product Range:	★★★	Express Delivery Option? (UK)	No
Price Range:	Medium	Gift Wrapping Option?	No
Delivery Area:	Worldwide	Returns Procedure:	Down to you

Also take a look at the following website for fashion accessories:

Website address	You'll find it in
www.aspinal.co.uk	Chapter 32: Christening Gifts

Chapter 12

Lingerie

Here are some great websites to point your other half to if you enjoy being given pretty lingerie (or perfect places to buy a treat for yourself). There's a good selection, much better than you can find in the shops, and what's really excellent here is that they make it so easy to find your size and what's in stock in your size, rather than you falling in love with something and then discovering that it's available only in a 32B.

Alongside the lingerie there's beautiful nightwear, lacy camisoles, swimwear, kaftans and wraps – so something for everyone. And most of these retailers are just waiting with their pretty packaging to make gift giving really special. Some also offer extra help for men (most of whom may well need it – sorry boys) to select something lovely and right for you.

Sites to Visit

www.belladinotte.com

This is a smiley website, with models in classic poses showing pretty nightwear, lingerie and other accessories. Italian silk-blend, lace-edged camisoles and tops come in modern colours depending on the season and they also offer attractive nightwear and a small range of lingerie.

You have the option of giving a gift voucher from Bella di Notte or alternatively selecting something yourself and having it wrapped into one of their burgundy gift boxes with your personal message.

Site Usability:	★★★★	Based:	UK
Product Range:	★★★★	Express Delivery Option? (UK)	Yes
Price Range:	Medium	Gift Wrapping Option?	Yes
Delivery Area:	Worldwide	Returns Procedure:	Down to you

www.bonsoirbypost.com

Here you'll find pretty nightwear from Bonsoir by Post, ranging from soft, dreamy cotton to Italian lace and pure silk in a range of colours. Be warned though, if your taste is for black or neutral you won't find much of it here, but rather colours such as ash, heather, pale blue and white. There's also a small range of loungewear, including Yoga pants, fluffy towels and bath robes, plus scented candles, mules, beaded slippers and bedsocks. There's a special gift section where they've picked their favourites, which can be boxed and sent out for you.

Site Usability:	★★★★	Based:	UK
Product Range:	★★★	Express Delivery Option? (UK)	Yes
Price Range:	Medium/Very Good Value	Gift Wrapping Option?	Yes
Delivery Area:	Worldwide	Returns Procedure:	Down to you

www.cku.com

This is the website for Calvin Klein's modern, minimal range of underwear and I should tell you right now that if you're looking for anything larger than a D (or in a very few styles a DD) cup, you should move on fast. If you're within their size range you'll probably find the collection of beautiful, sexy and not overpriced lingerie and basics quite irresistible. For guys there are the classic boxers, dressing gowns and other nightwear. This is an excellent place to buy for older teens, both boys and girls – certainly my kids – love it all.

Site Usability:	★★★★★	Based:	UK
Product Range:	★★★	Express Delivery Option? (UK)	No
Price Range:	Medium	Gift Wrapping Option?	No, but gift packaging at Christmas
Delivery Area:	Worldwide using their country-specific sites	Returns Procedure:	Free

www.contessa.org.uk

Contessa has a superb selection of bras and briefs in every colourway and style you can think of. You can choose by brand, style, size or colour, or to make matters even easier just click on your size on the Home Page and everything that they have in stock can be viewed straight away. The emphasis here is very much on price and they frequently have some excellent offers. They'll ship worldwide and gift wrap your order as well.

Site Usability:	★★★★★	Based:	UK
Product Range:	★★★★	Express Delivery Option? (UK)	Yes
Price Range:	Medium/Very Good Value	Gift Wrapping Option?	Yes
Delivery Area:	Worldwide	Returns Procedure:	Down to you

www.elingerie.uk.net

This is a calm, well-photographed and easy-to-navigate website, offering brands such as Rigby and Peller, Chantelle, Janet Reger, Huit, Freya, Splendour, Panache and lots more. The products are all very easy to see, although I suggest you search by size rather than pick on a range and find it's not available. There's also lots of help for men buying lingerie as gifts, plus a gift wrap service.

Site Usability:	★★★★	Based:	UK
Product Range:	★★★★	Express Delivery Option? (UK)	No
Price Range:	Luxury/Medium	Gift Wrapping Option?	Yes
Delivery Area:	Worldwide	Returns Procedure:	Down to you

www.figleaves.com

If you can't find it here, you may well not be able to find it anywhere as this is definitely one of the best collections of lingerie, swimwear and sportswear available online. Almost every lingerie brand name is offered, from DKNY, Dolce & Gabbanna and Janet Reger to Sloggi, Gossard and Wonderbra, and delivery is free worldwide. All sizes are covered, from very small to very large, and there's a huge choice in just about every category. The service is excellent and they offer gift wrapping and speedy delivery anywhere.

Site Usability:	★★★★★	Based:	UK
Product Range:	★★★★★	Express Delivery Option? (UK)	Yes
Price Range:	Luxury/Medium/Very Good Value	Gift Wrapping Option?	Yes
Delivery Area:	Worldwide	Returns Procedure:	Free in the UK

www.glamonweb.co.uk

This is quite an unusual website, with some slightly strange translations (probably due to the fact that they're electronic, rather than done by real people). It offers lingerie, hosiery and nightwear by La Perla, Marvel and Malizia. There's beautiful and luxurious lingerie, with prices to match, and I would suggest that you make sure you know the La Perla size you need before you order as the sizing is not standard. If in doubt you can email or call the customer service team.

Site Usability:	★★★★	Based:	UK
Product Range:	★★★★	Express Delivery Option? (UK)	Yes
Price Range:	Luxury/Medium	Gift Wrapping Option?	No
Delivery Area:	Europe	Returns Procedure:	Down to you

www.heavenlybodice.com

This is a lingerie website which is particularly good for gifts and especially from him to her. You can choose from a wide range of designers, from Charnos and Warners to Naughty Janet and Shirley of Hollywood. There's an excellent selection of bridal lingerie, a separate section for larger sizes, swimwear by Fantasie, Panache and Freya, and gifts by price band or in the 'Naughty' category. There's also a gift guide specifically for men.

Site Usability:	★★★★	Based:	UK
Product Range:	★★★★	Express Delivery Option? (UK)	No
Price Range:	Luxury/Medium	Gift Wrapping Option?	Yes
Delivery Area:	Worldwide	Returns Procedure:	Down to you

www.hush-uk.com

Hush-uk.com has a well-designed and beautifully photographed website where there are lots of clothes for going to sleep in or just for lounging around, with nightdresses, pyjamas and gowns, vest tops, t-shirts and sloppy-joes and also kaftans and sarongs for the beach and sheepskin slippers. In the gift ideas section you can combine various items to be wrapped up together and they offer gift vouchers as well.

Site Usability:	★★★★	Based:	UK
Product Range:	★★★★	Express Delivery Option? (UK)	Yes
Price Range:	Medium	Gift Wrapping Option?	Yes
Delivery Area:	Worldwide	Returns Procedure:	Down to you

www.janetreger.co.uk

On Janet Reger's beautiful, dark website, there's the most gorgeous selection of lingerie, where the prices are definitely not for the faint-hearted. Once you've picked the style you like you can immediately see all the other items in the range, plus colourways and size options (don't expect large sizes here). This brand is totally about luxe and glamour, so be prepared to spend a small fortune – but on absolutely wonderful quality and style. Everything is despatched in one of their chic ivory gift boxes.

Site Usability:	★★★★★	Based:	UK
Product Range:	★★★★	Express Delivery Option? (UK)	Yes
Price Range:	Luxury	Gift Wrapping Option?	Yes
Delivery Area:	Worldwide	Returns Procedure:	Down to you

www.ladybarbarella.com

Specialising in exclusive vintage pieces, decadent silks and burlesque styles, plus designs aimed at the many of us who can't fit into a 32B, at Lady Barbarella you can browse through a delightful selection of less available designers, including Damaris Evans, Emma Benham, Frankly Darling, FleurT, Spoylt and Yes Master, plus many more. This is a prettily and cleverly designed website, well worth a look if you like something a bit different. They offer gift wrap and gift certificates and there's a Gentlemen's Gift Guide with some excellent advice.

Site Usability:	★★★★	Based:	UK
Product Range:	★★★	Express Delivery Option? (UK)	Yes
Price Range:	Medium	Gift Wrapping Option?	Yes
Delivery Area:	Worldwide	Returns Procedure:	Down to you

www.lasenza.co.uk

La Senza is an own-brand lingerie retailer originally based in Canada and now well established in the United Kingdom. There's a good choice of lingerie and nightwear, ranging from beautiful basics to seriously sexy styles, as well as bra accessories. It's great to know that retailers are actually catering for those who want something larger than a C cup – sizes here go from 30A to 38F. There are lots of different colours and styles and in the Gift Ideas section there are suggestions for pampering gifts and accessories, plus an interactive gift advice guide for men. Interactive? Hmmm.

Site Usability:	★★★★★	Based:	UK
Product Range:	★★★★★	Express Delivery Option? (UK)	Yes
Price Range:	Very Good Value	Gift Wrapping Option?	Yes
Delivery Area:	Worldwide	Returns Procedure:	Down to you

www.myla.com

Of course, chocolate body paint may be just what you're looking for, along with some of the more risqué items offered on this sexy lingerie website (I'll say no more), but if what you're looking for is really beautiful feminine lingerie, then just click into their lingerie section and ignore the rest. They also offer suspenders, thongs, feather boas, silk mules, camis and baby dolls and sizing goes up to a 36E in some parts of the range.

Site Usability:	★★★★	Based:	UK
Product Range:	★★★	Express Delivery Option? (UK)	Yes
Price Range:	Luxury/Medium	Gift Wrapping Option?	No
Delivery Area:	Worldwide	Returns Procedure:	Down to you

www.rigbyandpeller.com

Rigby and Peller has always been about making sure that you're wearing the correct size bra. You may know their shop, just round the side of Harrods, where you can be properly fitted and choose from a chic selection of lingerie. On their website they not only give you lots of advice on fit, but also the choice from a wide range of brands such as Aubade, Lejaby, La Perla and Marie Jo. Gift services include luxury gift wrapping and vouchers, plus advice for men buying lingerie as a present.

Site Usability:	★★★★	Based:	UK
Product Range:	★★★★	Express Delivery Option? (UK)	Yes
Price Range:	Luxury/Medium	Gift Wrapping Option?	Yes
Delivery Area:	Worldwide	Returns Procedure:	Down to you

www.sassyandrose.co.uk

If you're a collector of gorgeous nightwear (and definitely one of those who likes to look glam when she goes to bed rather than the novelty t-shirt kind), you should have a browse here at this pretty range of camisoles, chemises, nightdresses, kaftans and pjs in high-quality but well-priced silk and embroidered cotton. Their clever 'Please buy me this' facility enables you to send an email to your other half, telling them what you would like to receive. No, I didn't say subtle, I said clever.

Site Usability:	★★★★	Based:	UK
Product Range:	★★★	Express Delivery Option? (UK)	No
Price Range:	Medium	Gift Wrapping Option?	No
Delivery Area:	UK and call them for worldwide	Returns Procedure:	Down to you

www.sophieandgrace.co.uk

Sophie and Grace offers top-quality lingerie, nightwear and swimwear, including the bridal ranges of Honeymoon Pearls and Verde Veronica where you'll find garters, bras and briefs, basques and nightgowns with touches such as embroidered lace and pearl straps. This is a different and luxurious range of lingerie and if you're about to get married you'll no doubt want some to take away on honeymoon as well. Delivery is free and everything is automatically tissue wrapped and gift boxed.

Site Usability:	★★★★	Based:	UK
Product Range:	★★★	Express Delivery Option? (UK)	Yes
Price Range:	Luxury/Medium	Gift Wrapping Option?	Yes
Delivery Area:	UK. Call them for overseas	Returns Procedure:	Down to you

Also take a look at the following websites for lingerie:

Website address	You'll find it in
www.agentprovocateur.com	Chapter 33: Valentine's Day
www.glamorousamorous.com	Chapter 33: Valentine's Day
www.silkstorm.com	Chapter 33: Valentine's Day

Chapter 13

Home Accessories

Before buying gifts from this department, stop and think for a moment about the person you're buying for. Is her home modern, minimalist and neutral? Traditional country and decorated in rich, deep colours? Or city chic with splashes of brights? (And, of course, there are lot of other styles.)

It's really important to do this first in order to get it right as most people are aiming for a certain theme within their homes - even if they don't really know they're doing it. You can choose something that will work in perfectly or something that will immediately be hidden - or worse, given away.

Once you've identified their style, the selection is so much easier and you'll be able to find gifts here that someone will be surprised and delighted to receive. If all of the above is something you already know, I apologise, but I've been so surprised by some of the things people have given me for my home (very old barn conversion, dark rugs, deep colours and extremely traditional) that I thought it might be of help.

Sites to Visit

www.baer-ingram.com

Baer and Ingram design and print their own exclusive fabrics which you can order online. The collection includes florals, Toile de Jouy, patchwork, polka dots and stripes in a choice of colourways. You'll also find some lovely gifts and home accessories such as lighting, painted furniture, table linen and gifts for tinies. You can order most of the products online, but if you want something made to order, such as blinds, headboards, curtains or cushions, you need to give them a call.

Site Usability:	★★★★	Based:	UK
Product Range:	★★★★	Express Delivery Option? (UK)	No
Price Range:	Luxury/Medium	Gift Wrapping Option?	No
Delivery Area:	Worldwide	Returns Procedure:	Down to you

www.biju.co.uk

Luxurious bathrobes and towels, cashmere blankets (at a faint-inducing price) and throws and a wonderful collection of table linen, Missoni tableware, mats and trays are just some of the items you can choose from on this treasure trove of a website where they also offer enchanting children's bedding and bedroom accessories. There's so much here you need to have time for a good browse. They also offer a personalisation embroidery service on their bathrobes and towels to help you create totally individual gifts.

Site Usability:	★★★★	Based:	UK
Product Range:	★★★★	Express Delivery Option? (UK)	No
Price Range:	Luxury/Medium	Gift Wrapping Option?	No
Delivery Area:	Worldwide	Returns Procedure:	Down to you

www.bodieandfou.com

Bodie and Fou is a home accessories company named after its co-founders, French sisters Elodie and Karine, who decided to fill a gap in the market for simple, contemporary and unique home interiors. You can buy handmade glass candlesticks, unusual table linens and accessories and a wide range of Cote Bastide home and bath products here. It's not a large range, but everything is extremely beautiful and gorgeously photographed, so it's well worth a browse.

Site Usability:	★★★	Based:	UK
Product Range:	★★★	Express Delivery Option? (UK)	Yes
Price Range:	Medium	Gift Wrapping Option?	No
Delivery Area:	UK	Returns Procedure:	Down to you

www.bombayduck.co.uk

This is a pretty home gifts and interiors website with a wide range of ideas, from their own beautifully packaged candles to candy-coloured leather accessories, crystal glass chandeliers, vintage-style bathroom accessories and printed cushions. There's a wealth of gift suggestions, some expensive – the gorgeous vintage-style chandelier at £275 – and others extremely reasonable. They also have a special Christmas area which you can browse in season.

Site Usability:	★★★★	Based:	UK
Product Range:	★★★★	Express Delivery Option? (UK)	Yes
Price Range:	Luxury/Medium	Gift Wrapping Option?	No
Delivery Area:	Worldwide	Returns Procedure:	Down to you

www.brissi.co.uk

Brissi began life as an interiors store in Marlborough, Wiltshire and has now grown up to have two stores in London plus an excellent online shopping facility. Although many of the products on offer have a retro feel, the overall mood is chic and modern, with beautifully clear photography and mainly neutral colours. The range includes crystal perfume bottles, black and white Limoges tableware and classic glass. In the Gifts section you can shop by recipient or by price and although they don't offer gift wrapping as such, everything is sent out ribbon tied in tissue paper.

Site Usability:	★★★★★	Based:	UK
Product Range:	★★★★	Express Delivery Option? (UK)	Yes
Price Range:	Luxury/Medium	Gift Wrapping Option?	No
Delivery Area:	Worldwide	Returns Procedure:	Down to you

www.cabane.co.uk

Here's another website offering a wide selection of ideas for the home, influenced by traditional French style yet with a practical, modern twist. Think of simply furnished cabins with crackling log fires, perched high on hillsides, or wooden beach houses full of light and you'll get the mood that's being created here. You'll find pretty bedspreads, cushions and blankets, Savon de Marseilles soaps and candles, colourful linen and cotton napkins and tablecloths.

Site Usability:	★★★★	Based:	UK
Product Range:	★★★★	Express Delivery Option? (UK)	Yes
Price Range:	Medium	Gift Wrapping Option?	No
Delivery Area:	Worldwide	Returns Procedure:	Down to you

www.coffeeandcream.co.uk

This is a beautifully calm website to visit, offering attractively photographed and unusual home accessories, mainly in neutral shades. Think animal print candles, faux fur throws, smoky glasses, almond-coloured velvet quilts, black ceramic canisters and pale French Provençal cushions. For anyone who likes natural colours and five-star chic in their home, this is the place to find it.

Site Usability:	★★★★	Based:	UK
Product Range:	★★★	Express Delivery Option? (UK)	No
Price Range:	Luxury/Medium	Gift Wrapping Option?	Automatic
Delivery Area:	Worldwide	Returns Procedure:	Down to you

www.designersguild.com

You'll find Tricia Guild's gorgeously coloured bedlinen here, both for grown-ups and children, plus very different towels, bedspreads and throws, small leather goods and Fragrant Home from Designers Guild – a beautiful collection of home fragrance and luxury body products. If you haven't come across Designers Guild until now but you like pretty, colourful designs, take a look here.

Site Usability:	★★★★	Based:	UK
Product Range:	★★★	Express Delivery Option? (UK)	Yes
Price Range:	Luxury/Medium	Gift Wrapping Option	Yes
Delivery Area:	UK	Returns Procedure:	Down to you

www.dianaforrester.co.uk

On Diana Forrester's website there's a good choice of quite unusual gifts and decorative accessories for the home and garden, mainly from France but also from other parts of the world. Items range from a cute mouse salt and pepper set to vintage-style French storage jars, unusual vases and photo frames, fine porcelain and an original expresso set. You can also see pictures from Diana's shop in Edinburgh, which will definitely make you want to go there.

Site Usability:	★★★	Based:	UK
Product Range:	★★★	Express Delivery Option? (UK)	No
Price Range:	Medium	Gift Wrapping Option?	Yes
Delivery Area:	Worldwide	Returns Procedure:	Down to you

www.dibor.co.uk

Dibor is an independent, UK-based company offering continental-style furniture, home accessories and gifts. For your bedroom they have a selection of delightful French-inspired, hand-painted furniture, including cupboards, chests of drawers and pretty bedside tables, plus small accessories such as jewelled perfume bottles, French photo frames and Victorian Rose-covered toiletry bags.

Site Usability:	★★★	Based:	UK
Product Range:	★★★	Express Delivery Option? (UK)	Yes
Price Range:	Medium	Gift Wrapping Option?	No
Delivery Area:	Worldwide	Returns Procedure:	Down to you

www.emmabridgewater.co.uk

Emma Bridgewater is well known for her high-quality pottery and clever and attractive designs such as Polka Dots, Hugs and Kisses and Hearts, as well as her mug collections which include dogs, cats, birds and flowers. Every season she's bringing out new products, such as cutlery, glass, preserves and teas, all with her signature script. Almost every kitchen has one or two pieces of her pottery. The only question is, can you resist the urge to collect?

Site Usability:	★★★★★	Based:	UK
Product Range:	★★★★	Express Delivery Option? (UK)	Yes
Price Range:	Medium	Gift Wrapping Option?	Yes
Delivery Area:	Worldwide	Returns Procedure:	Down to you

www.grahamandgreen.co.uk

Graham & Green is a long-established retailer of home and lifestyle products, including candles, tableware, silk cushions, pretty etched glasses and duvet covers and quilts. They're quite hard to really categorise as the products are so widespread, but if I tell you that some of their bestsellers are bevelled mirrors, Chinese lanterns, lavender-scented bags and Penguin (as in the books) mugs, you'll probably get the idea.

Site Usability:	★★★★	Based:	UK
Product Range:	★★★	Express Delivery Option? (UK)	Yes
Price Range:	Medium	Gift Wrapping Option?	No
Delivery Area:	UK	Returns Procedure:	Down to you

www.in2decor.com

In2decor is an easy-to-navigate home accessory and gifts website where you can choose from one of the prettiest selections of traditional-style cushions, Venetian glass mirrors, unusual vases and candle holders (such as the monkey nuts candle holder I'm after) and Chinese-influenced porcelain. This is a good place to find gifts – the choice isn't enormous but what is there is different and attractive.

Site Usability:	★★★★★	Based:	UK
Product Range:	★★★★	Express Delivery Option? (UK)	No
Price Range:	Medium	Gift Wrapping Option?	No
Delivery Area:	UK	Returns Procedure:	Down to you

www.janconstantine.com

This is a collection of hand-embroidered fabric, cushions and lavender bags with themes such as Bees and Bugs, Seaside Collection, Botanical,

Rose and Classic, described as 'designed for today and destined to be the heirlooms of the future'. These are unique textiles and accessories which you'll probably want to collect and you'll find extremely hard to give away, although their present-giving potential is excellent.

Site Usability:	★★★★	Based:	UK
Product Range:	★★★	Express Delivery Option? (UK)	Yes
Price Range:	Medium	Gift Wrapping Option?	No
Delivery Area:	Worldwide	Returns Procedure:	Down to you

www.locketts.co.uk

Locketts of Hungerford offers a high-quality range of modern and traditional photograph albums, plus photo frames which range from glass and silver to leather and padded travel frames, most of which are made in the company's workshops in the UK. They also have social and sporting books, leather games sets, such as cards and backgammon, and easel picture stands. Use this site also if you need to have faded photographs restored.

Site Usability:	★★★★	Based:	UK
Product Range:	★★★★	Express Delivery Option? (UK)	No
Price Range:	Medium	Gift Wrapping Option?	No
Delivery Area:	Worldwide	Returns Procedure:	Down to you

www.ninacampbell.com

As you would expect, the website of well-known interior designer Nina Campbell is beautifully designed. On it you can choose from a range of her home accessories, including glassware, linens, patterned lambswool throws, small items such as match strikers and pretty bonbon bowls. You can also order her stunningly packaged home fragrance collection, which includes candles and room sprays.

Site Usability:	★★★★	Based:	UK
Product Range:	★★★	Express Delivery Option? (UK)	No
Price Range:	Luxury/Medium	Gift Wrapping Option?	No
Delivery Area:	Worldwide	Returns Procedure:	Down to you

www.objects-of-design.com

Here you'll find British designed and made gift and home accessory ideas, with everything being made either in small runs or specially for you. There's the Penguin collection of mugs, Emily Readett-Bayley bookends, wonderful Ferguson's Irish Linen and Phil Atrill crystal stemware – and that's just a small selection to give you an idea. You can search by product type or by supplier and create a wish list as you go. You could spend a great deal of time here and you'll find gifts for everyone.

Site Usability:	★★★★	Based:	UK
Product Range:	★★★★★	Express Delivery Option? (UK)	Yes
Price Range:	Medium	Gift Wrapping Option?	Yes
Delivery Area:	Worldwide	Returns Procedure:	Down to you

www.oldeglory.co.uk

Having spent a great deal of time in the US due to the fact that my mother-in-law lives in Maryland, I've become really attached to the old-style quilts, Shaker boxes and cushions. For that reason I'm delighted to have found this website, established by an American who moved to the UK with her British husband and decided to bring a New England country store with her. For the quilts you'll have to wait a while as they are handmade; for other items you can immediately see the stock availability. If you need something urgently, give them a call and email them for international delivery prices.

Site Usability:	★★★★	Based:	UK
Product Range:	★★★★	Express Delivery Option? (UK)	No
Price Range:	Medium	Gift Wrapping Option?	No
Delivery Area:	Worldwide	Returns Procedure:	Down to you

www.polly-online.co.uk

Whereas on some websites you have to search for information about delivery and gift wrapping, at polly-online it's all clearly laid out for you, as are the items on offer, so buying is far easier. There's an eclectic, contemporary collection here – unusual sculptures and modern jewellery sit side by side with funky lighting, 'sculpted' cushions and pretty, reasonably priced sets of tableware, making this a good place for wedding gifts as well as gifts for other occasions.

Site Usability:	★★★★★	Based:	UK
Product Range:	★★★	Express Delivery Option? (UK)	No
Price Range:	Medium	Gift Wrapping Option?	Yes
Delivery Area:	Worldwide	Returns Procedure:	Down to you

www.queenshill.com

This is a family-run business offering a lovely selection of fabrics, wallpapers, gifts and home accessories from brands such as Mulberry, GP and J Baker, Harlequin and Fired Earth. The selection of mouthwatering gift ideas includes Mulberry candles, pot pourri, and James Brindley's range of faux fur (think leopard, llama, bear and cheetah) throws, cushions and hot water bottle covers. Resist if you can. You can request free samples of fabrics to help you finalise your choice.

Site Usability:	★★★★★	Express Delivery Option? (UK)	No
Product Range:	★★★★★	Gift Wrapping Option?	No
Price Range:	Luxury/Medium	Returns Procedure:	Down to you
Delivery Area:	Worldwide		

www.thefrenchhouse.net

Here's everything from France, from tableware, linen and cutlery to toiletries by Christian Lenart and Savon de Marseilles and elegant Anduze garden pots. Also a selection of pretty bedlinen in traditional French designs, such as Toile de Jouy, Fleurs de Champs and Monogram. The descriptions and information about every item are clear and well written and everything is beautifully photographed.

Site Usability:	★★★★	Based:	UK
Product Range:	★★★★	Express Delivery Option? (UK)	No
Price Range:	Medium	Gift Wrapping Option?	No
Delivery Area:	UK	Returns Procedure:	Down to you

Section 3
Strictly for Him?

S o why the question mark, you may be asking. Well, I thought that there had to be a question mark here as although these online retailers are very much geared for the man in the family, there are also ideas for everyone, from pampering 'experience days' (how I hate that expression) to gifts for girls even within some of the men's clothing websites.

There are also beautiful writing instruments, high-quality wallets and purses and games for all generations, so if you're looking for a gift for a girlfriend but you've run out of ideas, do take a look. Needless to say, if you're searching out something special for your man, this is a great place, along with the enthusiasts' websites in the section below.

Chapter 14

Gadgets, Games and Experience Days

ou may instinctively rush past this chapter, having previously given too many 'clever' gadgets and gizmos, which after the first rush of enthusiasm got put away, never to see the light of day again. Most of the gadget retailers have now wised up and offer, together with the 'silly' gifts, some useful and fun ideas, so do take a look.

With regards to specialist days out, do take care. You can spend a great deal of money here on something that gets forgotten and never used, ergo your money is completely wasted. Make sure that the person you're giving an 'experience' to is likely to want to use it and then check that they do – book it for them and go with if necessary. I say this because twice my family have been given this type of gift and twice they haven't organised themselves to use it. Daft or what?

Sites to Visit

http://eurostore.palm.com

At this worldwide specialist in hand-held computers you can purchase a wide range of products, from the newest, state-of-the-art compact models to all the essential accessories to link your hand-held to your PC. As the world of hand-held computers seems to develop by the day (and it seems to me you need to be something of a boffin to be able to use them properly), you'll need all the excellent information they give you here. GPS solutions and SmartPhones are available as well.

Site Usability:	★★★★★	Based:	UK
Product Range:	★★★★★	Express Delivery Option? (UK)	Yes
Price Range:	Luxury/Medium	Gift Wrapping Option?	No
Delivery Area:	Worldwide	Returns Procedure:	Down to you

www.chessbaron.co.uk

If you know someone who's a chess enthusiast, you'll almost certainly find something for them from this retailer based in Taunton, Somerset, offering just artisan-made chess boards and pieces, so if you're looking for any other type of game you'll need to go somewhere else. There are over 100 sets to choose from, from well-priced travel sets retailing for under £50 to exquisitely made rosewood or ebony sets at about £300.

Site Usability:	★★★★★	Based:	UK
Product Range:	★★★★	Express Delivery Option? (UK)	No
Price Range:	Luxury/Medium	Gift Wrapping Option?	No
Delivery Area:	Worldwide	Returns Procedure:	Down to you

www.greatexperiencedays.co.uk

Here if you're looking for a gift for an active person you can choose between driving a Ferrari or Porsche 996, dual-control flying lessons or clay pigeon shooting (to name just a few). Alternatively you can organise a pampering day out or simply purchase an original newspaper for the special date. They'll ship (items that can be shipped, of course) anywhere in the world and offer standard or express delivery for gifts and vouchers in the UK.

Site Usability:	★★★★★	Based:	UK
Product Range:	★★★★★	Express Delivery Option? (UK)	Yes
Price Range:	Luxury/Medium	Gift Wrapping Option?	Experiences arrive as a gift pack
Delivery Area:	Worldwide	Returns Procedure:	Down to you

www.iwantoneofthose.co.uk

An irresistible (and cleverly designed) gift and gadget shop with a huge choice and a well-designed website. You can search by price or product type and there's a wide range at all levels. With excellent animation for most products, you can choose from gadgets for garden, kitchen and office, plus the inevitable toys and games. They offer same-day delivery, free standard delivery on orders over £50 and are happy to ship to you anywhere in the world.

Site Usability:	★★★★★	Based:	UK
Product Range:	★★★★★	Express Delivery Option? (UK)	Yes
Price Range:	Medium/Very Good Value	Gift Wrapping Option?	Yes
Delivery Area:	Worldwide	Returns Procedure:	Down to you

www.microanvika.com

Here's an online site with an offline presence in Tottenham Court Road and Selfridges, offering the latest in computers, cameras and audio equipment, including ipods and all the accessories. Expect a good choice and excellent service – they do know what they're talking about and really want to help. Being a slightly less well-known retailer, Micro Anvika is a good place to look if you're trying to buy that hot new product just before Christmas.

Site Usability:	★★★★★	Based:	UK
Product Range:	★★★★	Express Delivery Option? (UK)	Yes
Price Range:	Medium	Gift Wrapping Option?	No
Delivery Area:	Worldwide	Returns Procedure:	Down to you

www.oregonscientific.co.uk

Oregon Scientific, established in the US in 1989, creates electronic products for modern lifestyles. Its innovative range is the combination of cutting-edge US technology and stylish European design. You've no doubt seen their stylish wireless weather stations and thermometers, but did you know that you can also find the world's slimmest radio-controlled alarm clock or a Barbie B Book learning laptop on this irresistible website? Plus there are loads more ideas, ranging from the very reasonable to the really quite expensive.

THE SHOPAHOLIC'S GUIDE TO BUYING GORGEOUS GIFTS ONLINE

Site Usability:	★★★★★	Based:	UK
Product Range:	★★★	Express Delivery Option? (UK)	Yes
Price Range:	Luxury/Medium	Gift Wrapping Option?	No
Delivery Area:	UK	Returns Procedure:	Down to you

www.paramountzone.com

Paramount Zone offers an extensive and carefully selected choice of gadgets, games, boys' toys, bar items, sports gadgets (a good selection), mp3 players, executive items/toys, bachelor pad stuff, gift ideas and lifestyle accessories – and these are just some of the items you'll find. The majority of UK address orders are despatched the same day for 1-2-day delivery and they're happy to deliver worldwide.

Site Usability:	★★★★	Based:	UK
Product Range:	★★★★	Express Delivery Option? (UK)	Yes
Price Range:	Luxury/Medium	Gift Wrapping Option?	No
Delivery Area:	Worldwide	Returns Procedure:	Down to you

www.redletterdays.co.uk

One of the best 'experience' day providers (you've probably seen their brochures and packs in some of the larger stores), Red Letter Days makes it easy for you to choose between flying, driving and some serious adventurer experiences. They also offer some great junior options, plus body and soul pampering and luxurious days out, such as lunch on the Orient Express. Once you've ordered what you want, it will be sent out in an attractive gift pack to the recipient.

Site Usability:	★★★★★	Based:	UK
Product Range:	★★★★★	Express Delivery Option? (UK)	Yes
Price Range:	Luxury/Medium	Gift Wrapping Option?	No
Delivery Area:	UK	Returns Procedure:	Down to you

www.sciencemuseumstore.com

Next time you go to London, pay a visit to the Science Museum, where you can take a Moon Walk, check out the Wild Safari or examine the Spy Car. If you can't get there you can find a number of fun and innovative products at the online shop. A rocket that flies using vinegar and baking soda to demonstrate Newton's Third Law of Motion, for example, and a light that floats in mid-air as if by magic. Just two of the interesting and fun gifts you can find here.

Site Usability:	★★★★★	Based:	UK
Product Range:	★★★★	Express Delivery Option? (UK)	Yes
Price Range:	Medium	Gift Wrapping Option?	No
Delivery Area:	UK	Returns Procedure:	Down to you

www.shopping-emporium-uk.com

This is a brightly coloured, unsophisticated website offering the highest quality Italian-made games sets for backgammon, dominoes and solitaire, bridge, roulette, poker and other games, contained in unique boxes and travel cases made of mahogany, walnut and high-quality leather. They also offer mini football and billiard tables and lots of other games. This is definitely the top end of the market, but the prices are not unreasonable for what you're buying.

Site Usability:	★★★★	Based:	UK
Product Range:	★★★	Express Delivery Option? (UK)	No
Price Range:	Luxury/Medium	Gift Wrapping Option?	No
Delivery Area:	Worldwide	Returns Procedure:	Down to you

www.thegadgetshop.com

Browse this online catalogue for some of the funniest, coolest gadgets you can buy, with everything from the frivolous to the functional, the digital to the downright silly. You'll find Big Boys' Toys, Retro Toys, Fun Stuff, Star Wars and iPod accessories here too. They'll ship all over the world and offer an express delivery service in the UK. This is a particularly good website for mid to older teenagers, so if you have one of those to buy for, take a good look round.

Site Usability:	★★★★★	Express Delivery Option? (UK)	Yes
Product Range:	★★★★★	Gift Wrapping Option?	Yes
Price Range:	Medium/Very Good Value	Returns Procedure:	freepost or via the customer services
Delivery Area:	Worldwide		department
Based:	UK		

www.thesharperedge.co.uk

Originally in the mobile phone industry, this retailer branched out into up-to-the-minute gadgets and gifts about five years ago and specialises in keeping you au fait with the latest ideas on the market. It's an excellent store offering you clever and unusual suggestions, plus innovative household accessories. It's a good place to look if you need a last-minute present as they despatch aiming for next-day delivery and offer to wrap your present as well.

Site Usability:	★★★★	Based:	UK
Product Range:	★★★★	Express Delivery Option? (UK)	Yes
Price Range:	Medium	Gift Wrapping Option?	Yes
Delivery Area:	Worldwide	Returns Procedure:	Down to you

www.trackday-gift-experiences.com

This is different from most of the 'experience' websites in that Trackday offers only driving experiences (at different venues in the South and Midlands) that you can select here for the boy racer in your life – if he hasn't got a fast enough car already. Send him rally driving, 4 x 4 off road, Formula 1 or off in a supercar, or even to learn how to manage a skid pan – excellent for everyone, particularly new drivers. You order vouchers, either open or for a particular experience, and they're valid for a year.

Site Usability:	★★★★	Based:	UK
Product Range:	★★★	Express Delivery Option? (UK)	Yes
Price Range:	Luxury/Medium	Gift Wrapping Option?	No
Delivery Area:	UK	Returns Procedure:	Down to you

Chapter 15

Cigars, Pens and Small Leathers

I f you know someone who smokes cigars, you almost certainly can't go wrong by buying them something from one of the two websites below, where you can find not just cigars but beautiful humidors, unusual cutters and lighters and other accessories. Just a word of warning: if you're not sure what type of cigar they smoke, either find out before you buy or, unless you're an expert, call one of these retailers and ask for advice.

With regards to pens and small leather gifts, there's a good choice below, from fun pens to Mont Blanc and high-quality wallets, purses and travel accessories. Also take a look in Chapter 18 for this type of present, where you'll find retailers such as Pickett, or Chapter 40 for Gucci and Smythson.

Cigars – Sites to Visit

www.simplycigars.co.uk

This is my favourite UK-based website offering cigars and humidors, plus some attractive accessories and gifts, wines and spirits. The cigars are expensive, as you would expect, however the site is beautifully designed, with clever drop-down menus and I know from experience that if you need a last-minute gift for a smoker (or wine lover), they will do their utmost to get it to you on time, so do have a look.

Site Usability:	★★★★★	Based:	UK
Product Range:	★★★★★	Express Delivery Option? (UK)	Yes
Price Range:	Luxury/Medium	Gift Wrapping Option?	No
Delivery Area:	Worldwide	Returns Procedure:	Down to you

www.topcubans.com

Buying cigars in the UK is an extremely expensive experience, particularly as you can buy from abroad and make a huge saving on superb quality products. Here is a wide choice, recommendations and advice you can trust and the delivery service is excellent. Not only that, but if you're a smoker you'll be bombarded with regular special offers and even recipes to match the time of year. This is a cigar smoker's paradise.

Site Usability:	★★★★★	Based:	Switzerland
Product Range:	★★★★★	Express Delivery Option? (UK)	No
Price Range:	Luxury/Medium	Gift Wrapping Option?	No
Delivery Area:	Worldwide	Returns Procedure:	Down to you

Pens and Small Leather Gifts – Sites to Visit

www.davidhampton.com

If you like to carry your cash and cards around in a superb quality leather wallet or purse, then this is the site for you. David Hampton of London has been supplying luxury leather goods to top hotels throughout the world for the last 20 years and now, for the first time, you can get your hands on some of the exquisitely crafted accessories online. Made out of the finest hides, items are available in colours such as aubergine and straw in addition to traditional black and brown.

Site Usability: ★★★★	Based:	UK
Product Range: ★★★	Express Delivery Option? (UK)	No
Price Range: Medium	Gift Wrapping Option?	No, but gift boxing is automatic
Delivery Area: Worldwide	Returns Procedure:	Down to you

www.filofax.co.uk

Your Filofax is now available in many different colours, sizes and styles, including mini, pocket, A5 and A4, black, red, pink, purple, pale blue and denim. And on this website you can see each and every one, plus all the refills and accessories such as calculators and pens. Together with this you can download their address software and also buy the luxury range of Yard O'Led pens here, making this a very good website for gifts.

Site Usability: ★★★★★	Based:	UK
Product Range: ★★★	Express Delivery Option? (UK)	Yes
Price Range: Medium	Gift Wrapping Option?	No
Delivery Area: Worldwide	Returns Procedure:	Down to you

www.mrpen.co.uk

Mr Pen has a clear website offering different ranges of pens, including Cross and Sheaffer, plus the gorgeously packaged Mount Everest Legacy. An engraving service is available for most pens for a small charge, while gift wrapping is free. Cut-glass inkwells, general cartridges and pen repairs are also available. If you're looking for a special nib, call them and you can expect a really personal service.

Site Usability: ★★★	Based:	UK
Product Range: ★★★★	Express Delivery Option? (UK)	Yes
Price Range: Luxury/Medium	Gift Wrapping Option?	Yes
Delivery Area: Worldwide	Returns Procedure:	Down to you

www.old.co.uk

Robert Old has an attractive and easy-to-navigate website, offering a high-quality range of men's gifts and accessories, including cashmere sweaters and scarves, leather gifts from cufflink boxes to travel alarm clocks, classic English briefcases and weekenders and shoes by Crockett and Jones. There's lots of clear information about each item and although standard delivery is the norm, they switch to express delivery towards Christmas.

Site Usability:	★★★★	Based:	UK
Product Range:	★★★★	Express Delivery Option? (UK)	Yes
Price Range:	Medium	Gift Wrapping Option?	No
Delivery Area:	Worldwide	Returns Procedure:	Down to you

www.penandpaper.co.uk

So what's different about this website, when you can find most of the same pens elsewhere? Well, apart from being well laid out and offering free delivery on orders over £50, it has a section for different and hard-to-find pens, including left-handed pens and the unusual Yoro pen. For gift ideas as well as the colourful Cross Morph Pens, there is a good range of the Fisher Space Pens, including lacquered Bullet Pens in bronze, Orange Slush, Purple Passion and Rainbow, Shuttle retractable pens, YK3 and Zero Gravity pens.

Site Usability:	★★★★	Based:	UK
Product Range:	★★★★	Express Delivery Option? (UK)	No
Price Range:	Luxury/Medium	Gift Wrapping Option?	No
Delivery Area:	Worldwide	Returns Procedure:	Down to you

www.penshop.co.uk

This is an attractive website offering one of the best selections of luxury pens, including Yard-o-Led's beautiful sterling silver fountain pens, ballpoints and pencils, Faber Castell pens in wood and silver, Mont Blanc (you need to phone to order) and Porsche Design steel pens. They also offer Lamy, Rotring, Shaeffer and Waterman, aim to send out the day you order and they'll deliver worldwide. There's a repairs service as well.

Site Usability:	★★★★	Based:	UK
Product Range:	★★★★	Express Delivery Option? (UK)	Yes
Price Range:	Luxury/Medium	Gift Wrapping Option?	No
Delivery Area:	Worldwide	Returns Procedure:	Down to you

www.peterdraper.co.uk

Offering Porsche design, Caran D'Ache and Lalex pens, plus Parker, Waterman, Lamy and Cross, and Filofax organisers and pen refills, Peter Draper has an unsophisticated website but one where you can expect to find very good service – free delivery on all orders over £25 and worldwide shipping. This is the kind of retailer where, if you have a query, you can call and speak to someone who really knows what they're talking about and can give you good advice, particularly if you're looking for a special gift.

Site Usability:	★★★	Based:	UK
Product Range:	★★★★	Express Delivery Option? (UK)	No
Price Range:	Luxury/Medium	Gift Wrapping Option?	No
Delivery Area:	Worldwide	Returns Procedure:	Down to you

Also check out these websites for pens and small leather gifts:

Website address	**You'll find them in:**
www.forzieri.com	Chapter 11: Fashion Accessories
www.gucci.com	Chapter 40: Luxury Gifts
www.pickett.co.uk	Chapter 18: For That Really Special Gift
www.smythson.co.uk	Chapter 40: Luxury Gifts

Chapter 16

Shirts and Accessories

No, I'm not suggesting that you give socks and handkerchiefs as presents – perish the thought. Even shirts are a risky gift unless it's your other half and you know exactly (and I mean exactly) what he likes. The times I've given my sons beautiful shirts for Christmas or birthdays and been accused of copping out; that clothes don't count as a present (ha ha) or that I've bought totally the wrong kind of stripe anyway. No, I wouldn't do that to you.

What you will find here, and what I think make excellent gifts, are the extra accessories – the clever cufflinks, high-quality belts and well-priced cashmere scarves and sweaters. Those I think are fine – now it's over to you.

Sites to Visit

www.albertthurston.com

If your man is of the brace-wearing variety, he'll love something from this retailer who's been in the business since 1820. Their collection has now evolved into a wonderful range which includes (as well as evening and regimental collections) 'huntin', shootin' and fishin', Patterns and Polka

Dots and the 'Jazz' collection, with its unique designs. Everything here is gift boxed and despatched worldwide free of charge. Prices are quoted in dollars until you check out in Worldpay, but they are based in the UK.

Site Usability:	★★★★	Based:	UK
Product Range:	★★★★	Express Delivery Option? (UK)	No
Price Range:	Luxury/Medium	Gift Wrapping Option?	No
Delivery Area:	Worldwide	Returns Procedure:	Down to you

www.ctshirts.co.uk

Well known for their colourful and well laid out printed catalogues, you can also order all their shirts, handmade shoes, ties and other accessories online. This website is extremely attractive and easy to navigate and the service offered is excellent. A range of shirt qualities and styles is available and they frequently have special offers. There's a good selection of casual shirts and knitwear, tailoring, ladies' shirts, cashmere knits and accessories and 'Tiny Tyrwhitt' clothing too.

Site Usability:	★★★★★	Based:	UK
Product Range:	★★★★★	Express Delivery Option? (UK)	Yes
Price Range:	Medium	Gift Wrapping Option?	Yes
Delivery Area:	Worldwide	Returns Procedure:	Down to you

www.gievesandhawkes.com

Situated at Number 1 Savile Row, London and established in 1785, Gieves and Hawkes has always stood for the very best in men's tailoring, whether for formal evening wear, suiting or casual wear. On this website you can now not only find out a great deal about the brand but also choose from the high-quality range of shirts, belts and braces, cufflinks, shoes and ties. Expect a classic selection, beautifully presented, and don't expect to find inexpensive prices, but you're definitely getting what you pay for here in terms of quality.

Site Usability:	★★★★	Based:	UK
Product Range:	★★★	Express Delivery Option? (UK)	No
Price Range:	Luxury/Medium	Gift Wrapping Option?	Yes
Delivery Area:	EU	Returns Procedure:	Down to you

www.harvieandhudson.com

Harvie and Hudson is a family-owned London shirtmaker and gentlemen's outfitter based in Jermyn Street, St James's and Knightsbridge. They offer a wide range of shirts online, from deep button-down to classic striped, plain and check shirts, unusual colour combinations and excellent country shirts. You can have your shirt custom made by selecting from their fabrics and then choosing your cuff and collar style and you can order too from their selection of ties, links, socks and evening wear shirts and accessories.

Site Usability:	★★★★	Based:	UK
Product Range:	★★★★★	Express Delivery Option? (UK)	No
Price Range:	Medium	Gift Wrapping Option?	No
Delivery Area:	Worldwide	Returns Procedure:	Down to you

www.hawesandcurtis.com

Hawes and Curtis was established in 1913 and is famous for being the creator of the backless waistcoat, which was worn under a tailcoat and was renowned for its comfort. Now on this excellently designed website you can choose from the range of classic and fashion shirts, ties, cufflinks, silk knots and boxer shorts. They also offer a range of women's classic, high-quality shirts in three different styles.

Site Usability:	★★★★	Based:	UK
Product Range:	★★★	Express Delivery Option? (UK)	No
Price Range:	Medium	Gift Wrapping Option?	No
Delivery Area:	Worldwide	Returns Procedure:	Down to you

www.hilditchandkey.co.uk

Recognised as one of the longest established Jermyn Street retailers of men's shirts and accessories (as well as some women's shirts), Hilditch manages to give you a top-of-the-range shopping experience without you having to leave home. Their shirts are not the cheapest, definitely, but if you order from them you can be absolutely certain that you'll get the high quality you're paying for. They also offer silk ties and some clothing.

Site Usability: ★★★★	Based:	UK
Product Range: ★★★★	Express Delivery Option? (UK)	No
Price Range: Luxury	Gift Wrapping Option?	No
Delivery Area: Worldwide	Returns Procedure:	Down to you

www.josephturner.co.uk

Joseph Turner offers men's shirts, ties, cufflinks, sweaters, shoes and accessories with a wide choice in all areas and regular special offers. Their shoes are made for them by Loake. There's much more information on sizing than is usual on other websites, together with an alterations service. As with all the men's clothing websites, they're extremely keen to offer something extra, so you'll find cashmere sweaters, socks and belts here as well.

Site Usability: ★★★★★	Based:	UK
Product Range: ★★★★★	Express Delivery Option? (UK)	No
Price Range: Medium	Gift Wrapping Option?	No
Delivery Area: UK	Returns Procedure:	Down to you

www.kjbeckett.com

K J Beckett has a good selection of accessories for men, including Regent Belt Company belts, cufflinks by Simon Carter, Ian Flaherty and Veritas, silk ties, cummerbunds, wallets and handkerchiefs – and that's just a few of the many items on offer. They'll deliver almost anywhere in the world using their priority service and UK delivery is free of charge. They offer gift wrapping as well.

Site Usability: ★★★★★	Based:	UK
Product Range: ★★★★★	Express Delivery Option? (UK)	Yes
Price Range: Luxury/Medium	Gift Wrapping Option?	Yes
Delivery Area: Worldwide	Returns Procedure:	Down to you

www.pakeman.co.uk

Here's an extensive range of good-quality, sensibly priced classic cloth-ing from this Cotswolds-based retailer. For men you can choose from black-tie tailoring, suits, flannels, cords, jeans, shirts and ties, belts, shoes, cufflinks and underwear. They offer a next-day delivery service for items in stock and the emphasis is on service and quality. This is not a complicated website but one where there is a high standard in every area, so don't be put off by the simplicity of the pictures.

Site Usability:	★★★★	Based:	UK
Product Range:	★★★★	Express Delivery Option? (UK)	Yes
Price Range:	Medium	Gift Wrapping Option?	No
Delivery Area:	Worldwide	Returns Procedure:	Down to you

www.perilla.co.uk

At Perilla you'll find 'the ultimate treat for feet', a range of high-quality, British-made alpaca socks in a choice of colours and styles, from the delux, lightweight City Sock to the sturdier, ribbed Country Sock. You can choose from a selection of gift boxes containing up to five pairs and select the colours and sizes you want to be included. You can also buy luxurious alpaca scarves and wraps plus some high quality leather bags, which will be automatically gift wrapped for you, so if you're looking for a special gift this could be the perfect place.

Site Usability:	★★★	Based:	UK
Product Range:	★★★	Express Delivery Option? (UK)	Yes
Price Range:	Luxury/Medium	Gift Wrapping Option?	Yes
Delivery Area:	Worldwide	Returns Procedure:	Down to you

www.thomaspink.co.uk

Thomas Pink has a slick and beautifully designed website offering shirts, clothing and accessories for men and women. There's an enormous amount of detail available for every product, plus clear pictures and a speedy search facility by pattern, style and finish. You can also buy scarves, knitwear, accessories and nightwear. You can always be sure that what you'll receive will be a high-quality product, beautifully packaged and extremely well made.

Site Usability:	★★★★	Based:	UK
Product Range:	★★★★	Express Delivery Option? (UK)	Yes
Price Range:	Luxury	Gift Wrapping Option?	Yes
Delivery Area:	Worldwide	Returns Procedure:	Down to you

Chapter 17

Men's Toiletries

Now that online retailers have wised up to the fact that toiletries of all kinds are really easy to offer online, there are some excellent special websites pretty much just for men (although most will try to tempt you too).

Particularly good for gifts if your man is a traveller are some of the travel packs and sets available here and be warned, there is a huge range. Wise up to what he likes and have a good browse round. It is too easy to buy all your male friends gifts from this area, but if you pick something that you know they'll appreciate and probably already use, you should be fine.

Sites to Visit

www.adonisgrooming.com

The first thing you think (or at least, I thought of) when you come across this website is just how easy on the eye it is. Not only that, but Adonis offers an excellent range of grooming products for men, from shaving, hair care and bodycare, from brands such as Dermalogica, Clarins for Men and Jose Eisenberg, to gifts and accessories - travel kits by California North, Jack Black and 4V00, D R Harris fragrances and Zirh products.

Site Usability: ★★★★★	Based:	UK
Product Range: ★★★★★	Express Delivery Option? (UK)	Yes
Price Range: Medium	Gift Wrapping Option?	Yes
Delivery Area: Worldwide	Returns Procedure:	Down to you

www.carterandbond.com

Carter and Bond was established in 2002 to bring together the finest male grooming products around. This simple-to-navigate, secure website is home to over 600 products from more than 40 brands, including Molton Brown, American Crew, Baxter of California, Geo F Trumper and Proraso. Whether you're looking for skincare, hair care, fragrance, shaving products or gift ideas, you'll find them all here. Orders received by 2.30pm are despatched the same day (to anywhere in the world) and gift wrapping is available for just 95p per item.

Site Usability: ★★★★★	Based:	UK
Product Range: ★★★★★	Express Delivery Option? (UK)	Available on orders over £100
Price Range: Medium	Gift Wrapping Option?	Yes
Delivery Area: Worldwide	Returns Procedure:	Down to you

www.czechandspeake.com

Czech & Speake is a worldwide luxury brand of bathroom and kitchen fittings and accessories, creating unique and timeless products that combine authentic English traditional style and modern design. You can view their products online only (and then call them to order), but you can buy their marvellous aromatic fragrances and shaving requisites, all of which are perfect for gifts. Choose from Cuba, Neroli, No 88, Oxford and Cambridge as bath oils, colognes and aftershaves.

Site Usability: ★★★★	Based:	UK
Product Range: ★★★	Express Delivery Option? (UK)	No
Price Range: Luxury/Medium	Gift Wrapping Option?	No
Delivery Area: Worldwide	Returns Procedure:	Down to you

www.hqman.com

If you've spent any time at all at thesiteguide.com, you (hopefully) will already have come across wonderful hair and accessories website hqhair.

com. Well now they've launched a website specifically for men and excellent it is too. Check out brands such as 4V00, Anthony Logistics, Calmia, Decleor Men, Malin+Goetz and Fred Bennett, plus lots more, and expect to find the full ranges across body, bath, skincare, hair care and accessories. Good service and speedy delivery are the norm here too.

Site Usability:	★★★★★	Based:	UK
Product Range:	★★★★★	Express Delivery Option? (UK)	No
Price Range:	Luxury/Medium	Gift Wrapping Option?	No
Delivery Area:	Worldwide	Returns Procedure:	Down to you

www.jasonshankey.co.uk

If you're a fan of American Crew, Baxters of California, Philip B or Redken for men's hair treatments, this is the place for you. There's also a phenomenal range of other products on this site for both men and women, from hair care and hair appliances including Coriolis and GHD, nail care, slimming products, men's grooming and hangover cures. There are so many brands and products here that you may find it takes you a while to get round the website, but persevere – it'll be well worth the effort.

Site Usability:	★★★★	Based:	UK
Product Range:	★★★★	Express Delivery Option? (UK)	Yes
Price Range:	Medium	Gift Wrapping Option?	Yes
Delivery Area:	Worldwide	Returns Procedure:	Down to you

www.mankind.co.uk

This is definitely a great men's website. It's modern, easy to navigate and has a good range of products on offer, showcasing the very best and most innovative shaving, skin and hair care brands – think Sean John, Remington, LAB Series and Ice – and offering them in a way that makes buying simple, fast and fun. There are shaving products, skin basics and problem skin solutions as well as gift ideas here, with far too many brands for me to even try to list. Take a look.

Site Usability:	★★★★★	Based:	UK
Product Range:	★★★★★	Express Delivery Option? (UK)	Yes
Price Range:	Medium	Gift Wrapping Option?	Yes
Delivery Area:	Worldwide	Returns Procedure:	Down to you

www.murdocklondon.com

Murdock London is a modern men's grooming product retailer with a slick, easy-to-navigate website offering brands such as D R Harris, Caron, Malin+Goetz and Kevin Murphy, plus aromatic candles and room scents by Mariage Frères. In the Gift Box section you'll find an excellent selection of pampering, beautifully presented hampers by Edwin Jagger and Santa Maria Novella, ranging from around £40 to over £100.

Site Usability:	★★★★★	Based:	UK
Product Range:	★★★★	Express Delivery Option? (UK)	Yes
Price Range:	Luxury/Medium	Gift Wrapping Option?	No, but beautifully wrapped gift boxes
Delivery Area:	Worldwide	Returns Procedure:	Down to you

www.theenglishshavingcompany.co.uk

At theenglishshavingcompany.co.uk you'll find the highest quality hand-crafted razors and shaving sets, plus travel sets, soaps, brushes and aftershaves from Geo Trumper, Edwin Jagger, D R Harris and Molton Brown. You can read the 'shaving tutorial' in Useful Information, plus razor-shaving tips, so if you're tired of using your electric razor and want to turn traditional, you'll definitely need this site.

Site Usability:	★★★★	Based:	UK
Product Range:	★★★★	Express Delivery Option? (UK)	No
Price Range:	Luxury/Medium	Gift Wrapping Option?	Yes
Delivery Area:	Worldwide	Returns Procedure:	Down to you

www.trumpers.com

Established in 1875 in Curzon Street, Mayfair, this famous traditional London barber is well known for superb exclusive men's fragrances and grooming products. Think of scents such as Sandalwood, Bay Rum and Spanish Leather, which all have matching soaps and body washes. Now you can buy the full range online, plus an exclusive collection of ties and cufflinks, and they'll be delighted to ship to you anywhere in the world.

Site Usability:	★★★★	Based:	UK
Product Range:	★★★★	Express Delivery Option? (UK)	Yes
Price Range:	Luxury/Medium	Gift Wrapping Option?	Yes
Delivery Area:	Worldwide	Returns Procedure:	Free

Chapter 18

For That Really Special Gift

You know: those occasions when you really want to push the boat out, when price ceases to matter so much and you want something really, really unique and special – that Cartier watch, for example, lucky him.

Anyway, here are some places to seek out that important gift, where you will, in many cases, be paying a premium for a designer label and luxury packaging but where you can be sure you'll find something wonderful and an investment that will last for years.

Sites to Visit

www.blitzwatches.co.uk

Browse through the best brands such as Tag Heuer, Tissot, Baume and Mercier, Rolex and Cartier, to name but a few. Place your order and you can have your delivery the next day. The pictures are beautifully clear and extremely tempting and on some watches there are substantial savings to be had, which are clearly shown with each model. For some premium watches you receive the manufacturer's warranty, for others the warranty is provided by Blitz, so check before you buy.

Site Usability:	★★★★★	Express Delivery Option? (UK)	Yes
Product Range:	★★★★★	Gift Wrapping Option?	Yes
Price Range:	Luxury/Medium	Returns Procedure:	Down to you/Complicated, but these are
Delivery Area:	UK		valuable items so it's understandable
Based:	UK		

www.cashmere.co.uk

Purely Cashmere is one of Scotland's longest-standing online cashmere retailers. They offer high-quality, single-, two- and three-ply knits for men and women in a good range of colours and there's a combination of truly classic designs and modern styles, plus some luxurious throws for the home. They also sell cashmere care products such as Cashmere Wash and clear zipped bags for storing and travelling.

Site Usability:	★★★★	Based:	UK
Product Range:	★★★	Express Delivery Option? (UK)	Yes if an item is in stock
Price Range:	Luxury/Medium	Gift Wrapping Option?	No
Delivery Area:	Worldwide	Returns Procedure:	Down to you

www.crombie.co.uk

The Crombie name has been synonymous for over 200 years with high-quality, hard-wearing cloth and while that continues, the Crombie brand has been developed into an excellent collection of clothing, particularly for men. The range includes the famous Crombie coat, blazers and jackets, shirts, ties and other accessories. There are some good gift ideas here, with high-quality silk ties, leather, cashmere-lined gloves in a range of colours, belts and wallets, cufflinks and braces.

Site Usability:	★★★★	Based:	UK
Product Range:	★★★★	Express Delivery Option? (UK)	No
Price Range:	Luxury/Medium	Gift Wrapping Option?	No
Delivery Area:	Worldwide	Returns Procedure:	Down to you

www.dalvey.com

Dalvey of Scotland has created a range of elegant and useful gifts which are attractively displayed on this extremely well laid out website. Suggestions such as beautifully made leather travel clocks and business card cases, cufflinks and cufflink cases, hipflasks and binoculars are all luxuriously presented and would make lovely gifts. It is a small range, but if you're looking for something for the man in your life (and it's something you know he needs or he'll use), then buy here. Most items can be engraved.

Site Usability: ★★★★★	Based:	UK
Product Range: ★★★	Express Delivery Option? (UK)	No
Price Range: Luxury	Gift Wrapping Option?	No
Delivery Area: Worldwide	Returns Procedure:	Down to you

www.dunhill.com

In 1893 Alfred Dunhill inherited his father's saddlery business on London's Euston Road and developed a luxurious line of accessories. The first collection included car horns and lamps, leather overcoats, goggles, picnic sets and timepieces. Over 100 years later Dunhill is one of the leading makers of English luxury accessories for men and here you can choose from the range which now includes luggage, briefcases, wash bags, wallets, diaries and belts, ties and cufflinks.

Site Usability: ★★★★	Based:	UK
Product Range: ★★★	Express Delivery Option? (UK)	No
Price Range: Luxury	Gift Wrapping Option?	No
Delivery Area: UK	Returns Procedure:	Down to you

www.haroldcox.com

Royal warrant holder Harold Cox and Sons has a beautifully laid out website offering the very highest quality jewellery, in particular for men. The gold and enamel cufflinks range in price between £100 and £1,000 and you can select from designs such as bars, flags and sporting themes, plus 'button' links with diamonds. The site also sells signet rings, money clips and other accessories such as tie pins, cigar cutters and tie slides. Contact them for express delivery.

Site Usability: ★★★★★	Based:	UK
Product Range: ★★★★★	Express Delivery Option? (UK)	Yes, call them
Price Range: Luxury/Medium	Gift Wrapping Option?	No
Delivery Area: Worldwide	Returns Procedure:	Down to you

www.launer.com

Launer small leather goods (and signature handbags for ladies) are handmade by skilled craftspeople in the softest calf, exotic lizard, ostrich and alligator skin. Every attention is paid to detail and the gold-plated fittings all feature the signature Launer rope emblem. Launer's trademark is understated, elegant and classic. This is not the place for an up-to-the-minute look but for really beautifully made investment pieces that will last a great deal of time.

Site Usability:	★★★★	Based:	UK
Product Range:	★★★	Express Delivery Option? (UK)	No
Price Range:	Luxury/Medium	Gift Wrapping Option?	No
Delivery Area:	Worldwide	Returns Procedure:	Down to you

www.longmire.co.uk

At Longmire you'll find what is probably the best selection of luxury cufflinks available online. Don't expect the inexpensive here as although silver cufflinks start at just over £100, the signature enamel and gold links are over £1,000 and art deco-inspired 18ct gold 'stirrup' links over £2,000 (not to mention the black and white diamond revolver cufflinks, which will set you back a mere £5,000). This is the place for a really, really special gift.

Site Usability:	★★★★★	Based:	UK
Product Range:	★★★★	Express Delivery Option? (UK)	Yes
Price Range:	Luxury/Medium	Gift Wrapping Option?	No
Delivery Area:	Worldwide	Returns Procedure:	Down to you

www.oliversweeney.com

Oliver Sweeney is best known for his high-quality 'classic with a twist' and fashion-forward footwear, which you can order online here. Alongside these and in the same mode, there are leather wallets and key holders, gloves and belts, edgy attaché cases and weekenders, plus a small range of outerwear. If the man in your life is a true traditionalist, this is probably not the place, but if he's into modern menswear, take a look.

Site Usability:	★★★★★	Based:	UK
Product Range:	★★★★	Express Delivery Option? (UK)	No
Price Range:	Luxury/Medium	Gift Wrapping Option?	No
Delivery Area:	Worldwide	Returns Procedure:	Down to you

www.penshop.co.uk

This is an attractive website offering one of the best selections of luxury pens, including Yard-o-Led's beautiful sterling silver fountain pens, ballpoints and pencils, Faber Castell pens in wood and silver, Mont Blanc (you need to phone to order), and Porsche Design steel pens. Lamy, Rotring, Sheaffer and Waterman are also available. They aim to send out the day you order and they'll deliver worldwide. They also offer a repair service.

Site Usability:	★★★★★	Based:	UK
Product Range:	★★★★★	Express Delivery Option? (UK)	No
Price Range:	Luxury/Medium	Gift Wrapping Option?	Yes
Delivery Area:	Worldwide	Returns Procedure:	Down to you

www.pickett.co.uk

Gloves, wallets, umbrellas, belts, briefcases and stud boxes are just some of the high-quality, beautifully made men's accessories available on Pickett's website. If you've ever visited one of their shops you'll know that everything is the best you can buy and most items would make lovely gifts. Couple this with their distinctive dark green and orange packaging and excellent service and you can't go wrong, whatever you choose.

Site Usability:	★★★★	Based:	UK
Product Range:	★★★★	Express Delivery Option? (UK)	No
Price Range:	Luxury/Medium	Gift Wrapping Option?	No, but luxury packaging is standard
Delivery Area:	Worldwide	Returns Procedure:	Down to you

www.sophiec.co.uk

At SophieC you can buy superb quality cashmere knitwear and accessories for women, plus a luxurious collection of scarves for men. Buy him the gorgeous Kishom winter-weight scarf or one of the Osprey plain or herringbone scarves, available in a choice of colours such as rust, chocolate, black or marsh, grey, morello or blue. It's a beautifully designed website with clear pictures of all the products on offer.

Site Usability:	★★★	Based:	UK
Product Range:	★★★	Express Delivery Option? (UK)	No
Price Range:	Luxury/Medium	Gift Wrapping Option?	No
Delivery Area:	Worldwide	Returns Procedure:	Down to you

www.swaineadeney.co.uk

If you know London well you're bound to have passed the elegant Swaine Adeney Brigg store at 54 St James's Street. They're well known as purveyors of the highest quality gentlemen's accessories, such as umbrellas with unique handles, wallets, attaché and document cases in a variety of styles and leathers, plus wonderful (and wonderfully priced) leather luggage. They have a good gift selection and many of the items can be personalised.

Site Usability:	★★★★★	Based:	UK
Product Range:	★★★★	Express Delivery Option? (UK)	No
Price Range:	Luxury	Gift Wrapping Option?	No
Delivery Area:	Worldwide	Returns Procedure:	Down to you

www.thewatchhut.co.uk

Buy your next watch from thewatchhut.co.uk and you'll know that you're buying from an authorised dealer with the full manufacturer's guarantee. On some of the watches there are excellent discounts, so it's worth having a good look through the brands on offer, such as Ebel, Accurist, Tissot, Seiko, Breil, Diesel and Fossil. All watches come with a 14-day money-back guarantee so that if you change your mind once your watch arrives you'll have no problem in returning or exchanging it.

Site Usability:	★★★★★	Based:	UK
Product Range:	★★★★	Express Delivery Option? (UK)	Yes
Price Range:	Medium	Gift Wrapping Option?	No
Delivery Area:	UK	Returns Procedure:	Down to you

Chapter 19

Gift Stores for Men

I'm not, as anyone who knows me will tell you, an advocate of general gift stores as I think that it's too easy to find something that isn't necessarily suited to the recipient. Just a 'gift' in other words.

However, I'm really impressed by the websites below which have put a great deal of thought into what they're offering, from luxury gifts such as Paul Smith accessories and Duchamp cufflinks to Hunter watches and high-quality small leathers. Have a good look through and find something special.

Sites to Visit

www.bloomsburystore.com

Bloomsbury is a particularly well laid out and carefully edited gift website where you can find something for everyone. I particularly like the men's section, where alongside fragrances by Czech and Speake there are modern radios and iPod speakers, colourful accessories by Paul Smith, Bangers and Mash (yes, really), Duchamp and Simon Carter and watches by Mondaine and Opex. There are great gifts for girls here, too.

Site Usability: ★★★★★	Based:	UK
Product Range: ★★★★	Express Delivery Option? (UK)	Yes
Price Range: Luxury/Medium	Gift Wrapping Option?	No
Delivery Area: Worldwide	Returns Procedure:	Down to you

www.h-s.co.uk

This is a name you may well never have heard of, but Harrison and Simmonds has been in business since 1928, offering pipes, cigar humidors and accessories and luxury gifts from companies such as Dalvey. There's also a wide range of Mont Blanc pens and accessories – you need to call them to order these – plus chess sets, Hunter pocket watches and shooting sticks. They're happy to ship to you anywhere in the world and if you phone them for advice you'll receive excellent service.

Site Usability: ★★★★	Based:	UK
Product Range: ★★★★	Express Delivery Option? (UK)	Yes
Price Range: Luxury/Medium	Gift Wrapping Option?	No
Delivery Area: Worldwide	Returns Procedure:	Down to you

www.menkind.co.uk

Dedicated to stylish gifts for men, Menkind offers a wide variety, including leather cufflink and watch boxes, shaving sets, executive 'toys' and gadgets, books on subjects such as sports facts and trivia, and watches by Kenneth Cole, Quiksilver, Ted Baker and Fossil. There are some very reasonably priced gifts ideas here and there's a gift wrapping and card service as well.

Site Usability: ★★★★	Based:	UK
Product Range: ★★★	Express Delivery Option? (UK)	Yes
Price Range: Medium	Gift Wrapping Option?	No
Delivery Area: UK	Returns Procedure:	Down to you

www.presentsformen.com

This is a small family business started in 1990 by Jane Hudson, whose impetus came from the difficulty in finding good quality, inexpensive and innovative presents for the male members of her family. The wide range on offer includes a good selection of books, clothing and accessories,

GIFT STORES FOR MEN

sporting gifts, pens and computing and electrical gadgets. Everything is
clearly pictured and well described.

Site Usability:	★★★★★	Based:	UK
Product Range:	★★★★★	Express Delivery Option? (UK)	Yes
Price Range:	Medium/Very Good Value	Gift Wrapping Option?	Yes
Delivery Area:	Worldwide	Returns Procedure:	Down to you

www.theinsideman.com

On a lot of general gift stores they make it too easy to move away from
thinking properly about your specific recipient. However, on this website
they've covered so many areas for men, such as art and design, leather
boxes and trays, smoking accessories, clocks, watches, pens, stationery,
sports, games and toiletries, that they've created an excellent, specifically
men's gift department store where you're unlikely not to find something.
Have a look and you'll see what I mean.

Site Usability:	★★★★	Based:	UK
Product Range:	★★★★	Express Delivery Option? (UK)	Yes
Price Range:	Medium	Gift Wrapping Option?	No
Delivery Area:	Worldwide	Returns Procedure:	Down to you

Section 4
For VSPs (Very Special People)

For VSPs you can't just wander off to a normal gift shop. You need to be taken somewhere dedicated to your chosen recipient where your gift will show a great deal of thought and care. This is particularly true with new babies and mothers who have just produced. Yes, by all means order that beautiful bouquet of flowers – you'll probably be doing the same as everyone else and for good reason. Then go on and buy a small, pretty treat, something that'll be different from the rest and that'll last a good bit longer than the flowers.

These websites are really good for those types of treats and if your other gift-giving friends aren't online shopaholics yet, they'll put you right ahead of the pack as the selection here is not one you'll find easily, if at all, in the shops.

The other VSPs, of course, are toddlers and kids who in the first case want large, colourful and non-breakable toys and games, and in the second case want you to spend loads of money on sets with tiny, easy-to-lose pieces like Lego and Playmobile. You can have lots of fun buying for children and the websites here help by enabling you to choose by age or price and whether you're buying for a boy or a girl. In other words, they've already done most of the research for you. Go on – it's now incredibly easy to be the favourite godmother/aunt/granny in town.

Chapter 20

Precious Gifts for New Babies

There are now a number of places online where you can find lovely baby gifts - beautifully designed, softly coloured websites with pretty pictures of selections of clothes, soft toys and baby toiletries all packaged together to make this type of gift giving almost too easy.

Here, too, you'll discover handmade baby bedding, personalised blankets and cushions and exquisite baby layettes, so be warned - it's easy to spend a small fortune, but you'll have great fun doing so.

Sites to Visit

www.babas.uk.com

All of Babas' beautiful handmade baby bedding and accessories are individually made for you and wrapped in their own unique calico packaging. You can choose sets for cribs, cots and Moses baskets or sleeping bags and towels in their range of contemporary designs, with names such as Noah's Ark, Teddy Triplets and Splashy Duck. Everything is really beautiful and different from what you'll find elsewhere and perfect for baby gifts.

Site Usability:	★★★★	Based:	UK
Product Range:	★★★	Express Delivery Option? (UK)	No
Price Range:	Medium	Gift Wrapping Option?	Yes
Delivery Area:	Worldwide	Returns Procedure:	Down to you

www.babiesbaskets.com

Babiesbaskets is a retailer offering (you guessed) 'basket' gift sets for new babies and they go right up to the luxury end of the spectrum, although prices start off quite reasonably. There's the 'Loveheart' baby basket containing a babygro, cardigan, pram shoes, fleece and photo album, and the ultimate 'Fudge' baby basket which offers as well a cableknit blanket, a hand-embroidered towel and babygro and handmade photo album. Everything is beautifully packaged.

Site Usability:	★★★★	Based:	UK
Product Range:	★★★★	Express Delivery Option? (UK)	Yes
Price Range:	Luxury/Medium	Gift Wrapping Option?	Yes
Delivery Area:	Worldwide	Returns Procedure:	Down to you

www.babybare.co.uk

Here's another prettily designed and easy-to-navigate website, specialising in gifts for the new baby. There are ready-to-send gift sets for boys and girls at a variety of price levels, china gifts such as cups and mugs, money boxes and piggy banks, soft, personalised fleece pram blankets and lots more. And if you aren't keen on their own ready-made sets, you can put together your own and include soft toys, bath wear, sleepsuits, blankets and shawls.

Site Usability:	★★★★	Based:	UK
Product Range:	★★★	Express Delivery Option? (UK)	Yes
Price Range:	Luxury/Medium	Gift Wrapping Option?	Yes
Delivery Area:	Worldwide	Returns Procedure:	Down to you

www.babyblooms.co.uk

At Baby Blooms you'll be ordering handmade bouquets, created from specially designed Baby Blooms garments. Small bouquets include a range of socks and a hat, while the larger bouquets also feature bodysuits and sleepsuits, creatively formed into flower buds. This may sound slightly strange but everything here is really pretty and, needless to say, will last much longer than flowers.

Site Usability: ★★★★	Based:	UK
Product Range: ★★★★	Express Delivery Option? (UK)	Yes
Price Range: Medium	Gift Wrapping Option?	Yes
Delivery Area: Worldwide	Returns Procedure:	Down to you

www.babycelebrate.co.uk

This is a Cheshire-based, high-quality baby gift retailer where there are delightful ideas for newborn and slightly older babies with names such as Baby Play Basket and Luxury Baby on the Go. For children aged up to two they have pretty printed cutlery sets and lunch boxes, plus colourful soft and wooden toys. As everything is designed to be a gift, the products are all beautifully presented so you could have them sent out direct on your behalf.

Site Usability: ★★★★	Based:	UK
Product Range: ★★★	Express Delivery Option? (UK)	Yes
Price Range: Luxury/Medium	Gift Wrapping Option?	Yes
Delivery Area: Worldwide	Returns Procedure:	Down to you

www.babygiftbox.co.uk

Babygiftbox offers a lovely range of ideas. You can choose from Welcome Home baby boxes with names such as Flower Power and Lullaby, soft lambswool or fleece and cashmere blankets and christening gifts such as silver charms, chiming spoons and hand-knitted heirloom cot blankets. There's also the Yummy Mummy Gift Set to make sure that the new mum isn't forgotten.

Site Usability: ★★★★	Based:	UK
Product Range: ★★★★	Express Delivery Option? (UK)	Yes
Price Range: Medium	Gift Wrapping Option?	Yes
Delivery Area: UK	Returns Procedure:	Down to you

www.babygiftgallery.co.uk

The range of baby gifts on offer here on this attractive website is huge, so be prepared to take your time. In particular take a look at the christening gifts of sterling silver bangles, Doudou et Compagnie House of Barbotine gift boxes, Emile et Rose keepsake boxes and photo albums. Then you might want to browse through baby gift boxes which you can customise yourself and babywear by Bob and Blossom, Emile et Rose, Inch Blue, Little Blue Dog, Toby Tiger and more.

Site Usability:	★★★★★	Based:	UK
Product Range:	★★★★★	Express Delivery Option? (UK)	Yes — call them
Price Range:	Luxury/Medium	Gift Wrapping Option?	Yes
Delivery Area:	Worldwide	Returns Procedure:	Down to you

www.balloonsweb.co.uk

Just looking at the pictures on this website, particularly in the Catamini and Pamplona sections, makes you want to buy something as they're absolutely enchanting. Balloonsweb specialises in designer children's clothing for the aforesaid brands and also Miss Sixty, Chipie, Jean Bourget, Ikks and Timberland. This is an excellent children's website offering clothes and accessories from newborn to 14 years, plus pretty baby gifts and christening wear.

Site Usability:	★★★★★	Based:	UK
Product Range:	★★★★★	Express Delivery Option? (UK)	No
Price Range:	Luxury/Medium	Gift Wrapping Option?	No
Delivery Area:	Worldwide	Returns Procedure:	Down to you

www.bellini-baby.com

Every time I think 'that's enough, no more baby gift websites' I come across another that you simply have to know about and this is one of those. Perfect for luxury, expensive gifts, Bellini Baby offers you the opportunity to buy absolutely beautiful baskets and hampers (most of which include champagne, so they're for you, too), with Takinou of France soft toys, Bebe-Jou soft cotton terry baby dressing gowns, pampering essentials and chocolates, all gorgeously wrapped and hand-tied with ribbon.

Site Usability: ★★★★★	Based:	UK
Product Range: ★★★★	Express Delivery Option? (UK)	They aim for next day for all UK orders
Price Range: Luxury	Gift Wrapping Option?	Yes
Delivery Area: Worldwide	Returns Procedure:	Down to you

www.blueberrybarn.co.uk

This is in the main a hamper and gift website for lots of different occasions. Just click through to the Mum and Baby department and you'll find a good range of suggestions, most of which can be wrapped and personalised (and they make those options very clear). Choose from such ideas as the 'Guess How Much I Love You' baby book, Peter and Jemima activity basket and Baby Welcome Gift Box, to name but a few.

Site Usability: ★★★★★	Based:	UK
Product Range: ★★★★	Express Delivery Option? (UK)	No
Price Range: Medium	Gift Wrapping Option?	Yes
Delivery Area: UK	Returns Procedure:	Down to you

www.boutiqueenfant.com

Boutique Enfant offers a collection of cashmere knitwear for 6-month to 12-year-old babies and children in a rich and vibrant colour selection for older children and marshmallow colours for the baby range. The emphasis is on traditional designs and you can mix and match from the collection of knits or buy blankets and toys. If you're looking for a special present they offer a high-quality gift wrapping service and they'll ship worldwide. There are exquisite hand-smocked girls' dresses here as well.

Site Usability: ★★★★★	Based:	UK
Product Range: ★★★★	Express Delivery Option? (UK)	No
Price Range: Luxury	Gift Wrapping Option?	Yes
Delivery Area: Worldwide	Returns Procedure:	Down to you

www.fuzzybuzzys.co.uk

Fuzzybuzzys produces personalised fleece blankets for babies, made from the softest lambskin fleece and 100% double-brushed cotton. The blankets are machine washable, quick-dry, colourfast (they promise) and will not shrink or fray with use. You choose from the range of colours, prints and appliqués and then personalise your blanket with the baby's name.

Site Usability:	★★★★	Based:	UK
Product Range:	★★★	Express Delivery Option? (UK)	No
Price Range:	Medium/Very Good Value	Gift Wrapping Option?	Yes
Delivery Area:	Worldwide	Returns Procedure:	Only if faulty

www.gltc.co.uk

A great range of gifts and ideas for babies and young children of all ages is available here, including personalised cutlery, clocks and adventure books, baby and toddler sleeping bags, magic lanterns, colourful wall hangings and also some innovative storage ideas. There's the Squishy, Squirty Bath Book, Jungle soft toy bowling set and Toy House play mat, plus loads more clever suggestions.

Site Usability:	★★★★★	Based:	UK
Product Range:	★★★★★	Express Delivery Option? (UK)	Yes
Price Range:	Medium	Gift Wrapping Option?	No
Delivery Area:	Worldwide	Returns Procedure:	Down to you

www.jojomamanbebe.co.uk

This is a pretty website offering a good choice for babies and young children. The drop-down menus on the Home Page take you quickly and clearly to everything you might be looking for, whether it's baby essentials, nightwear or towelling snugglers. They also have some excellent Polartec all-in-ones for colder weather. Delivery is free in the UK, there are some good gift ideas and they offer gift vouchers and gift boxes as well.

Site Usability:	★★★★★	Based:	UK
Product Range:	★★★★	Express Delivery Option? (UK)	No
Price Range:	Medium	Gift Wrapping Option?	Yes
Delivery Area:	Worldwide	Returns Procedure:	Down to you

www.letterbox.co.uk

Letterbox is more of a traditional toy shop, where you can buy gifts and toys for children of all ages. These include activity toys, dressing-up outfits, pretty room accessories (painted chests of drawers and fairy mobiles) and traditional games. There are also baby gifts such as personalised cushions and towels and bathrobes from ages 6–12 months upwards.

Site Usability:	★★★★	Based:	UK
Product Range:	★★★★★	Express Delivery Option? (UK)	Yes
Price Range:	Medium	Gift Wrapping Option?	No
Delivery Area:	Worldwide	Returns Procedure:	Down to you

www.morelloliving.co.uk

I was delighted to find this beautifully designed website, where you can browse a range of well-photographed, clear pictures of lovely accessories and gifts for children, including knitted animals, finger puppets, wooden letters, photo frames, scented candles and much more. Take a look round now, as from the personalised paintings to the Create-it Fairy Princess kit I'm sure you'll be as enchanted as I was.

Site Usability:	★★★★★	Based:	UK
Product Range:	★★★★★	Express Delivery Option? (UK)	No
Price Range:	Medium	Gift Wrapping Option?	No
Delivery Area:	UK	Returns Procedure:	Down to you

www.roomersgifts.com

Embroidered baby blankets, hand-painted, personalised toy boxes and door plaques, personalised bracelets and friendship rings, plus other unique gifts for babies and children are just some of the things you'll find here. This is not a traditional baby gift website, but one where you're more likely to find something they'll love to own a bit later on, such as a named treasure box.

Site Usability:	★★★	Based:	UK
Product Range:	★★★	Express Delivery Option? (UK)	No
Price Range:	Medium	Gift Wrapping Option?	No
Delivery Area:	Worldwide	Returns Procedure:	Down to you

www.thebaby.co.uk

This is a gorgeous baby website, offering so much you could get lost. Go past the essential equipment pages and click through to 'Getting Dressed',

121

where you'll find enchanting babygros, sleepsuits and accessories, or to 'Baby Furniture and Accessories', offering a wide range including decorated hangers and a John Crane mouse chair. If you're feeling really generous you could choose one of Stevenson Brothers' handmade rocking horses, made to last a lifetime.

Site Usability:	★★★★	Based:	UK
Product Range:	★★★★★	Express Delivery Option? (UK)	Yes
Price Range:	Luxury/Medium	Gift Wrapping Option?	Yes
Delivery Area:	Worldwide	Returns Procedure:	Down to you

www.thekidswindow.co.uk

The Kids Window is a real children's department store offering clothing brands from designers such as Catfish, Inside Out, Marie Chantal and Budishh, a full range of baby equipment, activity toys such as trampolines, swings and slides and lots of toys and games. You can search on this website by age, gender, season and brand or just click through to each section of the range.

Site Usability:	★★★★★	Based:	UK
Product Range:	★★★★★	Express Delivery Option? (UK)	Yes
Price Range:	Luxury/Medium	Gift Wrapping Option?	Yes
Delivery Area:	Worldwide	Returns Procedure:	Down to you

www.timetin.com

If you want to give something completely different from the normal run of baby gifts, take a look here. You can use your baby Timetin to gather information on what life was like around the time of your baby's birth, remind yourself of the names you considered and make predictions on how you think he or she will develop. The Timetin contains a specially designed 'Time Book', reminder card, sealing labels, Message for the Future envelope and advice on what to put in the tin.

Site Usability:	★★★★	Based:	UK
Product Range:	★★★	Express Delivery Option? (UK)	No
Price Range:	Medium	Gift Wrapping Option?	No
Delivery Area:	Worldwide	Returns Procedure:	N/A unless faulty

www.tinytotgifts.com

This is a beautifully laid out website where you can order musical soft toys, Asthma Friendly Cuddly Comforts and the Guess How Much I Love You gift set, which contains two Nut Brown hares and a story book. You can also buy delightful baby outfits, Funky Feet and Daisy Root baby shoes and bathtime accessories. There's a high-quality gift wrapping service and they'll ship worldwide.

Site Usability:	★★★★★	Based:	UK
Product Range:	★★★★	Express Delivery Option? (UK)	No
Price Range:	Medium	Gift Wrapping Option?	Yes
Delivery Area:	Worldwide	Returns Procedure:	Down to you

www.weegooseberry.com

Wee Gooseberry has definitely aimed itself at the tiny end of the designer market, with most of the clothes going up to 24 months. There's a wonderful choice of brands including Levi, Catamini, Bob and Blossom (love it), Ellepi, Kidorable rainwear (love that too), Mini Mink, Ickle Pickle and Snuggle Sac. They also have fancy-dress costumes for tinies, a wide range of shoes and some lovely gift ideas. Buy from them.

Site Usability:	★★★★★	Based:	UK
Product Range:	★★★★★	Express Delivery Option? (UK)	Yes
Price Range:	Luxury/Medium	Gift Wrapping Option?	Yes
Delivery Area:	Worldwide	Returns Procedure:	Down to you

Chapter 21

For New Mums

I f a friend of yours has just produced, you'll almost certainly want to send her some flowers, so choose from the florists below or within Chapter 4. Then pay a visit to the other websites here which specialise in pampering gifts for new mums (and they definitely need some pampering).

As well as browsing through the gift ideas below you might like to take a look at www.thewhitecompany.com, which is a particular favourite of mine for this type of gift. There you'll find soft towelling robes, luxury separates to lounge around in and fragrant toiletries, beautifully boxed. Take a look.

Sites to Visit

www.arenaflowers.com

Arena Flowers offers a pretty selection of hand-tied floral arrangements as new baby gifts which you can accompany with a teddy bear, Prestat chocolates or a balloon. As there's such a wide range over all the categories I suggest that you select by flower type or by the amount you want to spend. They offer a free UK next-day delivery service, plus a same-day service throughout the UK (which is free in London and the South East).

Site Usability:	★★★★★	Based:	UK
Product Range:	★★★★★	Express Delivery Option? (UK)	Yes
Price Range:	Medium	Gift Wrapping Option?	No
Delivery Area:	UK	Returns Procedure:	Down to you

www.babeswithbabies.com

This is definitely a lovely place to buy a gift for a new mum (or if you are one, to treat yourself). They offer pretty polka dot mama and baby pyjamas, chic nursing tops, super-fluffy alpaca slippers, pampering gift sets and incredibly elegant baby bags as just some of their ideas. You can book baby portrait sessions and buy gift vouchers here as well.

Site Usability:	★★★★★	Based:	UK
Product Range:	★★★★	Express Delivery Option? (UK)	Yes, but call to arrange
Price Range:	Medium	Gift Wrapping Option?	Automatic
Delivery Area:	Worldwide	Returns Procedure:	Down to you

www.cologneandcotton.com

This is a very special website, offering some unusual and hard-to-find bath and body products and fragrance by Diptyque (if you haven't already tried their candles you really should, they're gorgeous), Cath Collins, La Compagnie de Provence and Cote Bastide. There are also fragrances by Annik Goutal, Coudray and Rosine and for the bathroom they have lovely fluffy towels and bathrobes.

Site Usability:	★★★★★	Based:	UK
Product Range:	★★★★	Express Delivery Option? (UK)	Yes
Price Range:	Luxury/Medium	Gift Wrapping Option?	Yes
Delivery Area:	Worldwide	Returns Procedure:	Down to you

www.dreambabyuk.co.uk

There are lots of different types of new and expecting mum gifts on this website, so whether she's into natural, spa or the beautifully fragranced type of pampering, you'll find it here. There's also the Booties Keepsake Book, which comes in blue or pink (of course), Beatrix Potter My First Year book and Natalia New Parent Survival Kit. There are also other gift ideas, including teddies and champagne, new baby gifts and food hampers.

Site Usability:	★★★★★	Based:	UK
Product Range:	★★★★	Express Delivery Option? (UK)	Yes
Price Range:	Luxury/Medium	Gift Wrapping Option?	No
Delivery Area:	Worldwide except for container roses and bouquets	Returns Procedure:	Email them first

www.gorgeousthingsonline.com

This is a mixture of pampering gifts, including candles by Arco, bath melts and bath truffles by Di Palomo, Nougat London Body Shimmer and moisturising soap, plus pretty bathroom accessories, throws and blankets and attractive cushions. Everything is beautifully photographed and extremely tempting and nothing is overpriced. They'll ship anywhere in the world and offer a gift wrapping service as well.

Site Usability:	★★★★	Express Delivery Option? (UK)	No
Product Range:	★★★★	Gift Wrapping Option?	Yes
Price Range:	Medium	Returns Procedure:	Down to you
Delivery Area:	Worldwide		

www.hi-baby.co.uk

There are lots of items here to buy which are not necessarily gift related, such as TENS machines, morning sickness relief, lingerie and support and relaxation products, but there are also some good gift ideas in the (surprise) Pregnancy Gift section. These include jewellery and pampering products and best of all, they offer gift wrapping and boxing and pretty cards too.

Site Usability:	★★★★★	Based:	UK
Product Range:	★★★	Express Delivery Option? (UK)	Yes
Price Range:	Medium	Gift Wrapping Option?	Yes
Delivery Area:	Worldwide	Returns Procedure:	Down to you

www.janepackerdelivered.com

Here are the most beautifully presented, modern flowers to send as a gift or if you want to give yourself a treat, to yourself. The range in her stores is much larger than what's offered online, but here you'll find roses, hyacinths, pink parrot tulips, orchids and mixed bouquets, all presented in her unique, chic style. You can buy Jane Packer's books, fragranced bath and body gifts, champagne and chocolates and gift vouchers here as well.

Site Usability:	★★★★★	Express Delivery Option? (UK)	Yes
Product Range:	★★★	Gift Wrapping Option?	No, but everything is beautifully presented
Price Range:	Luxury/Medium		
Based:	UK	Returns Procedure:	Down to you

www.kennethturner.co.uk

White Flowers, Wild Garden, Magnolia Grandiflora and Rose (plus Original) are some of the fragrances you'll find on this pretty website, presented as candles, tea lights, shower gel and body lotions, room colognes and pot pourri. His packaging, in flower-printed blue and white boxes, turn his products into perfect gifts. You'll find travel sets and prepared gift boxes here too.

Site Usability:	★★★★	Based:	UK
Product Range:	★★★	Express Delivery Option? (UK)	Yes
Price Range:	Luxury/Medium	Gift Wrapping Option?	Yes
Delivery Area:	Worldwide	Returns Procedure:	Down to you

www.laline.co.uk

Laline is a new range of bath, bodycare and home accessories, handmade with natural oils and fragrances such as Shea butter, aloe and citrus oils, all sourced in France and beautifully packaged. The range includes soaps, body creams and souffles, body oils, face masks, plus products for men, babies and home. Prices start from around £4.

Site Usability:	★★★★	Based:	UK
Product Range:	★★★	Express Delivery Option? (UK)	Yes
Price Range:	Medium/Very Good Value	Gift Wrapping Option?	No
Delivery Area:	EU	Returns Procedure:	Down to you

www.lambertsflowercompany.co.uk

On this stylishly designed website Lamberts offers a small but cleverly thought out collection of bouquets and arrangements. There are gorgeous new baby gifts, special flowers for Valentine's Day and other occasions, plus teddies, chocolates and vases. Lamberts also specialises in wedding flowers, including bouquets, church and reception arrangements and buttonholes, plus stylish arrangements for the home.

Site Usability:	★★★★★	Delivery Area:	UK
Product Range:	★★★★	Based:	UK
Price Range:	Luxury/Medium	Express Delivery Option? (UK)	No

www.myfirstday.co.uk

There are so many wonderful gifts you can choose as a memento of a baby's birth, most of which fit into a specific category such as flowers, hampers or silver. Here's something totally different, which I think is a lovely idea: each day since mid-summer's day 2005, landscape photographer Gavan Goulder has taken stunning photographs of the Cornish coastline, so you can buy a beautifully framed photograph to mark the day of your (or a friend's) baby's birth. Take a look.

Site Usability:	★★★★★	Based:	UK
Product Range:	★★★	Express Delivery Option? (UK)	No
Price Range:	Luxury/Medium	Gift Wrapping Option?	No
Delivery Area:	Worldwide	Returns Procedure:	Down to you

www.passionleaf.com

If you'd like to give fruit as a gift but don't really want to send the same as everyone else, have a look round here. Passionleaf creates quite amazing, real fruit bouquets (which currently they can deliver only within the M25 area) using strawberries, melons, oranges and pineapples cut into pretty shapes and packed into wicker tubs. Just to look at this website will make your mouth water. You can add balloons and chocolate strawberries to your gift. Call to order.

Site Usability:	★★★	Based:	UK
Product Range:	★★★★	Express Delivery Option? (UK)	Yes
Price Range:	Luxury/Medium	Gift Wrapping Option?	No
Delivery Area:	UK within M25	Returns Procedure:	Down to you

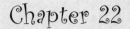

Chapter 22

For Toddlers up to 4

ere life gets a bit more interesting, as although you can carry on buying baby and infant clothes for gifts, you can give presents that are far more entertaining and interesting, as well as encouraging learning.

There are loads of ideas, some of which have an educational side and some of which are purely for fun. I suggest that you go for something in between which will be appreciated by the parents and enjoyed by the recipient as well.

Having said that, there are two types of present which have been given to my kids and are still remembered with great fondness and I really don't think you can go wrong with either. The first is a special soft toy - no, not educational, I know, but a gift which they will most likely treasure for many years. The second is a starter train set. I haven't yet come across a four year old who can't be entertained for many hours by one of those.

Take a look at the websites below and also in Chapter 23, where most of the retailers cover all ages as well.

Site to Visit

www.babydazzlers.com

This company aims to offer you toys that combine the elements of fun with teaching, so as well as lots of toys and craft kits to buy there's a great deal of advice on what you should be choosing for children at each stage and age, from birth to five years. It's an excellent resource (as well as a great shop) and I just wish it had been around when I had my kids.

Site Usability:	★★★★★	Based:	UK
Product Range:	★★★★★	Express Delivery Option? (UK)	Yes, but call them
Price Range:	Medium	Gift Wrapping Option?	Yes
Delivery Area:	UK and call for overseas	Returns Procedure:	Down to you

www.baby-toys.co.uk

Here in the well-stocked soft toys section you can find Imogene Rabbit, Twaddles Osgood and Thelonious Monkey, Ziggles, Garden to Go and Wrap Along Bee. So if the child you're buying for is not quite yet into the brainteasers and early learning ideas, you can find something charming for them that'll probably become a lifelong friend and it, and you, will be kept constantly in mind. Having said that, you'll also find interesting and creative gift ideas in the other sections of this very good website.

Site Usability:	★★★★★	Based:	UK
Product Range:	★★★★	Express Delivery Option? (UK)	No
Price Range:	Medium	Gift Wrapping Option?	No
Delivery Area:	Worldwide	Returns Procedure:	Down to you

www.beyondtherainbow.co.uk

This is a marvellous website to look round for toys and games for a pre-schooler. Not only is it colourful, fun and well laid out, but there's a wide selection, in sections such as Bashing and Banging (great for small boys), Pull and Push Along Toys and Activity Toys, as well as the straightforward learning variety. There are also some great wall charts to help to learn to tell the time and to spell, plus the Maths Bus. Delivery is free on orders over £50.

Site Usability: ★★★★★	Based:	UK
Product Range: ★★★★★	Express Delivery Option? (UK)	Yes
Price Range: Luxury/Medium	Gift Wrapping Option?	No
Delivery Area: UK	Returns Procedure:	Down to you

www.dillongreen.co.uk

Dillon Green specialises in soft toys and other treats for babies, with Steiff and Jelly Cat being the main brands. Then there are microwavable bears (they're filled with treated wheat grains and lavender flowers so you can warm them up safely), Minimink gorgeous fake fur scarves, hats and bootees, Miamoo products such as Cuddle Cream and Splashy Wash and finally, for mums, Mama Mio pregnancy body treats.

Site Usability: ★★★★★	Based:	UK
Product Range: ★★★	Express Delivery Option? (UK)	Yes
Price Range: Medium	Gift Wrapping Option?	No
Delivery Area: Worldwide	Returns Procedure:	Down to you

www.elc.co.uk

The baby and toddler section at the Early Learning Centre's colourful website is well worth having a look round, as you'll find a wide range perfect for starting your baby off, including bath toys, Blossom Farm baby toys, buggy and cot toys and just about every other type of baby toy you can think of. They make it easy for you to choose since, as well as selecting by type of toy, you can choose by themes such as Action and Adventure and Art and Music.

Site Usability: ★★★★★	Based:	UK
Product Range: ★★★★★	Express Delivery Option? (UK)	Yes
Price Range: Medium/Very Good Value	Gift Wrapping Option?	No
Delivery Area: UK	Returns Procedure:	Free – collection or freepost

www.gamleys.co.uk

Action Man, Bratz Dolls, Dora the Explorer (love that one), Little Tikes, My Little Pony, Peppa Pig, Pixel Chix (!?), Pocoyo, Polly Pocket and Power Rangers are just some of the brands on offer here. Then for tinies there are pre-school toys by Fisher Price, Mega Bloks, Teletubbies and Tomy.

Provided you stick to the clear menus of categories and brands you shouldn't get lost; go off on a tangent and you almost certainly will be.

Site Usability:	★★★★★	Based:	UK
Product Range:	★★★★★	Express Delivery Option? (UK)	No
Price Range:	Medium	Gift Wrapping Option?	No
Delivery Area:	UK	Returns Procedure:	Down to you

www.helenbroadhead.co.uk

If you like something completely different then take a look here, where Helen Broadhead offers her original and hand-painted range of furniture. What you need to do first is look on her designs page and choose from the collection, including Under the Sea, Teddy Bears, Jungle, Tank, Pirates or Fairy, then select the piece of furniture you'd like, from tables and chairs to mirrors and chests. Nothing is overpriced and most items would make lovely gifts.

Site Usability:	★★★★	Based:	UK
Product Range:	★★★★	Express Delivery Option? (UK)	No
Price Range:	Medium	Gift Wrapping Option?	Yes
Delivery Area:	Worldwide, but call for overseas deliveries	Returns Procedure:	No returns for bespoke items unless they're faulty

www.hippins.co.uk

The Hippins brand has been around for over a decade, offering a unique mix of groovy children's designer clothing, funky children's furniture, traditional handcrafted wooden toys, personalised presents, unusual ideas for christening gifts, children's birthday presents and everything for new babies, including stylish nursery furniture, baby bedding and nursery accessories. You'll also find the site's own-label children's designer clothing range for ages from birth to 8 years, including handmade leather baby shoes.

Site Usability:	★★★	Express Delivery Option? (UK)	No
Product Range:	★★★★★	Gift Wrapping Option?	No
Price Range:	Medium	Returns Procedure:	Down to you. Personalised items are not returnable
Delivery Area:	EU		
Based:	UK		

www.izziwizzikids.co.uk

I really like this website. When you reach one of those moments when you just can't look at another hugely colourful and busy online retailer, where there's (probably) too much choice, you can calm down here. Izzi Wizzi specialises in toys for babies up to the age of one. For each product (Tooting Teddy or Old MacDonald's Noisy Barn, for example) they give you just the right amount of information. You can browse by age, product type or category and they deliver throughout the EU.

Site Usability:	★★★★★	Based:	UK
Product Range:	★★★	Express Delivery Option? (UK)	Yes
Price Range:	Medium	Gift Wrapping Option?	No
Delivery Area:	EU	Returns Procedure:	Down to you

www.minimarvellous.co.uk

Don't be surprised when the address for this website changes to bloom-ingmarvellous.co.uk, as this is the 'mini' section of the excellent baby and maternity clothing company of the same name. They have a very good range of toys for kids of 2–8 years, including activity toys, arts and crafts, playsets, early learning, books and DVDs. Expect good prices, a good choice and really good service here.

Site Usability:	★★★★★	Based:	UK
Product Range:	★★★★★	Express Delivery Option? (UK)	No
Price Range:	Medium/Very Good Value	Gift Wrapping Option?	No
Delivery Area:	Worldwide	Returns Procedure:	Down to you

Chapter 23

Children from 4 to 11

If it wasn't almost impossible, bearing in mind the wide selection each of these website offers, I would divide them up into further age categories as really 4–11 is far too wide and you wouldn't dream of giving both the same kind of gift. Helpfully, most of these online retailers cater very well for the different age groups and when you visit their websites you can go directly to the age of your choice to see that particular range.

It seems so long ago now to me that my kids were 11 (let alone 4) that I would have found it impossible to remember what they liked to be given, were it not that I've had a 4-, 9- and 11-year-old living with me for a few weeks. No extra market research needed there, then.

Sites to Visit

www.accessorize.co.uk

Just about as well known on the High Street as its sister shop Monsoon, Accessorize is the essential destination if you're looking for a gift for a fashion-conscious girl or if your own early teen and upwards needs (as in I NEED) a new pair of earrings, flip-flops, party slip-on shoes, scarf or bag. Not only are the prices extremely reasonable but the products are fun and modern. The stores themselves are usually heaving, so take advantage of the fact that you (or they) can now shop online.

Site Usability:	★★★★★	Based:	UK
Product Range:	★★★★	Express Delivery Option? (UK)	No
Price Range:	Medium	Gift Wrapping Option?	No
Delivery Area:	UK	Returns Procedure:	Down to you

www.cosyposy.co.uk

This well thought out childrenswear website has gone straight into my list of favourites, as it's attractive to look at, easy to navigate and offers an original and reasonably priced range for boys and girls from 2 to 6, plus a separate babies' collection. Brands include Inch Blue, Cacharel, Elizabeth James and Butterscotch. There are also some good gift ideas for new babies and children, including gift sets and toys, and you can buy gift vouchers, which can be sent out on your behalf.

Site Usability:	★★★★★	Based:	UK
Product Range:	★★★★★	Express Delivery Option? (UK)	Yes
Price Range:	Medium	Gift Wrapping Option?	Yes
Delivery Area:	Worldwide	Returns Procedure:	Down to you

www.dollshouse.com

Whether you're new to the world of dolls' houses or a dedicated minia-turist, the Dolls House Emporium should fill you with inspiration. The site features fully decorated dolls' houses and thousands of miniatures in colour-coordinated room sets, plus carpets and flooring, lighting and wallpapers. You can also see a selection of 1:12-scale dolls' houses shown open and fully furnished to give you ideas.

Site Usability:	★★★★★	Based:	UK
Product Range:	★★★★	Express Delivery Option? (UK)	No
Price Range:	Luxury/Medium	Gift Wrapping Option?	No
Delivery Area:	Worldwide	Returns Procedure:	Down to you

www.hamleys.co.uk

If you've ever visited this world-famous Regent Street toy emporium (I hate the word but it's the only way to describe this store) you'll know that there's a huge range of gadgets, games, soft toys, puzzles, stocking fillers and every toy you can think of at all price levels and for all ages. In fact, it's a disastrous place to take more than one child at a time as there's so much to see. There's a highly edited range on the website, although the list of products on offer is growing all the time.

Site Usability:	★★★★★	Based:	UK
Product Range:	★★★★	Express Delivery Option? (UK)	No
Price Range:	Luxury/Medium	Gift Wrapping Option?	No
Delivery Area:	Worldwide	Returns Procedure:	Down to you

www.jigsaw-puzzles-online.co.uk

Personally I've never had the patience to tackle mega jigsaw puzzles, but I know that there are those who do and who keep them out year round for rainy-day entertainment. This site is aimed at puzzle enthusiasts of all ages as it caters for everyone, with 60-piece puzzles for children and going right up to the (horrendous to me) 13,000-piece puzzle by Clementoni. I wouldn't know where to start, would you?

Site Usability:	★★★★★	Express Delivery Option? (UK)	Yes
Product Range:	★★★★★	Gift Wrapping Option?	No
Price Range:	Luxury/Medium	Returns Procedure:	Down to you
Based:	UK		

www.lambstoys.co.uk

This is another of those toy websites that offers so many brands it's hard to know where to start. To help you I'll tell you that they have an excellent range of Meccano, Hornby and Scalextric, Lego, Schleich Models, Flashing Storm scooters and Power Rangers. Then for little girls there's Zapf Baby Annabel, Chou Chou and Colette, plus Miss Milly and My Model makeup and hair styling sets (and lots more). Phew.

Site Usability: ★★★★★	Based:	UK
Product Range: ★★★★★	Express Delivery Option? (UK)	Yes
Price Range: Medium	Gift Wrapping Option?	No
Delivery Area: Worldwide	Returns Procedure:	Down to you

www.lilyandagathe.com

Based in the Catalan region of France bordering on Spain, Lily and Agathe is a small English/French-speaking company with a love of all things beautiful, charming and vintage. Here you'll discover exceptional and timeless gifts and toys with a lean towards nostalgia. Many of the items here are one-offs, so if you see something you like, buy it quick. If you like the overall idea, keep checking back.

Site Usability: ★★★★	Based:	France
Product Range: ★★★★	Express Delivery Option? (UK)	No
Price Range: Medium	Gift Wrapping Option?	Yes
Delivery Area: Worldwide	Returns Procedure:	Down to you

www.littlefolk.co.uk

This is an excellent place for unusual gifts for children as just about everything in the kids' section would make a great present. They have some lovely, well-priced, personalised t-shirts, aged from 3 to 14, with the Little Folk (Twirl the Little Ballerina, Fizzly the Little Fairy and Squirt the Little Elephant are just a few), plus the alphabet letter and name of your choice. There are also personalised bags, bedding, place settings and pictures.

Site Usability: ★★★★★	Based:	UK
Product Range: ★★★	Express Delivery Option? (UK)	Yes, for some items
Price Range: Medium	Gift Wrapping Option?	No
Delivery Area: UK	Returns Procedure:	Down to you

www.mailorderexpress.com

Mail Order Express claims to be the largest toy website in Europe and who am I to argue? It's a hugely busy site with loads of offers and pre-order invitations on the Home Page but where, thankfully, you can shop by categories such as Music, Gadgets, Party, Science, Toy Vehicle, Dolls and Accessories, or by brand. Take a look for yourself.

Site Usability:	★★★★	Based:	UK
Product Range:	★★★★★	Express Delivery Option? (UK)	Yes
Price Range:	Medium/Very Good Value	Gift Wrapping Option?	No
Delivery Area:	Worldwide	Returns Procedure:	Down to you

www.mischiefkids.co.uk

At Mischief Kids you can find a great selection of designer clothing for kids, from labels such as Emile et Rose, Ikks, Mim-Pi, Marese, Trois Pommes and Quiksilver. Click on the brand you're interested in and you can immediately see everything they're offering, plus what's available right now (although this could be simplified). This is an excellent website for children's clothing and one that kids will enjoy looking through too, for its fun and quirky design.

Site Usability:	★★★★	Based:	UK
Product Range:	★★★★★	Express Delivery Option? (UK)	Yes
Price Range:	Luxury/Medium	Gift Wrapping Option?	No
Delivery Area:	Worldwide	Returns Procedure:	Down to you

www.modelhobbies.co.uk

Model Hobbies is the perfect place for the model enthusiast. It has an extremely well laid out website and offer models by more than 50 different manufacturers, plus all the paints, tools and brushes you could possibly need. There are miniature soldiers here as well. They cleverly highlight the newest kits to hit the market so that you keep coming back for more, and you can buy gift vouchers too.

Site Usability:	★★★★★	Based:	UK
Product Range:	★★★★★	Express Delivery Option? (UK)	No
Price Range:	Luxury/Medium	Gift Wrapping Option?	No
Delivery Area:	Worldwide	Returns Procedure:	Down to you

www.otherlandtoys.co.uk

Otherland Toys offers a wide selection and is particularly good for boys. I suggest when you're looking round that you click on 'only show items in stock' as there's so much to choose from anyway and at least you won't be looking at what they don't have. There are remote control cars at all levels, excellent gadgets, Meccano Magic and lots of outdoor ideas. Make sure you have your cup of coffee with you when you start – you'll need it.

Site Usability:	★★★★★	Based:	UK
Product Range:	★★★★★	Express Delivery Option? (UK)	Yes, Fedex worldwide
Price Range:	Luxury/Medium/Very Good Value	Gift Wrapping Option?	Yes
Delivery Area:	Worldwide	Returns Procedure:	Down to you

www.sayitwithbears.co.uk

This is one of those websites that obviously started off doing one thing and then branched out, because you can find not only bears here but elephants, rabbits, cats, labradors and dalmations, plus lots of other dogs. So if you know someone who collects soft toys or needs a feel-good gift, you should take a look. Oh yes, and you can buy Lovvie Bears, Thank you Bears and Anniversary Bears as well.

Site Usability:	★★★★	Based:	UK
Product Range:	★★★★★	Express Delivery Option? (UK)	Yes
Price Range:	Medium	Gift Wrapping Option?	Yes
Delivery Area:	Worldwide	Returns Procedure:	Down to you

www.shopping-emporium-uk.com

This is a brightly coloured, unsophisticated-looking website offering Italian-made sets for backgammon, dominoes and solitaire, bridge, roulette, poker and other games at a wide range of price levels. Then there are dart boards, billiard tables, mini football tables and a great deal more. Expect to spend a lot of time if you know someone who likes games as there's so much to see and choose from.

Site Usability:	★★★★★	Based:;	UK
Product Range:	★★★	Express Delivery Option? (UK)	No
Price Range:	Luxury/Medium	Gift Wrapping Option?	No
Delivery Area:	Worldwide	Returns Procedure:	Down to you

www.tansen.co.uk

Tansen is an eclectic, pretty and different range of clothes and accessories for women, girls and boys. Inspired by the East, the designs follow the traditions and beauty of Nepal, India and Japan, incorporating embroidery and vibrant colours, fabrics such as silk saris, chiffon, cord and cotton, hand-knit and crochet, and prints embellished with sequins, beads and jewels. There are some gorgeous clothes, particularly for little girls, which would make lovely gifts.

Site Usability:	★★★★	Based:	UK
Product Range:	★★★★	Express Delivery Option? (UK)	Yes
Price Range:	Medium	Gift Wrapping Option?	No
Delivery Area:	Worldwide	Returns Procedure:	Down to you

www.theentertainer.com

This is one of the largest independent toy retailers in the UK, with a huge range and an excellent, easy-to-navigate website with 'More Toys, More Value and More Fun' as their motto. Here you can search by brand, type of toy, age group or price and you can choose from so many, including Baby Annabel, Dr Who, Hornby, Mattel, Nintendogs and Playmobil. Find something you like and you'll be offered lots more like it, helping you to narrow down your choice quickly.

Site Usability:	★★★★★	Based:	UK
Product Range:	★★★★★	Express Delivery Option? (UK)	Yes
Price Range:	Luxury/Medium	Gift Wrapping Option?	No
Delivery Area:	Worldwide	Returns Procedure:	Down to you

www.toysbymailorder.co.uk

Toys by Mail Order specialises in toys, gifts, nursery items and jigsaw puzzles for children of all ages. The menus are easy to use as once you've clicked on Online Shop you can see all the brands and all the different types of toy, such as baby toys, puzzles, soft toys and arts and crafts. There's also a selection of games ranging from early learning games to murder mystery. They offer fast delivery and personalised messages for special occasions.

Site Usability:	★★★★	Based:	UK
Product Range:	★★★★★	Express Delivery Option? (UK)	Yes, 2-day service
Price Range:	Medium	Gift Wrapping Option?	No
Delivery Area:	Worldwide	Returns Procedure:	Down to you

www.toysdirecttoyourdoor.co.uk

Some general toy websites make you (me in any case) want to run away, they're so busy on the home page. On this website you're immediately drawn in, from the train running across the top of the screen to the clear menu, information and special offer details. They sell Playmobil, Thomas trains, Sylvanian Families, Lego and Duplo, Brio, Schleich animals and much more.

Site Usability:	★★★★★	Based:	UK
Product Range:	★★★★★	Express Delivery Option? (UK)	No
Price Range:	Medium	Gift Wrapping Option?	No
Delivery Area:	Worldwide	Returns Procedure:	Down to you

www.toysrus.co.uk

This one you'll definitely have heard of (or seen no doubt) as the UK branch of the US toy megastore. Personally I think the shops are just too huge to cope with, so it's great that they're online, although this website is one of the busiest around. There's a fantastic range of well-priced toys and equipment for children of all ages, including multimedia PCs, games, bikes and outdoor fun products. You can also click through to Babiesrus with its selection for the younger members of the family.

Site Usability:	★★★★	Based:	UK
Product Range:	★★★★★	Express Delivery Option? (UK)	No
Price Range:	Medium/Very Good Value	Gift Wrapping Option?	No
Delivery Area:	UK, but there are separate Canada and US websites	Returns Procedure:	Free by freepost or collection

Section 5
For the Enthusiast

I think we all know someone who loves to cook (not just has to, but loves to) or who spends their time looking after their garden, playing a specific type of sport, reading, taking pictures, painting, making music or travelling.

These people are easier than most to buy gifts for and I'm not just talking about the latest book (although those work too and if you think it's a good idea you can just go straight off to www.amazon.co.uk or www.waterstones.com). I'm talking about finding something just that little bit different, maybe something that they haven't come across before that they'll really appreciate as it fits in so well with what they love to do.

So if you do know this type of enthusiast, take a look here first - you won't be disappointed.

Chapter 24

Cook

The cooking enthusiast is almost the most difficult to buy for. Pots and pans may be a bit too mundane and you can't give them food (unless it's a very special type of ingredient). Often the latest cookery book is an all-too-easy answer.

On the websites below there are some clever ideas, such as 'designer' pepper mills (a good cook can never have too many, although if they're anything like my husband they'll use them up one by one and then wait for someone else – me – to do the refilling), high-quality knives, chopping boards, decorative containers and excellent small appliances.

There are also the specialist ingredients such as olive oils and spices. I suggest that you don't go for the boxed sets of ingredients, which certainly in our house seem to sit around for months, but large and probably decorative bottles of the best olive oils and most used herbs and spices will always go down well.

Sites to Visit

www.agacookshop.co.uk

If you know someone who has an Aga and likes cooking then this would be a great place to find them the latest Aga cookery book or some of the attractive Aga textiles. If it's someone you know very well you could even give them a new Aga kettle and you can be sure it would be used. There are other excellent products here, such as high-quality wooden chopping boards, bowls, chefs' knives and Kitchen Aid blenders.

Site Usability:	★★★★★	Based:	UK
Product Range:	★★★★	Express Delivery Option? (UK)	No
Price Range:	Luxury/Medium	Gift Wrapping Option?	No
Delivery Area:	UK	Returns Procedure:	Down to you

www.carluccios.com

You may have been lucky enough to eat in one of Antonio Carluccio's restaurants or to receive some of his wonderful regional Italian delicacies as a gift, such as his high-quality Italian olive oils in stone or glass flasks. You can be certain that anything you buy here will be just about as good as it gets. Everything is packaged beautifully, with lots of information about where the product originated and what you can use it for. Gift vouchers are available as well.

Site Usability:	★★★★★	Based:	UK
Product Range:	★★★★	Express Delivery Option? (UK)	No
Price Range:	Luxury/Medium	Gift Wrapping Option?	No
Delivery Area:	UK	Returns Procedure:	Down to you

www.cooksknives.co.uk

Essential for any cooking enthusiast is a set of really good quality sharp knives and you'll definitely find them here. You can buy individual knives or sets by Global, Henckels, Sabatier, Haiku and Wusthof (and more), professional knife sharpeners and OXO 'good grip' tools. You will pay quite a lot for a really good set of knives and knife block, but they will last you for years and be worth every penny. These are excellent gifts for real cooks.

Site Usability:	★★★★★	Based:	UK
Product Range:	★★★★★	Express Delivery Option? (UK)	No
Price Range:	Luxury/Medium	Gift Wrapping Option?	No
Delivery Area:	EU	Returns Procedure:	Down to you

www.cucinadirect.co.uk

Everything for the kitchen is beautifully displayed here, including the highest quality knives and chopping boards, pots and pans, unusual bar tools, glasses and serving dishes, picnic equipment, general housekeeping items and a selection of gift ideas. You'll also find a small but high-quality range of kitchen electrical appliances, plus some attractively packaged hampers, particularly at Christmas.

Site Usability:	★★★★★	Based:	UK
Product Range:	★★★★	Express Delivery Option? (UK)	Yes
Price Range:	Medium	Gift Wrapping Option?	Yes
Delivery Area:	Worldwide	Returns Procedure:	Down to you

www.diningstore.co.uk

There are some quite unusual products on this website, such as the ZapCap bottle opener, Escali Cibo nutritional scale and CaddyO bottle chiller, alongside the designer kitchen and tableware with collections from Eva Solo, Cuisinox Elysee, Le Creuset, Mauviel, Couzon and Jura. This is not the normal kitchen and cookware selection, so have a look round – you're certain to find something very different and some great gifts for the enthusiastic cook.

Site Usability:	★★★★	Based:	UK
Product Range:	★★★	Express Delivery Option? (UK)	No
Price Range:	Medium	Gift Wrapping Option?	No
Delivery Area:	Europe	Returns Procedure:	Down to you

www.divertimenti.co.uk

This famous London-based cookery equipment site offers over 5,000 items, from hand-painted tableware, including decorated and coloured pottery from France, to a comprehensive range of kitchen essentials, in-cluding knives, boards and bakeware. Then there are the Italian products (parmesan graters and ravioli trays), copper bowls and pans, children's baking sets, a wedding gift service, knife sharpening and copper re-tin-ning. This has always been and remains one of the best kitchen and dining shops around.

Site Usability:	★★★★	Based:	UK
Product Range:	★★★★★	Express Delivery Option? (UK)	No
Price Range:	Luxury/Medium	Gift Wrapping Option?	No
Delivery Area:	Worldwide	Returns Procedure:	Down to you

www.johnlewis.com

There are so many gifts you could buy from John Lewis that it's extremely difficult to know where they belong in this book. I've put them here because they offer so many wonderful ideas for the kitchen, not just the basics but clever and attractive accessories, unusual tableware, different textiles and excellent equipment. So if you're in any doubt about what to buy, you simply need to click through here and your problems will be solved.

Site Usability:	★★★★★	Based:	UK
Product Range:	★★★★★	Express Delivery Option? (UK)	Yes
Price Range:	Luxury/Medium	Gift Wrapping Option?	No
Delivery Area:	UK	Returns Procedure:	Down to you

www.oliviers-co.com

For those who love cooking and good food and want to use only the best, don't miss this wonderful site offering special olive oils (and other pantry goods). You'll discover olive oils infused with basil, lemon and chilli or pepper, mandarin and truffles, plus information and advice on how to use them and which foods they complement. There are also some attractive gift selections. They'll deliver throughout Europe and you need to allow ten days for your order to arrive.

Site Usability:	★★★★★	Based:	France
Product Range:	★★★★	Express Delivery Option? (UK)	No
Price Range:	Luxury/Medium	Gift Wrapping Option?	No
Delivery Area:	Europe	Returns Procedure:	Down to you

www.rickstein.com

You may well have heard of Rick Stein, eaten at his restaurant in Padstow if you're very lucky or bought or cooked from one of his many excellent recipe books. Now at his online shop you can order the items in his cook shop, such as utensils and original tea towels, send one of his hampers as a gift, buy his Chilli Chutney, tapenade or homemade Florentines, choose from his personal wine selection or buy gift vouchers. There's a good collection here and some great gift ideas for the cook, but of course only if he or she likes fish.

Site Usability:	★★★★★	Based:	UK
Product Range:	★★★★	Express Delivery Option? (UK)	No
Price Range:	Luxury/Medium	Gift Wrapping Option?	No
Delivery Area:	Worldwide for most items	Returns Procedure:	Down to you

www.silvernutmeg.com

Here's an A–Z of high-quality kitchen equipment, with professional-quality cookware, kettles, knives, pasta makers, toasters, pancake pans, workstations and bread-making machines being just a few of the products offered from brands such as Cuisinart, Gaggia and Magimix. You can also take a look through the home interiors section for candles, rugs, floor cushions and planters. The pictures are very clear and there are lots of products here that would make excellent gifts for cooks.

Site Usability:	★★★★	Based:	UK
Product Range:	★★★★★	Express Delivery Option? (UK)	No
Price Range:	Medium	Gift Wrapping Option?	No
Delivery Area:	Worldwide	Returns Procedure:	Down to you

www.steenbergs.co.uk

This is an attractive website offering a wide choice of organic salts and peppers and herbs and spices, from succulent vanilla to the heady Herbs de Provence. Most of the herbs and spices are offered in three or four different jar sizes and you can buy the spice collections here as well. There's a small selection of Fairtrade teas and tea gifts and accessories such as unusual salt and pepper mills.

Site Usability:	★★★★★	Based:	UK
Product Range:	★★★★★	Express Delivery Option? (UK)	Yes
Price Range:	Medium	Gift Wrapping Option?	No
Delivery Area:	Worldwide	Returns Procedure:	Down to you

Chapter 25

Gardener

This is an area where I'm definitely not an expert, so I've had to take advice from the gardeners in my life as to what to suggest for the enthusiast. I have to confess that I was surprised that there were so many 'gardeners' paradise' websites, but delighted to be able to offer them all to you here.

The only thing I'm certain about is that you can't have too many pairs of really good flower shears and would the person who has pinched mine, yet again, please own up? It's just so annoying. There are some excellent ones here – time to shop.

Sites to Visit

www.baileys-home-garden.co.uk

Baileys offers a wonderfully eclectic mix of home and garden accessories, from pretty Welsh blankets and paint buckets to big sinks, garden lighting, Bailey's Bath Soak and Carrot Hand Cream. There are ideas for junior gardeners' gifts, including tools, watering cans and buckets (all in a gorgeous cherry red), and vintage-style garden forks, pots and twine reels. To order anything on this website you need to phone them – hopefully that will change soon.

Site Usability:	★★★★	Based:;	UK
Product Range:	★★★	Express Delivery Option? (UK)	No
Price Range:	Medium	Gift Wrapping Option?	No
Delivery Area:	UK	Returns Procedure:	Down to you

www.birstall.co.uk

Here you can buy absolutely everything for the garden and gardening enthusiast, from seeds to recliners, barbecues to poultry houses and swimming pool lighting. There are so many products bursting out from the site that it looks a bit confusing, but it's well worth the effort. As far as gifts are concerned, they sell high-quality Felco secateurs, decorative brass Haws watering cans and Leatherman knives, plus loads of other items.

Site Usability:	★★★★	Based:	UK
Product Range:	★★★★	Express Delivery Option? (UK)	No
Price Range:	Medium	Gift Wrapping Option?	No
Delivery Area:	Worldwide	Returns Procedure:	Down to you

www.bradleysthetannery.co.uk

Bradleys is an independent leather tannery based in Shropshire and specialising in the design and manufacture of a unique, high-quality range of garden, gift, leisurewear and lifestyle products. Everything is handmade in the UK using traditional methods and local craftsmen and all the leathers are tanned in-house. If I were a gardener I'd definitely want a pair of their unique gloves or leather-trimmed topiary shears which come in a range of colours.

Site Usability:	★★★★	Based:;	UK
Product Range:	★★★	Express Delivery Option? (UK)	No
Price Range:	Medium	Gift Wrapping Option?	No
Delivery Area:	Worldwide	Returns Procedure:	Down to you

www.crocus.co.uk

Crocus is one of the best gardeners' websites. It offers you not only attractive flowers and plants, giving you more information than most sites, but just about everything else you might need for the garden, all presented in an attractive and informative way. If you want some advice, they're just waiting to give it and they'll always have clever ideas for gifts for occasions such as Mother's Day and Easter. Take a look round now, it's definitely *the* gardener's paradise online.

Site Usability:	★★★★★	Based:	UK
Product Range:	★★★★★	Express Delivery Option? (UK)	Yes
Price Range:	Medium	Gift Wrapping Option?	No
Delivery Area:	UK	Returns Procedure:	Down to you

www.davidaustin.com

David Austin is famous for developing new types of English roses, with his first, 'Constance Spry', launched in 1963. On his website you can find many varieties, including Modern Hybrid Tea Roses and Floribundas, Climbing Roses, Ramblers, Modern Shrub Roses and Wild Species Roses. You'll also find his new fragrant English Roses created specially for the home. You can order his gift-boxed container roses and exquisite rose bouquets here as well for UK delivery.

Site Usability:	★★★★★	Based:	UK
Product Range:	★★★★	Express Delivery Option? (UK)	Yes
Price Range:	Luxury/Medium	Gift Wrapping Option?	Yes for container roses
Delivery Area:	Worldwide except for container roses and bouquets	Returns Procedure:	Down to you

www.franceshilary.com

Here's a wonderful place to find gifts for the gardener in your life. The site is produced by a husband and wife team inspired by visits to long-established working gardens around the country. The products combine practicality with style and most would make excellent presents, although if you're the gardener in your family you'll no doubt want a treat as well. There are beautifully made, classic tools, gloves, aprons and wonderful boots, dibbers, tampers and twine, plus carefully thought out gift sets.

Site Usability:	★★★★★	Based:	UK
Product Range:	★★★★	Express Delivery Option? (UK)	No
Price Range:	Medium	Gift Wrapping Option?	Yes
Delivery Area:	Worldwide	Returns Procedure:	Down to you

www.gardentrading.co.uk

There's a wide range of prices here as Garden Trading offers some unusual pieces of furniture, such as the Broomstick Bench, through to interesting canisters and glassware and the Lisa Stickley collection of cushions, enamel mugs and matchbox covers. There are suggestions in the Gift Ideas section but personally I would recommend having a browse round the whole site as there's a lot to see.

Site Usability:	★★★★	Based:	UK
Product Range:	★★★★	Express Delivery Option? (UK)	No
Price Range:	Medium/Very Good Value	Gift Wrapping Option?	No
Delivery Area:	UK	Returns Procedure:	Down to you

www.grandillusions.co.uk

There's a great deal to look at on this attractive website, but it's easy to navigate and the pictures are really clear. You can choose from the ranges of reasonably priced accessories, including candelabra, storm lanterns, votive glasses, French scented candles and guest soaps, plus a wide selection of small, pretty items for outdoors, from traditional watering cans to bird feeders, glass carriers and sconces.

Site Usability:	★★★★	Based:	UK
Product Range:	★★★★	Express Delivery Option? (UK)	No
Price Range:	Medium	Gift Wrapping Option?	No
Delivery Area:	UK	Returns Procedure:	Down to you

www.grovelands.com

Grovelands is a large garden centre in Berkshire which has managed to transfer just about all its products onto its website. You'll find a wide range of barbecue equipment, including brands like Weber and The Australian Barbecue Company, garden furniture from the highest quality teak to well-priced garden sets, and equipment from pond pumps to propagators. There's also an excellent range of gifts, plus Christmas trees, lights and ornaments. Delivery is free to the UK and they'll also ship most items worldwide.

Site Usability:	★★★★	Based:	UK
Product Range:	★★★★	Express Delivery Option? (UK)	Yes
Price Range:	Medium	Gift Wrapping Option?	No
Delivery Area:	Worldwide	Returns Procedure:	Down to you

www.plantstuff.com

This is not as it sounds to me – a plant website – but a great place to find lifestyle products and gardening gifts. It's beautifully laid out and easy to navigate and you can buy braziers and hammocks, candles in metal pots, slate cheeseboards, lead ducks and Hunter clogs and wellies. There's also a wonderful gardener's hamper, although most gardeners would almost certainly already have some of the items. Returns are free.

Site Usability:	★★★★★	Based:	UK
Product Range:	★★★★	Express Delivery Option? (UK)	No
Price Range:	Medium	Gift Wrapping Option?	No
Delivery Area:	EU	Returns Procedure:	Down to you

www.rhs.org.uk

On the Royal Horticultural Society's website you can become a member of the RHS or give someone else membership, which brings with it the monthly magazine, reduced entry into RHS flower shows and free entry into RHS and partner gardens. You can click through to RHS Shopping Online, which will invite you to the Wisley Bookshop (where you'll find gifts as well as books) and to the other online shopping areas. Alternatively you can go straight through to the main directory which links to other gardening websites.

Site Usability:	★★★★	Express Delivery Option? (UK)	No
Product Range:	★★★	Gift Wrapping Option?	No, but they will send some items as gifts for you
Price Range:	Medium		
Delivery Area:	Worldwide	Returns Procedure:	Down to you
Based:	UK		

www.rkalliston.com

This is an exceptional website offering perfect gifts for the gardener, from wasp catchers and storm lanterns to dibbers and twine, hammocks (to rest in after a hard day) and fairy vases, as well as gardeners' gift sets, china for alfresco dining and pretty flower baskets. These are just a few of the eclectic collection of gardening items available here.

Site Usability:	★★★★★	Based:	UK
Product Range:	★★★★	Express Delivery Option? (UK)	Yes
Price Range:	Medium	Gift Wrapping Option?	No
Delivery Area:	Worldwide	Returns Procedure:	Down to you

www.thecuttinggarden.com

Sarah Raven specialises in teaching people how to grow flowers that can be cut and used indoors and her first book, The Cutting Garden, won The Specialist Garden Book of the Year Award. On her colourful and attractively designed website you'll find a wonderful collection of seeds, seedlings and bulbs, her books and annual diary (a great gift), plus plenty of other ideas such as florists' scissors, flower-arranging gloves and outdoor tableware and glass.

Site Usability: ★★★★	Based:	UK
Product Range: ★★★★	Express Delivery Option? (UK)	No
Price Range: Medium	Gift Wrapping Option?	No
Delivery Area: UK	Returns Procedure:	Down to you

www.thegluttonousgardener.co.uk

Beautifully packaged and hand-tied with raffia, here's a wide selection of well-photographed gifts for any of your friends who like to garden and eat as well. So you'll find sloe gin accompanying young sloe trees, a bottle of Macon with a white grape vine and champagne with terracotta pots planted with sage, thyme, oregano and rosemary. This is an excellent website and something just that little bit different.

Site Usability: ★★★★★	Based:	UK
Product Range: ★★★★	Express Delivery Option? (UK)	Yes
Price Range: Medium	Gift Wrapping Option?	Yes
Delivery Area: UK	Returns Procedure:	Down to you

www.treesdirect.co.uk

Fruit and nut trees, ornamentals and aromatic, evergreen bays are just some of the unusual gift ideas you will find here. The trees are chosen for their colour, blossom, shape and size to suit all types of gardens and patios and they arrive dressed in a hessian sack tied with green garden string, planting instructions and handwritten message card. You can request that your tree arrives on a specific date and if you want advice just give them a call.

Site Usability: ★★★★	Based:	UK
Product Range: ★★★★	Express Delivery Option? (UK)	Yes
Price Range: Medium	Gift Wrapping Option?	No
Delivery Area: Europe	Returns Procedure:	Down to you

Chapter 26

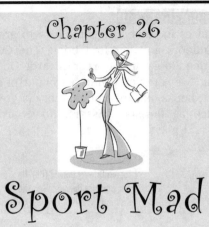

Sport Mad

This is an area where I'm a sort of indirect expert as although I have inexpertly - and badly - played and taken part in lots of types of sport (yes Calum, I said badly, I think they'll understand what that means), I have been involved, through my kids, in most sports, from golf, rugby and rowing to sailing and everything in between.

You do have to be careful with sporting gifts as you can go too far - that fishing rod that's for the wrong sort of fish or golf club that is absolutely not what he or she wants will be an expensive disaster. If you want to have a splurge of that sort I would give a gift voucher so that they can select their own.

On the other hand there are some very clever gifts to be found. I'm sure I've left out some people's sport and if you let me know I'll make sure that I include it next time. For the moment you'll have to make do with the following: garden sports and equipment, walking and hiking, fishing, golf, riding, rugby, football, cricket, sailing, skiing, tennis and squash.

Garden Games and Equipment
– Sites to Visit

www.gardengames.co.uk

Whether you're looking for trampolines, climbing frames, swings and slides, junior and full-sized croquet sets, snooker and pool tables, table tennis tables, aqua slides or an old-fashioned wooden sledge, you'll find everything on this friendly website. All the items are well photographed, they offer speedy UK delivery and will also ship to the US, Canada and Spain.

Site Usability:	★★★★★	Based:	UK
Product Range:	★★★★	Express Delivery Option? (UK)	Yes
Price Range:	Medium	Gift Wrapping Option?	No
Delivery Area:	UK, US, Canada and Spain	Returns Procedure:	Down to you

www.mastersgames.com

At Masters Traditional Games you'll find a wide range of traditional indoor and outdoor games such as Chinese Checkers with a solid teak board and a hand-crafted bagatelle board. Everything is made only in high-quality materials. You'll also find outdoor draughts, table football, table tennis, roulette, croquet, rounders and bar games such as skittles, Aunt Sally and bar billiards.

Site Usability:	★★★★	Based:	UK
Product Range:	★★★★	Express Delivery Option? (UK)	Yes if you contact them
Price Range:	Medium	Gift Wrapping Option?	No
Delivery Area:	Worldwide	Returns Procedure:	Down to you

For the Walking and Hiking Enthusiast – Sites to Visit

www.blacks.co.uk

If you or any member of your family has ever done any camping, walking, hiking or climbing, you'll probably already have visited Blacks, where they offer a well-priced (rather than 'designer') range of clothing and accessories and good-value skiwear in season. You'll find waterproof jackets and trousers, lots of fleece, tents, poles, footwear and socks and great gifts such as Cybalite torches, Kick and Huntsman knives and tools, and Garmin compasses.

Site Usability:	★★★★★	Based:	UK
Product Range:	★★★★★	Express Delivery Option? (UK)	No
Price Range:	Medium/Very Good Value	Gift Wrapping Option?	No
Delivery Area:	UK	Returns Procedure:	Down to you

www.completeoutdoors.co.uk

Everything for walking, trekking, rambling, camping, climbing and many other activities is available here. There is a wide range of tents, rucksacks, sleeping bags, navigation equipment, boots, walking poles and general camping accessories from well-known brands such as Paramo, Berghaus, Brasher, Meindl, Bushbaby, Victorinox, Leki, Karrimor, Leatherman, Rohan, Nomad Medical, Regatta. There's plenty more, plus a good gift section.

Site Usability:	★★★★	Based:	UK
Product Range:	★★★★★	Express Delivery Option? (UK)	No
Price Range:	Medium	Gift Wrapping Option?	No
Delivery Area:	UK	Returns Procedure:	Down to you

For the Fisherman – Sites to Visit

www.fly-fishing-tackle.co.uk

From a full range of rods and reels by manufacturers such as Snowbee, Fulling Mill, Loop and Fladen to waders, hats, caps and gloves - everything for the keen fisherman is available here. If you're looking for a gift, go past the fly-tying kits unless you're sure they'll be welcome and concentrate more on fly boxes, tackle bags and rod carriers or fly-tying tools, lamps and magnifiers.

Site Usability:	★★★★	Based:	UK
Product Range:	★★★★	Express Delivery Option? (UK)	Yes
Price Range:	Luxury/Medium	Gift Wrapping Option?	No
Delivery Area:	Worldwide	Returns Procedure:	Down to you

www.gifts4fishing.co.uk

This is a really good website offering gifts for fishermen that don't get in the way of the rods, reels and flies. You'll find sterling silver fish cufflinks, Barbour scarves and hip flasks, humorous mugs, limited-edition prints, note cards, barware, Richard Wheatley fly boxes and silk ties. They use first-class post for all deliveries and ship worldwide.

Site Usability:	★★★★	Based:	UK
Product Range:	★★★	Express Delivery Option? (UK)	Yes
Price Range:	Medium	Gift Wrapping Option?	No
Delivery Area:	Worldwide	Returns Procedure:	Down to you

For the Golfer – Sites to Visit

www.118golf.co.uk

With its excellent delivery service offering standard, express and Saturday delivery, plus international delivery, and its diverse range of products for the golfer, this is an excellent website for gifts. Check through the golf accessories where you'll find the range from Callaway and Nike, golf gadgets including swing trainers and ball retrievers, DVDs and books.

There's also a gift finder which offers you a selection depending on how much you want to spend.

Site Usability:	★★★★★	Based:	UK
Product Range:	★★★★★	Express Delivery Option? (UK)	Yes
Price Range:	Luxury/Medium	Gift Wrapping Option?	No
Delivery Area:	Worldwide	Returns Procedure:	Down to you

www.gleneagles.com

I probably don't need to tell you that this is a five-star hotel and championship golf course and it offers five-star products in its shop. So, it's expensive. But if you want something really special then this could be a good place to visit (online, I mean). I wouldn't, personally, go for the Gleneagles embroidered clothing unless whoever you're searching for a gift for has actually played there. However, take a quick look at the accessories and you may find something that'll be a success.

Site Usability:	★★★★	Based:	UK
Product Range:	★★★	Express Delivery Option? (UK)	No
Price Range:	Luxury/Medium	Gift Wrapping Option?	No
Delivery Area:	Worldwide	Returns Procedure:	Down to you

www.hattiesmart.com

Hattie Smart designs golf gloves, but not just any old golf gloves – these are designer items, made from the finest leather and available in a range of colours, including pistachio, violet, fuchsia and cranberry for women and kangaroo, bay leaf and vanilla for men. All the gloves are reasonably priced and arrive beautifully packaged, so they'd be the perfect gift for your golf-playing friend or relative.

Site Usability:	★★★	Based:	UK
Product Range:	★★★	Express Delivery Option? (UK)	No
Price Range:	Medium	Gift Wrapping Option?	Yes
Delivery Area:	Worldwide	Returns Procedure:	Down to you

For the Rider – Sites to Visit

www.mad4ponies.com

This is a great site for pony-mad children as unlike lots of other eques-
trian websites aimed at all riders of all ages, this website is just for
kids (girls really) aged 5 to 16 who love to ride. They have funky pink
or purple nubuck jodhpur boots, glitter whips, vibrant grooming kits,
sparkly diamante hat covers, colourful jodhpurs and bright and brilliant
products for your favourite pony. There's also pony-themed gear for
school bags, bedrooms, the bathroom and casual wear.

Site Usability:	★★★★	Based:	UK
Product Range:	★★★	Express Delivery Option? (UK)	Yes
Price Range:	Medium	Gift Wrapping Option?	No
Delivery Area:	Worldwide, but email for a delivery quote for overseas	Returns Procedure:	Down to you

www.theequestrianstore.com

This well-designed and easy-to-navigate website offers express worldwide
delivery and sells just about everything for horse and rider. You'll find a
comprehensive clothing section offering jodhpurs and hard hats, jackets
and boots and in the horse section all you need including saddles, bridles,
horse rugs and accessories. The gift, books and DVD section should give
you some great ideas for gifts for the rider.

Site Usability:	★★★★	Based:	UK
Product Range:	★★★★	Express Delivery Option? (UK)	Yes
Price Range:	Medium	Gift Wrapping Option?	No
Delivery Area:	Worldwide	Returns Procedure:	Down to you

www.thelwell-horsey-gifts.com

Norman Thelwell's wonderfully funny cartoons first appeared in Punch
magazine more than 40 years ago. His portrayals of country life, sporting pursuits and in particular horses and riders are known and loved
the world over. This is not a sophisticated website with sophisticated
pictures, but if you know someone, whatever age, who rides or loves
horses (and has a sense of humour, of course), you'll doubtless find a

gift for them, from cards, diaries, gift wrap and pictures to 'get off my foot!' socks, printed t-shirts, The Riding Academy money box and cross stitch kits.

Site Usability:	★★★	Based:	UK
Product Range:	★★★★★	Express Delivery Option? (UK)	Yes
Price Range:	Luxury	Gift Wrapping Option?	No
Delivery Area:	Worldwide	Returns Procedure:	Down to you

For the Rugby, Football or Cricket Enthusiast – Sites to Visit

www.cartoonstock.com

Cartoonstock is a searchable database of over 60,000 quality gag cartoons, political cartoons, cartoon pictures and illustrations and sporting cartoons by more than 290 of the world's best cartoonists. Once you've chosen your area, e.g. sporting, you just have to put the type of sport (football, for example) into the search box and click 'search'. You'll then have loads of cartoons to choose from which you can add to your shopping basket. Once you've done that you can choose whether you want your selected cartoon as a print or on a mug, t-shirt or mouse mat.

Site Usability:	★★★★	Based:	UK
Product Range:	★★★★★	Express Delivery Option? (UK)	No
Price Range:	Medium/Very Good Value	Gift Wrapping Option?	No
Delivery Area:	Worldwide	Returns Procedure:	Down to you

www.cricketbits.co.uk

This is the one-stop shop for cricket novelties and gifts, with best sellers such as a cricket-ball clock, cricket letter rack and a framed, limited-edition picture commemorating the birth of the Ashes in 1882, showing the handwritten batting orders, scorecard and original scorers' sheet. There are simply loads of ideas, from the cheap and cheerful to the not so cheap (although most things are well priced), so take a look around here for stocking fillers and attractive gifts for all ages of cricketer.

Site Usability:	★★★★	Based:	UK
Product Range:	★★★★	Express Delivery Option? (UK)	No
Price Range:	Medium/Very Good Value	Gift Wrapping Option?	No
Delivery Area:	UK	Returns Procedure:	Down to you

www.kitbag.com

Kitbag is one of the best websites for football and rugby clothing, equipment and accessories. It's clear and quick to navigate, has a wide range of products and offers fast delivery. It keeps well up to date with the latest kit from your favourite team and offers a full range of shoes and balls from all the top brands. As they ship worldwide and offer European shirts as well, there's a quick currency converter ready and waiting for you to use. You can choose from Royal Mail standard or Special deliveries.

Site Usability:	★★★★★	Based:	UK
Product Range:	★★★★★	Express Delivery Option? (UK)	Yes
Price Range:	Medium	Gift Wrapping Option?	No
Delivery Area:	Worldwide	Returns Procedure:	Down to you

www.owzat-cricket.co.uk

Here are bats by Gunn and Moore, Kookaburra and Gray-Nichols, plus loads of other brands. Then there are gloves, pads, kitbags, body protection, accessories and balls. This is a website obviously designed for real cricketers and they're proud of the fact that they've sold to some of the world's top players, such as Phil Defreitas, Karl Krikken and Paul Franks. You'll definitely find something for the cricketer, including junior players, for whom they have an excellent range.

Site Usability:	★★★★★	Based:	UK
Product Range:	★★★★★	Express Delivery Option? (UK)	Yes
Price Range:	Medium	Gift Wrapping Option?	No
Delivery Area:	Europe	Returns Procedure:	Down to you

www.rugbymegastore.com

This is just as it sounds, a huge, busy website offering a total range for the rugby player, including bags, balls, team kit, books and rugby boots by brands such as Mizuno, Puma, Adidas and Nike, plus team t-shirts, protection, videos and news direct from the BBC. In the gift and souvenirs section you'll find ideas such as limited-edition prints, signed photos and rugby balls and World Cup souvenirs.

Site Usability:	★★★★	Based:	UK
Product Range:	★★★★★	Express Delivery Option? (UK)	No
Price Range:	Medium	Gift Wrapping Option?	No
Delivery Area:	UK	Returns Procedure:	Down to you

www.rugbyrelics.com

Rugby Relics is a family business based in Neath in North Wales where you'll find the most amazing collection of rugby gifts and memorabilia. If you want to buy a gift for a rugby-mad friend there's probably no better place to visit. You'll almost certainly find something from the collection of official programmes, prints and clothing or by clicking through to its sister website rugbygifts.com.

Site Usability:	★★★	Based:	UK
Product Range:	★★★	Express Delivery Option? (UK)	Yes
Price Range:	Medium	Gift Wrapping Option?	No
Delivery Area:	Worldwide	Returns Procedure:	Down to you

For the Sailor – Sites to Visit

www.chandlerystore.co.uk

Musto, Henri Lloyd and Gill are the three main brands on offer here for the sailor, including the clothing, accessories, footwear and luggage ranges. You'll also find deck shoes and chandlery, Kahuna watches, Leatherman knives, Silva compasses and charts and marine books, plus the clever Sea Shore six-speed Marine folding bike which stows away on board or in the boot of your car.

Site Usability:	★★★★	Based:	UK
Product Range:	★★★★	Express Delivery Option? (UK)	No
Price Range:	Medium	Gift Wrapping Option?	No
Delivery Area:	Europe	Returns Procedure:	Down to you

www.crewclothing.co.uk

This is an attractive and modern website with a constantly expanding range. It offers all the Crew gear, from the full collection of sailing-inspired clothing to lots of other choices, including hard-wearing footwear, faux fur jackets and gilets and excellent travel bags, gloves, hats and socks. The site offers standard and next-day UK delivery and same day in central London if you order by 12pm.

Site Usability:	★★★★	Based:	UK
Product Range:	★★★★	Express Delivery Option? (UK)	Yes
Price Range:	Medium	Gift Wrapping Option?	No
Delivery Area:	Worldwide	Returns Procedure:	Down to you

For the Skier or Boarder – Sites to Visit

www.ellis-brigham.com

On its wonderful, clearly photographed website for mountaineers and skiers, Ellis Brigham offers brands such as The North Face, Patagonia, Ice Breaker and Lowe Alpine. Every possible type of equipment is clearly shown and there are some good sporting gift ideas as well, including items by Leatherman, Victorinox, Maglite and Toollogic. In the ski section you'll find lots of different makes of ski clothing, colourful beanies and humorous ski socks, plus boots and skis by all the great brands.

Site Usability:	★★★★★	Based:	UK
Product Range:	★★★★★	Express Delivery Option? (UK)	No
Price Range:	Luxury/Medium	Gift Wrapping Option?	No
Delivery Area:	Worldwide	Returns Procedure:	Down to you

www.snowandrock.com

Snow and Rock is a well-known retailer for skiers, snowboarders and rock climbers, with a full range of equipment and clothing and accessories by brands such as Animal, Billabong, Ski Jacket, Helly Hanson, O'Neill, Quiksilver, Salomon and Oakley. There's lots of advice on what to buy and on fit. In the gift and gadget section you'll find ideas including books and films, watches, two-way radios, solar chargers and compasses.

Site Usability:	★★★★★	Based:	UK
Product Range:	★★★★★	Express Delivery Option? (UK)	Yes
Price Range:	Luxury/Medium/Very Good Value	Gift Wrapping Option?	No
Delivery Area:	Worldwide	Returns Procedure:	Down to you

For the Tennis or Squash Player – Sites to Visit

www.pwp.com

Calling itself 'Europe's No 1 racket specialist for tennis, squash and badminton', you can see the reason clearly when you browse this site. There's a great deal for the tennis player, with rackets by Wilson, Dunlop, Head, Slazenger and Prince, tennis shoes, well-priced balls and lots of accessories, including the ITP series of DVDs. If you're thinking of buying a gift for a player you would need to know exactly what they want or you could, of course, buy them the huge Wilson-logo umbrella.

Site Usability:	★★★★	Based:	UK
Product Range:	★★★★★	Express Delivery Option? (UK)	No
Price Range:	Luxury/Medium	Gift Wrapping Option?	No
Delivery Area:	Worldwide	Returns Procedure:	Down to you

www.racquetlink.com

This is another excellent tennis website retailing racquets by Prince, Wilson, Babolat and Yonex among others, ball baskets and ball lobbers by Lobster, Tennis Tower and Shotmaker, and everything else for the tennis enthusiast. There is also a Unique Gifts section where you'll find things like tennis bookends, coin trays, bottle openers and letter racks and they offer gift certificates as well.

Site Usability:	★★★★★	Based:	UK
Product Range:	★★★★★	Express Delivery Option? (UK)	Yes
Price Range:	Luxury/Medium	Gift Wrapping Option?	No
Delivery Area:	Worldwide	Returns Procedure:	Down to you

Chapter 27

Bookworm

I think that just about everyone I know enjoys a good read. I certainly do and we have far too many books in our house that no one seems inclined to sort through – do they ever? Books make excellent gifts provided you put a bit of extra thought into your choice. Below you'll find the places where you can buy not just the everyday read but also some special first editions and signed copies. Expensive, I know, but a fabulous gift for a collector.

I've also listed a couple of websites where you can search for specific books, just in case the major bookstores don't have them in stock when you need them. Most books are so heavily discounted these days that it's rare you'll have to pay the full price online. However, it can be frustrating if you know what you want but it's not available for a few weeks, so give these sites a try.

Sites to Visit

www.abebooks.co.uk

This is the worldwide marketplace for rare, secondhand and out-of-print books. You just need to know the title or the author and if it's available it'll be found immediately. You can then narrow your search to see only first editions, or signed copies, among other options. For special gifts this would be an excellent website as you can choose from a selection of real collectors' items. Alternatively you can simply track down that book you lost some years ago and always wanted to read again.

Site Usability:	★★★★★	Based:	UK
Product Range:	★★★★★	Express Delivery Option? (UK)	No
Price Range:	Luxury/Medium	Gift Wrapping Option?	No
Delivery Area:	Worldwide	Returns Procedure:	Down to you

www.amazon.co.uk

At Amazon you can buy not only books but so much more, including your new Kenwood food mixer or digital camera, baby products and tools for your garden, which can make life rather confusing. They have probably the most comprehensive range of books, music, movies and games available anywhere, frequently at the best price, and the service is excellent.

Site Usability:	★★★★★	Based:	UK
Product Range:	★★★★★	Express Delivery Option? (UK)	Yes
Price Range:	Medium/Very Good Value	Gift Wrapping Option?	Yes
Delivery Area:	Worldwide	Returns Procedure:	Down to you

www.best-book-price.co.uk
www.bookbrain.co.uk

These are two excellent places where you can compare book prices and see who has the book you're looking for in stock to send out immediately. They're both very easy to use. They're not really for buying ordinary paperbacks, although you can use them for that if you want to, but when you've found a special hardback that you want to give as a gift next week and you're being quoted 4-6 weeks' delivery, you may be able to find another bookshop which has it ready to send out. At the same time you can compare the prices across bookstores.

Site Usability:	★★★★★	Price Range:	Luxury/Medium/Very Good Value
Product Range:	★★★★★	Based:	UK

www.blackwells.co.uk

If you prefer a less busy book website then pay a visit to Blackwell's of Oxford, established in 1879 and an online store for over 10 years. What you'll find here is an excellent and more personal service with a clear path through to the various departments: Fiction, Leisure and Lifestyle, Science, Humanities, Arts, Medical, Business Finance and Law. There are some good discounts to be found and shipping is free to the UK on orders over £20.

Site Usability:	★★★★★	Based:	UK
Product Range:	★★★★★	Express Delivery Option? (UK)	Yes
Price Range:	Luxury/Medium	Gift Wrapping Option?	No
Delivery Area:	Worldwide	Returns Procedure:	Down to you

www.bookdepository.co.uk

The Book Depository claims to be the fastest growing book distributor in Europe and there's certainly a huge selection available through this easy-to-navigate website. This is also one of the best places to search out books you've been unable to find elsewhere. If you just want a browse here you can take a look at the editors' blogs and catch up on the latest book news and reviews. They offer free delivery to most countries worldwide.

Site Usability:	★★★★★	Express Delivery Option? (UK)	No
Product Range:	★★★★★	Gift Wrapping Option?	No
Price Range:	Medium/Very Good Value	Returns Procedure:	Down to you but contact them first by
Delivery Area:	Worldwide		email
Based:	UK		

www.bookgiant.com

Next time you're looking for a new book, take a quick look at bookgiant. com. They don't have anything like the range of some other bookstores, but what they do have are very good special offers, with special editions (usually small hardbacks) of brand new titles at up to 60% off the normal price. Postage and packing are free if you order three items or more; otherwise it's just £1. You need to register to order (so they can send you regular updates and keep your details to make your next order even quicker).

Site Usability:	★★★★★	Based:	UK
Product Range:	★★★	Express Delivery Option? (UK)	No
Price Range:	Very Good Value	Gift Wrapping Option?	No
Delivery Area:	Worldwide	Returns Procedure:	Down to you

www.borders.co.uk

Here you can sign up for Borders Email which means you'll be the first to find out about the in-store promotions, take part in the competitions, find out about events near you and join the new Book Group. Books Etc is also part of the Borders group and is featured here. If you want to order a book online you can just click straight through to the partner website at www.amazon.co.uk.

Site Usability:	★★★★	Based:	UK
Product Range:	★★★★★	Express Delivery Option? (UK)	Yes
Price Range:	Medium/Very Good Value	Gift Wrapping Option?	Yes
Delivery Area:	Worldwide through amazon.co.uk	Returns Procedure:	Free

www.compman.co.uk

This site started off as a computer books website but has moved into general educational books and fiction. So you can buy the latest John Grisham alongside Selected Papers on Particle Image Velocimetry. Help! The site is clearly laid out and you can see exactly what's in stock or on limited availability. Some of the discounts are very good. Standard delivery is 1-2 days and is free on orders over a small amount, which varies.

Site Usability:	★★★★	Based:	UK
Product Range:	★★★	Express Delivery Option? (UK)	Yes
Price Range:	Medium	Gift Wrapping Option?	No
Delivery Area:	Worldwide	Returns Procedure:	Down to you

www.hatchards.co.uk

Hatchards, booksellers since 1797, is the oldest surviving bookshop in London and is now based in its luxurious quarters at 187 Piccadilly, right next door to Fortnum and Mason. Not only do they offer a good choice of titles in hardback and paperback, from fiction, children's books, art and architecture, biography, food and wine, gardening, history and humour, but they also specialise in signed and special editions and what they call VIPs (Very Important Publications) - their recommendations for the season.

Site Usability:	★★★★★	Based:	UK
Product Range:	★★★★★	Express Delivery Option? (UK)	Yes
Price Range:	Luxury/Medium	Gift Wrapping Option?	No
Delivery Area:	Worldwide	Returns Procedure:	Down to you

www.jonkers.co.uk

Jonkers specialises in modern first editions, fine illustrated books, classic children's fiction and 19th-century literature. So if you have a goddaughter who might appreciate a first edition of Michael Bond's Paddington Goes to Town, you'll find it here, plus AA Milne, Enid Blyton, Lewis Carroll and many more. Because some of these books are very expensive and precious (up into the £1,000s), you can't order online but need to phone them using their freephone number.

Site Usability:	★★★★	Based:	UK
Product Range:	★★★	Express Delivery Option? (UK)	No
Price Range:	Luxury	Gift Wrapping Option?	No
Delivery Area:	Worldwide	Returns Procedure:	Down to you

www.redhouse.co.uk

Red House specialises in children's books for all ages, from babies to young adults. They produce a catalogue each month featuring an introduction from a leading author and their bright and colourful website carries a wide selection of handpicked books which is updated regularly. There's even a safe, fun online community for children, including competitions, things to do and a moderated message board. Every book is discounted and P&P is free when you buy four or more books.

Site Usability:	★★★★	Based:	UK
Product Range:	★★★★	Express Delivery Option? (UK)	Yes
Price Range:	Medium/Very Good Value	Gift Wrapping Option?	No
Delivery Area:	UK	Returns Procedure:	Down to you

www.thebookplace.com

If you want a new bookshop to look at you could have a browse on this very clear site, which offers an extremely wide range and shows availability as soon as you search for your book. They also have a good selection of signed copies which would make excellent gifts and you can read the weekly press reviews on the latest releases. Postage is £2.75 per single book order, plus 50p for each additional book, and they offer worldwide shipping and express delivery.

Site Usability:	★★★★	Based:	UK
Product Range:	★★★★	Express Delivery Option? (UK)	Yes
Price Range:	Medium	Gift Wrapping Option?	Yes
Delivery Area:	Worldwide	Returns Procedure:	Down to you

www.waterstones.com

Waterstone's website is extremely clear and easy to navigate and a lot less cluttered than many of the online bookstores. You can browse categories from the Home Page menu which includes areas such as Business, Finance and Law, Computing, Education and Comics and Graphic Novels alongside the more usual Fiction, Children's Books, Food and Drink and Sport. Delivery is free on orders over £15 within the UK and they offer surface or courier services for international orders.

Site Usability:	★★★★★	Based:	UK
Product Range:	★★★★★	Express Delivery Option? (UK)	Yes
Price Range:	Medium	Gift Wrapping Option?	Yes
Delivery Area:	Worldwide	Returns Procedure:	Down to you

www.whsmith.co.uk

On W H Smith's easy-on-the-eye website you can buy books (often at very good discounts), all the latest DVDs, music and computer games, plus a small selection from the stationery ranges. There's also a wide selection of gift ideas, including original historic newspapers and commemorative sporting books, and you can subscribe at a discount to all your favourite magazines. The difference between this and a lot of book/music/games websites is that it's clear and simple to navigate but also has an excellent choice.

Site Usability:	★★★★★	Based:	UK
Product Range:	★★★★★	Express Delivery Option? (UK)	No
Price Range:	Medium	Gift Wrapping Option?	No
Delivery Area:	UK	Returns Procedure:	Down to you

Chapter 28

Music, Movies and Games

There are literally hundreds of places you can buy CDs, DVDs and computer games online and I wouldn't dream of trying to tell you about them all. I've selected a few that I have tried and found to be very good, plus the essential price comparison sites best-cd-price, dvdpricecheck and uk.gamestracker. On these sites you can, having selected the DVD, CD or game you're looking for, compare prices and click through to order.

As many of the websites you'll be offered don't charge postage, you can select the place where you get the best deal for each item and place as many orders as you like. You can also, of course, go to www.amazon.co.uk where you can order all of them even more quickly using the one-click setting, which I find far, far too tempting.

Sites to Visit

www.best-cd-price.co.uk

Know the CD you want to buy but want to make sure you get the best price? Use this price comparison website, which not only shows where you'll find the best deal but includes the postage details as well so you absolutely know where you are. This website is almost unbelievably quick to use and you can use it for DVDs and games as well. As an example, if you do a search on Take That's 'Beautiful World', you'll be given 11 places where you can buy it online, with prices from £8.79 to £12.60. Quite a difference, I'm sure you'll agree.

Site Usability:	★★★★★	Price Range:	Luxury/Medium/Very Good Value
Product Range:	★★★★★	Based:	UK

www.cdwow.com

You'll find some of the best prices around here and again this site covers all mediums, from CDs and DVDs to computer games. Because the prices are so good it would be worth purchasing gift vouchers here as you can be sure that the recipient will get a good deal, whatever they choose to spend them on. They offer free delivery worldwide for all items and regular special offers.

Site Usability:	★★★★★	Based:	UK
Product Range:	★★★★★	Express Delivery Option? (UK)	No
Price Range:	Medium/Very Good Value	Gift Wrapping Option?	No
Delivery Area:	Worldwide	Returns Procedure:	Down to you

www.dvdpricecheck.co.uk

If you're looking for a DVD, this is the place to start as you can see what's available throughout all the world regions. With so many places to buy films online it's hard to know without spending hours which is the best site, and with different sites charging different amounts, things get even worse. So here it is, the website that'll compare prices for you worldwide. Just key in your title and region (UK is Region 2) and you'll get all the answers. Many of the websites they offer don't charge you delivery on top, so you can order from as many as you want and as often as you like. Sounds tempting? It's hard to know when to stop.

Site Usability:	★★★★★	Price Range:	Luxury/Medium/Very Good Value
Product Range:	★★★★★	Based:	UK

www.game.co.uk

Whether you have an Xbox 360, Gamecube, Gameboy Micro, or Sony PS3 (or whatever the latest gaming station is), you'll find a huge range of games here for all of them, plus the consoles themselves and accessories. I have to be careful here as things will no doubt have moved on by the time you're reading this, so check out this site to find out what's new and hot. They also offer a reward points system – a good idea as loyalty to game sites is thin on the ground due to the amount of competition.

Site Usability:	★★★★★	Based:	UK
Product Range:	★★★★★	Express Delivery Option? (UK)	Yes for the UK
Price Range:	Medium/Very Good Value	Gift Wrapping Option?	No
Delivery Area:	Worldwide	Returns Procedure:	Down to you

www.hmv.co.uk

The HMV shops on Oxford Street and within Selfridges are usually the first places that my kids want to hit on a trip to London and I quite understand why. No matter whether you're looking for chart CDs or DVDs or something a bit harder to find, they're bound to have it. Up till now their online store has not matched their offline presence, but that's all changed. The website is super easy to navigate and there's a superb choice. As this is a retailer you're almost bound to know, you may well want to buy here.

Site Usability:	★★★★★	Based:	UK
Product Range:	★★★★★	Express Delivery Option? (UK)	Yes and Worldwide Express
Price Range:	Medium/Very Good Value	Gift Wrapping Option?	No
Delivery Area:	Worldwide	Returns Procedure:	Down to you

www.play.com

Music, movies, games and books at very good prices with delivery included are available from this Channel Islands-based website. They offer a huge range of films on DVD, CDs and games for all systems, plus special offers such as two DVDs for £12, 30% off specific boxed sets and 40% off a wide choice of current releases. Because delivery is included you can order individual disks as often as you want to rather than having to group orders together to save on postage.

Site Usability: ★★★★★	Based:	Channel Islands
Product Range: ★★★★★	Express Delivery Option? (UK)	No
Price Range: Medium/Very Good Value	Gift Wrapping Option?	No
Delivery Area: Worldwide	Returns Procedure:	Down to you

www.sendit.com

The difference here, as this is yet another website offering games consoles, games, DVDs and computer peripherals and software, is the service. They offer not only a courier service within the UK to make sure your order arrives when you need it, free UK delivery and speedy worldwide delivery, but also gift certificates and gift wrapping on most items with which they can include your personal message – and you can even choose your wrapping paper.

Site Usability: ★★★★★	Based:	Northern Ireland
Product Range: ★★★★★	Express Delivery Option? (UK)	Yes
Price Range: Medium/Very Good Value	Gift Wrapping Option?	Yes
Delivery Area: Worldwide	Returns Procedure:	Down to you

www.uk.gamestracker.com

However much you may dislike those extremely noisy (and too often violent) computer games, you won't want your precious ones spending more of their not-so-hard-earned pocket money than they need to. If you want to get them the latest game for Christmas or they want to choose one themselves, send them to Games Tracker, where you/they can compare the prices with all the retailers for any specific game and get the deal of the moment.

Site Usability: ★★★★★	Based:	UK
Product Range: ★★★★★	Express Delivery Option? (UK)	No
Price Range: Medium/Very Good Value	Gift Wrapping Option?	No
Delivery Area: Worldwide	Returns Procedure:	Down to you

www.virginmegastores.co.uk

On its sleek, gunmetal-grey website Virgin makes it easy for you to order all the latest releases and pre-order the next 'must-have' CDs, DVDs and games. They don't, as most music websites do, always give you the full and discounted price information and they may not be the cheapest, but if you compare prices you'll find they're not at the top end either. The benefit here is that all the information is very clear and UK delivery is free of charge.

Site Usability:	★★★★	Based:	UK
Product Range:	★★★★★	Express Delivery Option? (UK)	No
Price Range:	Medium/Very Good Value	Gift Wrapping Option?	No
Delivery Area:	UK and ROI	Returns Procedure:	Down to you

Chapter 29

Photographer

In these days of digital photography – and, it seems, digital everything – just about everyone appears to have a camera, a computer and an internet connection, enabling them to take pictures, download them and send them rushing across the world. The first step is obviously the camera and if you know someone who hasn't yet gone the digital route, one of the new tiny but incredibly efficient megapixel cameras will not only do the job perfectly but will make a marvellous present.

In our family we have two types of photographer – firstly there's my husband, who is a keen and very good sports photographer and has all the kit, from the high-tech Canon camera to all the different lenses. Then there are my 16-year-old daughter and myself, who make do very happily with the extremely compact cameras I've mentioned above, only hers is purple and mine is orange. They take excellent pictures and are great fun to use (and you can carry them around in your handbag). Go shop.

One further word – if you want to give someone who already has a camera a photographic-inspired gift, consider buying them Photoshop Elements, which enables them to crop, resize, join together and generally play with their pictures (and I'll admit right here and now that it was my eldest son who had to teach me how to use it). It's a great piece of software, but you'll have to go somewhere like www.amazon.co.uk or www.software.co.uk to buy it.

Sites to Visit

www.cameraking.co.uk

There are, of course, lots of places you can buy a camera online, but you might like to take a look here as this is a great place for real enthusiasts. They not only offer a huge range of cameras and show you straight away what's in stock, but the menu is very clear and there are some excellent accessories, including camera bags and cases and tripods of all shapes and sizes. I wouldn't recommend that you come here if you're looking for the latest pink, pocket-sized marvel, but for real equipment this is a great place.

Site Usability:	★★★★★	Based:	UK
Product Range:	★★★★★	Express Delivery Option? (UK)	Yes
Price Range:	Luxury/Medium/Very Good Value	Gift Wrapping Option	No
Delivery Area:	UK	Returns Procedure:	Down to you

www.cameras2u.com

This is an excellent website where you'll find all the new models at very good prices. Compare the prices on a comparison website such as kelkoo. co.uk and you'll find they're nearly always the lowest. There's a lot of advice on digital photography in general, such as linking up with your PC and printer, plus photo-taking tips. Couple this with free UK next-day delivery on orders over £100 placed before 1pm and this is definitely somewhere you should visit.

Site Usability:	★★★★	Based:	UK
Product Range:	★★★★	Express Delivery Option? (UK)	Yes
Price Range:	Luxury/Medium/Very Good Value	Gift Wrapping Option	No
Delivery Area:	UK	Returns Procedure:	Down to you in agreement with them

www.cameras.co.uk

This website will certainly take you to the places where you can buy your chosen digital camera for less, but it is, first and foremost, a review and advice centre on digital photography in general and on all the new camera ranges. Once you've had a good read and selected your camera, it will give you the price comparisons for the retailers offering that specific model and you can see some amazing differentials in price. It's a good place to check out if you're not sure which camera you want to buy or you want to compare prices.

Site Usability:	★★★	Based:	UK
Product Range:	★★★★	Express Delivery Option? (UK)	No
Price Range:	Luxury/Medium/Very Good Value	Gift Wrapping Option	No
Delivery Area:	UK	Returns Procedure:	Down to you in agreement with them

www.digitalfirst.co.uk

Here you'll find the latest cameras from all the major brand names, including Pentax, Canon, Nikon, Olympus and Fuji, plus scanners and printers. It's an extremely quick and easy website to navigate, with clear pages and easy buying instructions. It also offers two years' warranty, three months' free helpline, a gift wrapping service and free shipping to the UK mainland.

Site Usability:	★★★★	Based:	UK
Product Range:	★★★★	Express Delivery Option? (UK)	No
Price Range:	Luxury/Medium/Very Good Value	Gift Wrapping Option	Yes
Delivery Area:	Worldwide	Returns Procedure:	Down to you

www.digitalframesdirect.com

Having been given one of these frames by my son for Christmas (yes, lucky me), I can definitely recommend them as a gift for any photographer. They beat sticking pictures into albums as far as I'm concerned, are easy to update with your latest pics and provide a constant reminder of the people, places and events you want to keep in mind. Here you'll find a good selection in a range of sizes, right up to 10 inches, plus a selection of memory cards.

Site Usability:	★★★★★	Based:	UK
Product Range:	★★★★	Express Delivery Option? (UK)	Yes
Price Range:	Medium	Gift Wrapping Option	No
Delivery Area:	UK	Returns Procedure:	Down to you

www.expansys.co.uk

This website specialising in wireless technology is an excellent place to find out about the latest mobile phones, smartphones and pocket PCs, plus GPS navigation systems. In the Digital Camera department you can immediately see the best sellers (and how long you'll have to wait for delivery), then browse the list which is clearly sub-sectioned by brand. For some excellent gifts check out the Ora and Cullmann tripods and accessories – they're just that little bit different.

Site Usability:	★★★★★	Based:	UK
Product Range:	★★★★★	Express Delivery Option? (UK)	Yes
Price Range:	Luxury/Medium	Gift Wrapping Option	No
Delivery Area:	Worldwide	Returns Procedure:	Down to you

www.fotosense.co.uk

Fotosense offers an excellent range of the latest cameras, plus everything you need for digital video, MP3 players, binoculars, printers and studio lighting from a list of over 50 manufacturers. In addition it has one of the largest photographic accessory lists available in the UK. If you need advice on what to buy you can just give them a call and they'll be delighted to help. They deliver to the UK only but offer extremely fast delivery options.

Site Usability:	★★★★★	Based:	UK
Product Range:	★★★★★	Express Delivery Option? (UK)	Yes
Price Range:	Luxury/Medium/Very Good Value	Gift Wrapping Option	No
Delivery Area:	Worldwide	Returns Procedure:	Down to you in agreement with them

www.fototech.co.uk

At Fototech you can buy the latest digital photo frames by Digiview, Coskin, Brilliance and more (including three- and four-screen frames), plus kits that enable you to transfer your digital pics onto marble coasters, tiles, canvas and, using the Image Transfer Kit, onto practically any paintable surface. You'll need to go somewhere else for your memory cards, but the range of frames here is exceptional, so it's well worth having a look.

Site Usability:	★★★★	Based:	UK
Product Range:	★★★★	Express Delivery Option? (UK)	Yes
Price Range:	Luxury/Medium	Gift Wrapping Option	No
Delivery Area:	EU	Returns Procedure:	Down to you

www.pixmania.co.uk

Pixmania has a wonderfully slick, colourful and user-friendly website and tells you straight away about the best sellers and the newly released models. You can become a VIPix and receive a discount and free delivery for a year, plus 20% off extended warranties, or give one of their gift certificates. The range of products is huge and very much specialises in the latest 'must-have' camera. The site is also nearly always one of the best for price.

Site Usability:	★★★★★	Based:	France
Product Range:	★★★★★	Express Delivery Option? (UK)	Yes
Price Range:	Medium/Very Good Value	Gift Wrapping Option	No
Delivery Area:	Worldwide	Returns Procedure:	Down to you

Chapter 30

Artist and Musician

There are lots of clever gift ideas available online for everyone from junior artists and musicians to the more experienced kind. This is an area where once again I would suggest that if you want to give quite a big gift you need to find out exactly what would be the best thing or give a gift voucher, rather than making the choice yourself. I'm only trying to stop you from going out and buying that Buffet clarinet just as your godchild is about to give up - and I really, really do know about these things.

Quite a few of the websites below offer gift suggestions, particularly at Christmas, although they're not, in the main, gift retailers. You'll find all the specialised kit alongside ideas for beginners and most of it at some surprisingly good prices.

For the Artist – Sites to Visit

www.artboxdirect.co.uk

Artboxdirect offers discount art supplies, providing artists with a wide range of art materials from Winsor & Newton and Daler Rowney. There are good discounts off the prices of all paints and brushes, pastels, sets, pads and cases. It's best if you already know which colours you want to order, although you can download the full colour charts for each range of paints should you need to.

Site Usability:	★★★★	Based:	UK
Product Range:	★★★★	Express Delivery Option? (UK)	No
Price Range:	Medium/Very Good Value	Gift Wrapping Option?	No
Delivery Area:	Europe	Returns Procedure:	Down to you

www.lawrence.co.uk

Here are grown-up artists' materials for the grown-up artist. The site carries a huge range and offers a full advisory service and quick delivery. You can buy acrylics, art boards, glass paints and palettes, gold and silver leaf, papers, cards and envelopes, everything for printmaking, plus storage and packaging (and loads more). You can also buy gift vouchers for the artist in your life or choose from the site's suggestions.

Site Usability:	★★★★	Based:	UK
Product Range:	★★★★★	Express Delivery Option? (UK)	No
Price Range:	Luxury/Medium	Gift Wrapping Option?	No
Delivery Area:	Worldwide	Returns Procedure:	Down to you

www.yorkshireartstore.co.uk

Discover a wonderful treasure trove of artists' and craft supplies, from paints, pencils, brushes and inks, to clay, craft paper and adhesives, fabric, art and needlecraft equipment and accessories including frames, tapestry wools, stranded cotton and fantasy threads. This is not one of the most highly sophisticated websites (and even more confusingly it now calls itself The Picture Place), but it's easy to navigate and quick to order from. Expect a high level of service and speedy delivery and call them if you need advice.

Site Usability:	★★★★	Based:	UK
Product Range:	★★★★	Express Delivery Option? (UK)	No
Price Range:	Medium	Gift Wrapping Option?	No
Delivery Area:	UK	Returns Procedure:	Down to you

For the Musician – Sites to Visit

www.dawsonsonline.com

Once you arrive at this website you need to choose whether you want to go to the piano and orchestral instrument department, where you'll find an excellent range including sheet music, or through to rock and hi tech, which offers electric and acoustic guitars, microphones, mixers, synthesizers and the like. It's an extremely well laid out website, all prices and delivery times are clearly shown and it carries a full range of accessories.

Site Usability:	★★★★★	Based:	UK
Product Range:	★★★★★	Express Delivery Option? (UK)	No
Price Range:	Luxury/Medium	Gift Wrapping Option?	Yes
Delivery Area:	UK	Returns Procedure:	Down to you

www.musicroom.co.uk

Established in 1995, Musicroom is a global retailer, shipping products out to over 100 countries and offering one of the largest selections of sheet music, song books, books about music and tutor methods in the world. At Christmas time they offer a gift selection, including Christmas music, learning guides for different instruments, CDs and instrument accessories. It really is an excellent website, so if you know any young musicians, do stop off here.

Site Usability:	★★★★★	Based:	UK
Product Range:	★★★★	Express Delivery Option? (UK)	No
Price Range:	Luxury/Medium	Gift Wrapping Option?	No
Delivery Area:	Worldwide	Returns Procedure:	Down to you

www.signetmusic.com

This is quite a confusing site to look at, probably because the range is so big, but if you're in the market for a new or secondhand musical instrument you must look here as the prices can be very good. Because there's such a wide choice it's very helpful that they have a manufacturer index showing almost 100 brands, so you can go easily to the make and product you're looking for. They offer online live support (which you may well need) and worldwide delivery for just about everything.

Site Usability:	★★★	Based:	UK
Product Range:	★★★★	Express Delivery Option? (UK)	Yes
Price Range:	Luxury/Medium	Gift Wrapping Option?	No
Delivery Area:	Worldwide	Returns Procedure:	Down to you

www.themusiccellar.co.uk

Choose from a fantastic selection of musical instruments on this clear and easy-to-navigate website, from clarinets to grand pianos to acoustic and electric guitars. They offer a repair service and you can buy sheet music here as well. The instruments are discounted (check the price with your local supplier and/or a price comparison website to make sure) and some of the prices look excellent. Prices for UK shipping are supplied online but you need to call them for overseas.

Site Usability:	★★★★★	Based:	UK
Product Range:	★★★★★	Express Delivery Option? (UK)	No
Price Range:	Luxury/Medium	Gift Wrapping Option?	No
Delivery Area:	Worldwide	Returns Procedure:	Down to you

www.woodwindandbrass.co.uk

Woodwind and Brass has an attractive website which draws you into the wide range of products, including saxophones from Yanagisawa and Selmer, clarinets from Buffet, LeBlanc and Jupiter, flutes and piccolos from Trevor J James and Buffet, bass clarinets from Jupiter and Besson, and bassoons from Oscar Adler. Accessories include mouthpieces, reeds, stands, gig bags, cases and care and maintenance materials.

Site Usability:	★★★★★	Based:	UK
Product Range:	★★★★★	Express Delivery Option? (UK)	No
Price Range:	Luxury/Medium	Gift Wrapping Option?	No
Delivery Area:	Worldwide	Returns Procedure:	Down to you

Chapter 31

Traveller

K, I'll admit it: this is one of my favourite areas as I love to travel. I book absolutely everything online, first getting details of flights and checking out hotels, down to the rooms themselves, and then going for it. I rarely book flights, hotels and car hire all together as I prefer to be absolutely sure that I'm getting the type of room I want and the best car hire deal. That's not to say that you shouldn't book everything together, I just prefer not to (and I probably drive my family mad in the process).

For those, like me, who are travel addicts, having the right kit (and by right I mean in terms of efficiency rather than 'of the moment') is essential, as is having the latest information, so if you know someone who's like me, take a look below and get some ideas.

Sites to Visit

www.cntraveller.com

For an excellent (and reasonably priced) gift for the travel lover just click onto the website for Condé Nast's luxury travel magazine, then go through to subscribe. You can give the gift of 3 or 12 months' subscription, which (at time of writing) comes with the CN Traveller Privilege Card, enabling the recipient to save on luxury holidays worldwide. While you're on this website you'll no doubt want to have a browse too through the mouthwatering lists of wonderful places to go next.

Site Usability:	★★★★★	Based:	UK
Product Range:	★★★★★	Express Delivery Option? (UK)	No
Price Range:	Medium	Gift Wrapping Option?	No
Delivery Area:	Worldwide		

www.essentials4travel.co.uk

This is one of the best travel product and luggage websites, offering everything from classic and well-priced luggage by brands such as Antler, Travelpro and Skyflite to business cases and laptop bags, travel wallets, backpacks and wheeled duffles. You can also order your Michelin Red Guides and road atlases here, plus electric and PDA adaptors. They do have a small Gift Ideas section, but you might like also to look in Gadgets and Electronics for something for the traveller in your family.

Site Usability:	★★★★★	Based:	UK
Product Range:	★★★★★	Express Delivery Option? (UK)	No
Price Range:	Medium	Gift Wrapping Option?	No
Delivery Area:	Worldwide	Returns Procedure:	Down to you

www.goplanetgo.co.uk

If you don't find something here to give as a gift to someone who's addicted to travel, it would be really surprising as the range, of both products and prices, is enormous. There's everything from mini compact ipod speakers and DVD players to clever chargers and gadgets, essentials from leather organisers to stylish toiletry bags and the site's own well-edited selection of gifts, such as tiny camera tripods, aluminium travel games, TVR multi-function tools and spirit-level cufflinks.

Site Usability:	★★★★★	Based:	UK
Product Range:	★★★★	Express Delivery Option? (UK)	No
Price Range:	Medium/Very Good Value	Gift Wrapping Option?	No
Delivery Area:	Worldwide	Returns Procedure	Down to you

www.kikijames.com

Alongside her high-quality photo albums and frames, baby books, purses and leather-covered ring binders, Kiki James has some very good products for the traveller, including passport covers, leather luggage tags, journals, wash bags and tidy trays, all of which are available in a wide range of colours and all of which can be personalised. Products here are automatically wrapped and gift boxed, then you can choose her cream and sapphire bespoke outer wrap as well.

Site Usability:	★★★★★	Based:	UK
Product Range:	★★★★	Express Delivery Option? (UK)	Yes
Price Range:	Medium	Gift Wrapping Option?	Yes
Delivery Area:	Worldwide	Returns Procedure:	Down to you

www.moltonbrown.co.uk

The range of Molton Brown's bath, skincare, make-up and spa products seems to increase daily and you want to try every single one (at least I always do). The packaging is lovely and the products not only look and smell wonderful but they are not overpriced. Delivery is quick and you quite often get sent delicious trial-sized products with your order. This is a great site for gifts and travel-size products – which they specialise in – and that extra body lotion and bath gel you simply won't be able to resist.

Site Usability:	★★★★★	Based:	UK
Product Range:	★★★★★	Express Delivery Option? (UK)	Yes
Price Range:	Medium	Gift Wrapping Option?	Yes
Delivery Area:	Worldwide	Returns Procedure:	Down to you

www.nomadtravel.co.uk

If you know someone who's about to take off on safari or into the jungle, first introduce them to this website, which offers a good, highly edited range of efficient and well-priced travel clothing. They'll find lightweight trousers, zip-offs and vented shirts, base layer fleece and thermals, lots of advice on health abroad and on travelling with children. Then you could buy them a Nomad gift voucher, so they can buy anything they like, or choose for them from the wide range of travel essentials such as maps, compasses, binoculars and guides.

Site Usability:	★★★★★	Based:	UK
Product Range:	★★★★	Express Delivery Option? (UK)	Yes
Price Range:	Medium	Gift Wrapping Option?	No
Delivery Area:	Worldwide	Returns Procedure:	Down to you

www.sandstormbags.com

If you're looking for a luxury gift for someone who likes to travel a lot, then stop off here as you'll find a great range of bags and luggage that not only works well but has a high degree of authenticity. Sandstorm is the only range of authentic, premium, safari-style bags out of Africa. These beautiful bags are handcrafted in Kenya and are perfect for taking on safari, walking in the Cotswolds or for weekend city breaks in five-star hotels – they look good anywhere and deliver a combination of luxury, style and durability.

Site Usability:	★★★★★	Based:	UK
Product Range:	★★★★	Express Delivery Option? (UK)	Yes
Price Range:	Luxury/Medium	Gift Wrapping Option?	No
Delivery Area:	Worldwide	Returns Procedure:	Down to you

www.timetospa.com

Time to Spa offers Elemis face and body products in excellent travel collections, perfect for those on the go. This is not a general retailer so much as a beauty salon. You can register for an online consultation by one of the team of therapists for advice on your beauty regimen, find out about food and fitness for health and have your beauty questions answered. If you purchase from the online shop you'll find lots of gift ideas and can take advantage of the gift wrapping service.

Site Usability:	★★★★★	Based:	UK
Product Range:	★★★★	Express Delivery Option? (UK)	Yes
Price Range:	Medium	Gift Wrapping Option?	Yes
Delivery Area:	Worldwide	Returns Procedure:	Down to you

www.travelsmith.com

This US-based website must be the ultimate online travel store. It offers a comprehensive and well-priced range of travel clothing and accessories, from outerwear, including washable suede, tailoring and safari jackets to easy-care separates, hats, swimwear and luggage. There's also a good gift section with lots of different and innovative ideas. You can't place your order directly online for international delivery, but you can fax it to them, email or call them and they'll send it to you anywhere in the world.

Site Usability:	★★★★★	Based:	US
Product Range:	★★★★★	Express Delivery Option? (UK)	No
Price Range:	Medium	Gift Wrapping Option?	No
Delivery Area:	Worldwide	Returns Procedure:	Down to you

www.viator.com

Viator is a US-based travel company offering lots of information and advice on where to go and what to do when you arrive just about anywhere in the world. You can buy their gift certificates which can be used to purchase any of the 4,500-plus suggested activities that you'll find here. A helicopter tour in Las Vegas? You bet. A hot-air balloon ride in Italy? Of course. Swimming with sharks in Australia? Absolutely. Simply choose the gift certificate you want in the recipient's local currency and let them do the rest.

Site Usability:	★★★★	Based:	UK
Product Range:	★★★★★	Express Delivery Option? (UK)	No
Price Range:	Luxury/Medium	Gift Wrapping Option?	No
Delivery Area:	Worldwide		

www.zpm.com

If you know someone who does a lot of travelling, you'll find a perfect gift here, as ZPM specialises in pretty and useful make-up bags – everything from small cosmetic purses to hanging weekenders, all in a range of patterns. As well as these you'll find ideas for kids and babies and some attractive laundry and kitchen accessories. There's also a gift finder by occasion or personality to make life even easier.

Site Usability:	★★★★	Based: UK	
Product Range:	★★★	Express Delivery Option? (UK)	Yes
Price Range:	Medium	Gift Wrapping Option?	No
Delivery Area:	Worldwide	Returns Procedure:	Down to you

Section 6
Gifts by Occasion

*A*lthough many of the websites in this book will provide you with presents for different types of occasions, I've selected some of my favourites, which in my opinion offer gifts that are just that little bit more special, for weddings, Valentine's Day, Mother's Day and so on.

These will be particularly helpful when you need something that shows a lot of thought but you have little time to spare, which, if you're anything like me, will be most of the time. Although you won't find a huge number of websites here for each type of occasion, you may well find that perfect gift.

One word of caution - although more and more retailers are offering express delivery, and even express delivery worldwide, for some of the items here you will need to allow a little more time for your order to arrive. You'll be able to place your order in just a few clicks, so much less time than it would take you to buy something comparable offline, but to get it really right you need to think ahead.

Chapter 32

Christening Gifts

Having had three children (and three christenings) I am now completely straight in my mind as to what makes a really great christening gift. I would suggest that you steer away from the normal suggestions – the napkin rings, silver pushers and feeders and egg cups, which they won't appreciate as babies nor when they are older (and neither will you) – and choose something that they'll love to own a bit later on – a silver bracelet perhaps, a print for their room or a beautiful photo frame.

I certainly know which of my children's gifts are in use now and which still rest at the bottom of a cupboard, beautifully boxed as they are. I know for sure what I would buy as a christening gift – something to be loved, used and treasured for the future and a constant reminder of the giver. What could be better?

Sites to Visit

www.andreabrierley.com

This is a lovely place to buy something special and quite different. Andrea Brierley has created a range of prints of illustrated names decorated with gorgeous colourful designs of animals, roundabouts, farmyards, fairytale castles and the like. They're not expensive and something you can't buy anywhere else. She'll also undertake an original watercolour commission for you if you get in touch with her. You need to email or call to order.

Site Usability:	★★★★	Based:	UK
Product Range:	★★★	Express Delivery Option? (UK)	No
Price Range:	Medium	Gift Wrapping Option?	No
Delivery Area:	UK	Returns Procedure:	Down to you

www.aspenandbrown.co.uk

On this pale blue, prettily designed website, Aspen & Brown offers a range of gifts. In the Christening section there are lots of reasonably priced ideas, from personalised blankets and first china, baby shoes and silver bangles to charm bracelets, hand-painted initial canvases and named pictures. My advice would be to stay with the personalised items and the silver as there's a great choice and these are definitely the most special and unique.

Site Usability:	★★★★★	Based:	UK
Product Range:	★★★★★	Express Delivery Option? (UK)	No
Price Range:	Medium/Very Good Value	Gift Wrapping Option?	No
Delivery Area:	UK	Returns Procedure:	Down to you

www.aspinaloflondon.com

There are some lovely gift ideas here for babies, all in Aspinal's signature high-quality leather and well thought out designs. Choose from contemporary and traditional photo albums covered in pretty pastel shades, baby shower gift books, suede photo frames, photo wallets and keepsake boxes. Most items can be personalised and everything can be beautifully gift boxed and sent out with your personal message.

Site Usability:	★★★★★	Based:	UK
Product Range:	★★★★★	Express Delivery Option? (UK)	Yes
Price Range:	Luxury/Medium	Gift Wrapping Option?	Yes
Delivery Area:	Worldwide	Returns Procedure:	Down to you

www.bbr.com

Berry Bros & Rudd is Britain's oldest wine and spirit merchant, having traded from the same shop for over 300 years. Today members of the Berry and Rudd families continue to own and manage the family-run wine merchant. You can not only find out about the wines you should be drinking but you can also start a BBR Cellar Plan, use the Wedding List services and join the Wine Club. For a wonderful christening present give them a call and ask their advice on buying port to lay down – hopefully you'll be invited to share it later on.

Site Usability:	★★★★★	Based:	UK
Product Range:	★★★★★	Express Delivery Option? (UK)	Yes
Price Range:	Luxury/Medium	Gift Wrapping Option?	No
Delivery Area:	Worldwide	Returns Procedure:	Down to you

www.littlepresentcompany.co.uk

There is quite a variety of gifts on offer here for all sorts of occasions, including christenings and birthdays. Go straight to the christening gifts section, where there are screen-printed photograph albums, children-sized traditional wooden chairs, silver spoons and bowls and gorgeous horn and silver accessories which they'll want to use later on. In my opinion you couldn't go wrong with the beautiful hammered silver bowl they have here and which I haven't seen anywhere else. The only problem is you'll probably want to use it first.

Site Usability:	★★★★★	Based:	UK
Product Range:	★★★★	Express Delivery Option? (UK)	Yes
Price Range:	Luxury/Medium	Gift Wrapping Option?	No, but they will engrave items for you
Delivery Area:	UK	Returns Procedure:	Down to you

www.mariechantal.com

This is an exquisite collection of baby and childrenswear designed by Marie Chantal of Greece. As you would expect, the prices are quite steep, but you'll be hard put to find this quality of fabric and modern use of colour and design in many other children's stores. The clothing is available in two sections: babies and toddlers (although some of these go up to age 8). If you want something really special you should have a look here.

Site Usability:	★★★★	Based:	UK
Product Range:	★★★★	Express Delivery Option? (UK)	No
Price Range:	Luxury/Medium	Gift Wrapping Option?	No
Delivery Area:	Worldwide	Returns Procedure:	Down to you

www.murrayforbes.co.uk

Based in Inverness in the Scottish Highlands, Murray Forbes has an unusual selection of not overpriced jewellery online, plus some lovely gifts for children, perfect for christenings. My favourites are definitely the sterling silver fairy box, angel bangle and gold charm bracelet which any tiny will almost certainly want to use when they're old enough. If you'd like your gift engraved, they'll do it for you. The pictures are very clear and the details and information excellent. They offer free shipping and shipping insurance in the UK and will deliver worldwide.

Site Usability:	★★★★	Based:	UK
Product Range:	★★★	Express Delivery Option? (UK)	No
Price Range:	Medium	Gift Wrapping Option?	Yes
Delivery Area:	Worldwide	Returns Procedure:	Down to you

www.nurserywindow.co.uk

Once you arrive at this website you'll find it very hard to leave. There are some seriously lovely things here for children's rooms, from unusual bedding, moses baskets and high-quality cots and furniture to gift baskets for new babies and everything is beautifully photographed. Just click on the area of the online shop you're interested in, enter, and you'll certainly be hooked. Nothing is cheap but it's all beautiful quality.

Site Usability:	★★★★★	Based:	UK
Product Range:	★★★★	Express Delivery Option? (UK)	No
Price Range:	Luxury/Medium	Gift Wrapping Option?	No
Delivery Area:	UK	Returns Procedure:	Down to you

www.rachelriley.com

The next time you're asked where someone could find a really special outfit for your little one, point them in the direction of Rachel Riley, where you'll discover a truly lovely collection for infants, teens and grown-ups as well. Everything there is exquisite, with marvellous attention to style and detail, and as you'd expect nothing is inexpensive. So if you can't afford to kit out your child totally from here, at least you could ask a godmother or granny to contribute something really special.

Site Usability:	★★★★	Based:	UK
Product Range:	★★★★	Express Delivery Option? (UK)	Yes
Price Range:	Luxury	Gift Wrapping Option?	No
Delivery Area:	Worldwide	Returns Procedure:	Down to you

www.richmondsilver.co.uk

In its Christening Gifts section Richmond Silver has quite a wide selection of ideas, ranging from a hallmarked, sterling silver bear necklace at under £20 to a heavy gauge, handmade silver cup for around £200. There are some very good, classic ideas here with which you're unlikely to go wrong, although I would recommend staying with the sterling silver which is in most cases very reasonably priced, rather than straying off into silver plate, no matter how pretty it looks.

Site Usability:	★★★★	Based:	UK
Product Range:	★★★★	Express Delivery Option? (UK)	Yes
Price Range:	Medium	Gift Wrapping Option?	Yes
Delivery Area:	UK	Returns Procedure:	Down to you

www.thewoolcompany.co.uk

There's no question that most people give silver or beautiful baby clothes for christenings. Here's something slightly different that will almost certainly be used for a long time. The Wool Company's 100% pure new merino wool blankets have whip-stitched edges and come in a variety of colours, from polar ice check (soft blue) and natural cream to wonderful guava check and carmine red. You can also buy nursery sheepskin here and pastel-checked 'cuddle' blankets, plus blankets for the home.

Site Usability:	★★★★★	Based:	UK
Product Range:	★★★	Express Delivery Option? (UK)	No
Price Range:	Medium	Gift Wrapping Option?	No
Delivery Area:	UK	Returns Procedure:	Down to you

Chapter 33

Valentine's Day

Flowers, flowers, flowers, of course – what else is there for Valentine's Day? Well, diamonds, silly – and did you know that roughly 35% of the diamonds bought throughout the year are given on Valentine's Day? Or that approximately 1 billion Valentine cards and messages are sent each year worldwide, making the day the second largest card-sending holiday of the year behind Christmas?

You (or he) may not be going to invest in that five-carat diamond this year, but if you're looking for cards, flowers, chocolates, fragrance, lingerie or a trip to somewhere special to give next Valentine's Day, you'll enjoy a browse through the websites below – and you can find the diamond, too.

Sites to Visit

www.agentprovocateur.com

Joseph Corre and Serena Rees opened the first Agent Provocateur shop in December 1994 and have never looked back. The look is overt and sexy and you'll find just that on this extremely unusual website, where their gorgeous lingerie is displayed with attitude on the most perfect bodies. Don't come here if you're looking for something in a size larger than a 36E or if you want a website where ordering is easy – it's not, until you get used to it. Do come here if you love their products and don't want to go out to find them.

Site Usability:	★★★	Based:	UK
Product Range:	★★★★	Express Delivery Option? (UK)	Yes
Price Range:	Luxury/Medium	Gift Wrapping Option?	No, but packaging is very attractive
Delivery Area:	Worldwide	Returns Procedure:	Down to you

www.boodles.co.uk

Gorgeous modern jewellery: the real thing. Some things you might just imagine buying for yourself and others you'd probably rather have bought for you, like the divine Asscher cut-diamond earrings that they don't even tell you the price for. Have a look round anyway, you might just be tempted. I should warn you though, there's almost nothing here for under £1,000. Everything is gift wrapped and they'll ship all over the world.

Site Usability:	★★★★	Based:	UK
Product Range:	★★★★	Express Delivery Option? (UK)	Yes
Price Range:	Luxury	Gift Wrapping Option?	Yes
Delivery Area:	Worldwide	Returns Procedure:	Down to you

www.chouchoute.co.uk

I have to confess it took me a while to get past the wonderful picture of the chocolate ginger I came across here – and only real strength of will made me resist rushing for my credit card. This Birmingham-based chocolatier, created by ex Fauchon (Paris) traiteur Pierre Soualah, offers fabulous pampering chocolates from gift boxes to hampers. Although the range is quite small, I'm sure, like me, you'll find it hard to resist.

Site Usability:	★★★★	Based:	UK
Product Range:	★★★	Express Delivery Option? (UK)	Yes
Price Range:	Medium	Gift Wrapping Option?	No
Delivery Area:	UK	Returns Procedure:	Down to you

www.echocs.com

Echocs has selected some of the best chocolate, food and drink gifts and combined them to create a range of mouthwatering presents, most of which they can deliver anywhere in the UK within 48 hours. There are classic hampers and organic gifts, wines and champagne with chocolates, chocolate messages, gorgeous flowers, scented candles and special suggestions for Valentine's Day. If you're at a loss as to what to buy this year, for any celebration, take a good look here.

Site Usability:	★★★★★	Based:	UK
Product Range:	★★★★	Express Delivery Option? (UK)	Yes
Price Range:	Medium	Gift Wrapping Option?	Yes, automatic
Delivery Area:	UK	Returns Procedure:	Down to you

www.expedia.co.uk

With Expedia, rather than looking at a variety of short breaks, you really do need to know where exactly you want to go. Take Paris, for example, the perfect city for a luxury break for Valentine's Day. Just go to Flights and Hotels, type in Paris and your dates and you'll get a wide selection plus availability. For the best results also select the hotel class. You won't find the tiny, hidden-away boutique hotels here, but this is an excellent place to book a last-minute trip away.

Site Usability:	★★★★★	Delivery Area:	Worldwide
Product Range:	★★★★★	Based:	UK
Price Range:	Luxury/Medium		

www.fastflowers.co.uk

Just about every online florist offers flowers for Valentine's Day – it would be strange if they didn't – but I particularly like this website for its innovative designs, which range from the classic bunch of a dozen red roses to rose hearts, gorgeous white roses, hand-tied red tulips and other romantic bouquets. You can also choose from their bouquets of the month and gift packages of roses and champagne. Prices here are reasonable and they have a diary reminder service as well.

Site Usability:	★★★★★	Based:	UK
Product Range:	★★★★	Express Delivery Option? (UK)	Yes
Price Range:	Medium	Gift Wrapping Option?	No
Delivery Area:	UK	Returns Procedure:	Down to you

www.glamorousamorous.com

You'll find some quite different lingerie here. Think animal print and
scarlet trim from Fifi Chachnil, sequin and silk camisoles from Guia La
Bruna and a lace bustier and thong from Bacirubati and you'll get the kind
of idea – extremely glam in other words. There's the Lingerie and Gift
Guide which offers help for men buying presents, and everything arrives
in a silk organza bag, wrapped in tissue paper scented with Provençal
lavender. UK mainland delivery is free.

Site Usability:	★★★★★	Based:	UK
Product Range:	★★★★	Express Delivery Option? (UK)	Yes
Price Range:	Luxury/Medium	Gift Wrapping Option?	Yes
Delivery Area:	Worldwide	Returns Procedure:	Down to you

www.imogenstone.co.uk

Imogen Stone is an exclusive online florist and luxury gift store, creating
beautiful floral designs using the finest fresh flowers combined with
scented herbs and interesting foliages. The flower and plant collection includes hand-tied bouquets, Fairtrade flowers, scented flowers and
seasonal plants, plus special designs for Valentine's Day, Mother's Day,
Easter and Christmas. You can include Rococo Chocolate Truffles, Abahna
Toiletries, Nougat and LSA vases with your order. Call before 1pm for
same-day delivery.

Site Usability:	★★★★★	Delivery Area:	Worldwide
Product Range:	★★★★	Based:	UK
Price Range:	Luxury/Medium	Express Delivery Option? (UK)	Yes

www.kirstengoss.com

After studying jewellery design in South Africa, Kirsten Goss moved to
London and launched her own company where she currently creates
exclusive, modern collections of jewellery using semi-precious stones
and sterling silver. Having been featured by Harpers, Elle, Glamour and
In Style, and described as 'the next big thing' by the Sunday Times
magazine, this site is definitely one to watch and a great place for an
unusual jewellery gift.

Site Usability:	★★★★	Based:	UK
Product Range:	★★★	Express Delivery Option? (UK)	Yes
Price Range:	Medium	Gift Wrapping Option?	No
Delivery Area:	Worldwide	Returns Procedure:	Down to you

www.laprovence.co.uk

La Provence sells beautiful French cloths, fabrics, Lampe Berger and designer giftware in its shops and online. It's a pretty collection, with wonderful gifts for girls, including Swarovski crystal-adorned heart necklaces, chic hand-painted porcelain, exquisite glassware and Margaret Loxton limited-edition prints of French scenes. They ship free of charge to mainland UK on all items except Lampe Berger perfumes.

Site Usability:	★★★★★	Based:	UK
Product Range:	★★★★	Express Delivery Option? (UK)	No
Price Range:	Medium	Gift Wrapping Option?	No
Delivery Area:	UK	Returns Procedure:	Down to you

www.mkn.co.uk/flower/

This retailer has determinedly stayed with its techie-inspired design which may put you off at first, but do persevere as the range they offer is always very good. Flowers for Valentine's Day include the traditional single or 12 red roses or you could send one or their mini fruit trees (crab apple, pear and mulberry) or ornamentals. Other gift ideas include personalised champagne, pampering boxes and chocolates.

Site Usability:	★★★	Delivery Area:	UK
Product Range:	★★★★	Based:	UK
Price Range:	Medium	Express Delivery Option? (UK)	Yes

www.moonpig.com

There's a wide selection of Valentine's Day cards here, from the traditional heart and flower decorated variety to sentimental themes and cards where you can download your own picture (not trying to hide your identity there, then). One of the best things here is that you can order your card and have them send it out for you so that it arrives in time.

Site Usability:	★★★★★	Delivery Area:	Worldwide
Product Range:	★★★★★	Based:	UK
Price Range:	Medium	Express Delivery Option? (UK)	Yes

www.silkstorm.com

The next time you're looking for something out of the ordinary, take a look at Silk Storm, an online lingerie boutique offering luxury French and Italian brands, with collections including Aubade, Valery, Argentovivo, Cotton Club and Barbara. Everything is beautifully photographed and the sizing help is excellent, although don't expect anything to go much above a 36D. They're aiming this very much at men buying lingerie for their ladies, with sexy pictures and gorgeous gift wrapping.

Site Usability:	★★★★	Based:	UK
Product Range:	★★★	Express Delivery Option? (UK)	Yes
Price Range:	Medium	Gift Wrapping Option?	Yes
Delivery Area:	Worldwide	Returns Procedure:	Down to you

www.viamichelin.co.uk

To find the perfect restaurant near you for a special Valentine's Day dinner, pay a visit to viamichelin.co.uk. Here you need to click on Maps, enter the city or town of your choice and then ask for Restaurants under Michelin Guides. If this sounds complicated, it really isn't and it's one of the best ways of finding a good range of restaurants in your area, from three Michelin rosettes to something a little simpler. Most restaurants have their own website, so once you find something that sounds appealing, click through and take a look at the décor and menus.

Site Usability:	★★★★★	Delivery Area:	Europe
Product Range:	★★★★★	Based:	UK
Price Range:	Luxury/Medium		

205

Chapter 34

Mother's Day

There's no doubt that Mother's Day is an important occasion in the family calendar, but sandwiched as it is between Valentine's Day and Easter it's easily overlooked or left until the last minute when flowers or chocs are most likely the only option.

Here are some online retailers offering unique and innovative gifts to make next Mother's Day just that little bit more special, plus exceptional flowers and plants quite different from those you can find on the high street.

Sites to Visit

www.farleylane.co.uk

Farley Lane has an eclectic range of British-made accessories for home and garden - think birds' feeding boxes and bee nesters, gardeners' hampers and gift boxes, unusual planters and gardening gloves, plus charming mirrors and handmade doorstops. This is quite a move away from the normal flower and fragrance gifts and will definitely last longer. You need to email them for overseas deliveries and normal UK delivery takes 3-5 working days.

Site Usability:	★★★★	Based:	UK
Product Range:	★★★	Express Delivery Option? (UK)	No
Price Range:	Medium	Gift Wrapping Option?	No
Delivery Area:	Overseas on request	Returns Procedure:	Down to you

www.frenchsoaps.co.uk

This is the home of Durance en Provence in the UK, where you can purchase their beautifully fragranced soaps made with rose petal pieces, lavender flowers and verbena, scented, rose-trimmed and ribbon-tied satin cushions and boules, prettily packaged Provençal candles and fabric-lined gift baskets. The packaging makes everything here extra special and they offer their next-day delivery service free of charge if your order is over £25.

Site Usability:	★★★★★	Based:	UK
Product Range:	★★★	Express Delivery Option? (UK)	Automatic on orders over £25
Price Range:	Medium	Gift Wrapping Option?	No, but packaging is gorgeous
Delivery Area:	UK	Returns Procedure:	Down to you

www.maddiebrown.co.uk

On this pretty, pale blue website, you'll find an excellent selection of Mother's Day gift ideas, from Emma Bridgewater china mugs and teapots, books on antiques and address books to vine tomato-scented candles, cologne French soaps and handcrafted handbags. Most of the prices are extremely reasonable, so this would be a good place to point your teenage children at for them to choose something special. You need to allow 14 days for delivery, so call them if you need your order urgently.

Site Usability:	★★★★	Based:	UK
Product Range:	★★★	Express Delivery Option? (UK)	No
Price Range:	Medium	Gift Wrapping Option?	No
Delivery Area:	UK	Returns Procedure:	Down to you

www.meltons.co.uk

Meltons was established over 20 years ago by international interior designer Cecilia Neal. She and her team work on residential projects both in the UK and abroad and have brought together on this attractive website some lovely and different gifts and accessories for the home. You'll find Limoges boxes, luxurious throws, mother-of-pearl spoons, horn beakers and unusual candlesticks. This is just a small part of the range, where you'll fine excellent presents for anyone who loves their home.

Site Usability:	★★★★★	Based:	UK
Product Range:	★★★★	Express Delivery Option? (UK)	Call them if you're in a hurry
Price Range:	Luxury/Medium	Gift Wrapping Option?	On some items
Delivery Area:	Worldwide on application	Returns Procedure:	Down to you

www.parkscandles.com

Parks Candles has an easy-to-navigate website offering a beautiful range of scented candles in decorative containers. Three-wick candles in silver bowls, perfumed candles in glass containers with silver lids and scented dinner candles in green, burgundy or cream are just some of the selection. Delivery is excellent and the prices are lower than you find in most shops.

Site Usability:	★★★★★	Based:	UK
Product Range:	★★★	Express Delivery Option? (UK)	Automatic
Price Range:	Medium	Gift Wrapping Option?	No
Delivery Area:	Worldwide	Returns Procedure:	Down to you

www.parseme.com

Based in Kensington Church Street, London, Parseme offers an exclusive range of home fragrance and bath and body products, including scented candles and room sprays in fragrances such as Lavande, Vanille, Verveine and Gardena Blossom. They also make wonderful, simple and beautifully boxed pot pourri in Fleurs Sauvages, Symphonie de Couleurs, Champe de Lavande and Les Orangerais, all of which would make beautiful gifts. (Are you listening, children?)

Site Usability:	★★★★★	Based:	UK
Product Range:	★★★	Express Delivery Option? (UK)	Recorded, 2–3 days
Price Range:	Medium	Gift Wrapping Option?	Yes
Delivery Area:	Worldwide	Returns Procedure:	Down to you

www.plants4presents.co.uk

Plants make wonderful gifts on Mother's Day (and most other occasions) because whereas that beautiful bunch of flowers will be gone within a week, plants of course last much, much longer. Here you can order from a good selection, including pink roses, early clematis, fruiting lemon and kumquat trees, jasmine, azaleas and beautiful moth orchids. Each plant is hand-wrapped and packed with care instructions and a handwritten, full-size greeting card.

Site Usability:	★★★★★	Based:	UK
Product Range:	★★★	Express Delivery Option? (UK)	Yes or you can select a date
Price Range:	Medium	Gift Wrapping Option?	No
Delivery Area:	UK	Returns Procedure:	Down to you

www.rosesonly.co.uk

Actually here they don't, surprisingly, sell only roses but a lovely selection of boxed flowers, such as gerberas, lilies and varieties of seasonal flowers, attractive bouquets plus the signature boxed roses. The choice available to you depends on where you live, with the largest selection being in London. The boxed flowers are gorgeous and different and you can add chocolates, champagne and small hampers to your gift.

Site Usability:	★★★★★	Based:	UK
Product Range:	★★★	Express Delivery Option? (UK)	Yes
Price Range:	Medium	Gift Wrapping Option?	No
Delivery Area:	Worldwide	Returns Procedure:	Down to you

www.thecandlecollection.co.uk

Here's a choice of scented candles and home fragrances from several quite hard to find brands such as Arco, Kenneth Turner, Menu of Copenhagen, Fragrance Boutique and TJ of West Hollywood. You need to click through the range to get a good idea of what's available as there's much more than immediately appears. There are some quite unusual ideas – elegant pink floating roses, grapevine candle lanterns and black candles being just three – so you're sure to find some excellent gifts.

Site Usability:	★★★★★	Based:	UK
Product Range:	★★★★	Express Delivery Option? (UK)	No
Price Range:	Medium	Gift Wrapping Option?	No
Delivery Area:	Worldwide	Returns Procedure:	Down to you

www.thelittlepicturegallery.com

There are some lovely prints at The Little Picture Gallery by artists including Annabel Fairfax, Claire Davies, Maureen Jordan and Nicholas St John Rosse. You can read up about each of them and I suggest that if you buy something here you print off the artist's information and include it with your gift. Choose from landscapes and animal prints, plus attractive seaside views. You can have your picture mounted or just buy the print on its own.

Site Usability:	★★★★★	Based:	UK
Product Range:	★★★★	Express Delivery Option? (UK)	Call if urgent
Price Range:	Medium	Gift Wrapping Option?	No
Delivery Area:	Worldwide on request	Returns Procedure:	Down to you in agreement with them

Chapter 35

Easter

We may have only just recovered from Christmas but Easter always seems to approach at high speed, with never enough time to get ready. Easter eggs are everywhere. Buy them early and you feel a bit foolish. Leave it too late and the best ones are all gone. Consider the fact that Easter accounts for 10% of the total chocolate sales for the year in the UK and that an average of 80 million Easter eggs are sold each year at a cost of over £500 million and you can understand why Easter is one of the most important trading periods for retailers.

To find the perfect Easter egg for your family chocoholic or the mini ones for your egg hunt you do need to start early. Then you can avoid the mad Good Friday rush when anything decent has disappeared from the shelves and feel really proud of yourself when the holiday weekend comes round. You're prepared, relaxed and ready to eat more chocolate than you would dream of doing at any other time of year.

Alongside all the chocolate you can buy beautifully scented soap eggs, fresh fruit baskets and your essential Simnel cake, without which no Easter celebration would be complete - at least in my family it wouldn't.

Sites to Visit

www.amara.co.uk

This is a lovely home accessories and gift website with some quite unusual products, such as the deliciously scented and beautifully packaged Gianna Rose Atelier soaps (robin's egg soaps in a porcelain dish and ducks in a gift box are just two), Millefiori candles, Mulberry Home and de Le Cuona throws and shawls, Missoni tableware and lots of other ideas. It's a beautifully designed website and you can see all the products very clearly.

Site Usability:	★★★★★	Based:	UK
Product Range:	★★★★	Express Delivery Option? (UK)	Yes
Price Range:	Medium	Gift Wrapping Option?	Yes
Delivery Area:	Worldwide	Returns Procedure:	Down to you

www.bettysbypost.com

At bettysbypost.com you can order handmade Christmas cakes in a variety of sizes, their family-recipe Christmas pudding with fruit soaked in brandy and ale, and seasonal favourites such as the delicious Simnel Cake, Pannetone and Stollen. Hand-decorated chocolate Easter eggs and gifts, miniature florentines and peppermint creams are just a few of the goodies on offer in the confectionary section. You'll also find lovely stocking fillers for children and preserves for the Christmas larder.

Site Usability:	★★★★★	Based:	UK
Product Range:	★★★★	Express Delivery Option? (UK)	No
Price Range:	Medium	Gift Wrapping Option?	No
Delivery Area:	Worldwide	Returns Procedure:	Down to you

www.chococo.co.uk

This is a small husband and wife-led team based in Purbeck in Dorset. Passionate about proper chocolate, they've developed their own, totally unique, award-winning range of fresh chocolates in vibrant, stylish packaging. Alongside their celebration hampers and chunky chocolates you'll find goodies such as Chilli Tickles and Raspberry Riots. There are always wonderful ideas for Easter, including giant goodie boxes, chocolate hens and colourful eggs for adults and kids.

Site Usability: ★★★★	Based:	UK
Product Range: ★★★	Express Delivery Option? (UK)	Yes
Price Range: Medium	Gift Wrapping Option?	No
Delivery Area: Europe	Returns Procedure:	Down to you

www.fortnumandmason.com

As you would expect, everything on this website is beautiful and expensive, so if you're buying Easter treats for a large family you may want to move straight on. However, if you're not buying for the masses, do have a look here, it's a real feast for the eyes. You'll find charmingly packaged cakes and biscuits, delightful eggs and novelties for children and serious, truffle-filled eggs for adults. Resist if you can. If you're going to order, make sure you do it early enough.

Site Usability: ★★★★★	Based:	UK
Product Range: ★★★★	Express Delivery Option? (UK)	No
Price Range: Luxury/Medium	Gift Wrapping Option?	No
Delivery Area: Worldwide	Returns Procedure:	Down to you

www.groovychocolate.co.uk

As well as offering boxes of chocolates you can choose a design from the wide range to suit any occasion and Groovy Chocolate will paint it onto a chocolate bar with the message of your choice. These are great for children who may be bored with the usual Easter egg or stocking fillers. They also offer luxury truffles and boxes of chocolates with names such as Seven Deadly Sins, chocolate beer mugs and chocolate champagne truffles and specialities for all types of occasion.

Site Usability: ★★★★★	Based:	UK
Product Range: ★★★★	Express Delivery Option? (UK)	Yes
Price Range: Medium	Gift Wrapping Option?	No, but beautifully presented
Delivery Area: Worldwide	Returns Procedure:	Down to you

213

www.megrivers.com

If, like me, your Easter isn't quite the same without a perfect Simnel cake with the 11 small balls of marzipan on top, but you simply don't have the time to make one, order yours here. Meg Rivers produces simply delicious cakes, including celebration cakes and her wonderful chocolate cake and brownies (be warned, they don't last long). Don't leave it too late to order as they do run out, particularly of seasonal cakes.

Site Usability:	★★★★★	Based:	UK
Product Range:	★★★★	Express Delivery Option? (UK)	No
Price Range:	Luxury/Medium	Gift Wrapping Option?	Yes
Delivery Area:	Worldwide	Returns Procedure:	Down to you

www.sofresh.co.uk

On this website you'll find beautifully photographed hampers and baskets of fresh fruit, to which you can add chocolates, flowers and plants and a personalised card. This would be a perfect place to order something for someone you can't get to see over Easter rather than just sending a traditional chocolate egg. Everything is offered in different sizes, from the reasonably priced to, quite frankly, gorgeously extravagant. Despatch is by overnight courier.

Site Usability:	★★★★★	Based:	UK
Product Range:	★★★★	Express Delivery Option? (UK)	Yes
Price Range:	Medium	Gift Wrapping Option?	No
Delivery Area:	UK	Returns Procedure:	Down to you

www.theobroma-cacao.co.uk

Forget your usual last-minute hunt for a chocolate egg this Easter and click straight through here, where you can order fine, hand-crafted chocolates developed by specialist patissier Philip Neal. You can buy wonderful gift selections, from seasonal boxes to heart-shaped gifts for Valentine's Day as well, but I would suggest that (at the right time of year, of course) you take a good look at his Marbled Finished and 'Spun' eggs, prettily wrapped mini eggs and unique, red, hand-painted eggs. Definitely one for grown-up chocoholics.

Site Usability:	★★★★★	Based:	UK
Product Range:	★★★★	Express Delivery Option? (UK)	No
Price Range:	Luxury/Medium	Gift Wrapping Option?	No
Delivery Area:	UK	Returns Procedure:	Down to you

www.thorntons.co.uk

Thorntons is ideal for Easter, birthdays, anniversaries and weddings, or simply when you want to treat yourself. You can buy their delicious chocolate hampers, choose 800g of continental chocolates or one of Thorntons' classic boxes and you'll also find gifts to add such as wine, flowers and Steiff bears. As well as all of this they have a small collection of cards which they'll personalise for you and send out with your gift.

Site Usability:	★★★★★	Based:	UK
Product Range:	★★★★★	Express Delivery Option? (UK)	Yes
Price Range:	Medium/Very Good Value	Gift Wrapping Option?	No
Delivery Area:	Worldwide for most products	Returns Procedure:	Down to you

Also take a look in the following chapters for Easter treats:

Chapter 3: Chocolates for Chocoholics
Chapter 4: Flowers

Chapter 36

Weddings

For weddings there are two options: firstly you can select something from the bride and groom's own list and secondly you can choose something entirely different.

I personally am not very good at buying from lists and prefer to try to find something really special that I can be as sure as possible the happy couple will like and use. There are gifts that my husband and I were given at our wedding that we use regularly 20 (yes really, 20) years on and each time I remember who gave them to us. They were definitely not on any list.

I think it depends on how well you know the pair getting married. Obviously if they say 'please stick to our list', then that's what you'll (probably) do, but if you know their taste and style and want to do your own thing, you can.

There are several websites below that I particularly like and some others, such as Pruden and Smith, in the Silver Weddings chapter below. You could also take a look at Chapter 40: Luxury Gifts for that extra special wedding present.

Sites to Visit

www.albumania.com

Here's a website where you can find a unique kind of present. At Albumania you design your own photo album, box file, guest book, wine book, address book or diary. You just download a photograph (digitally), choose the colour of binding and ribbon, all online, and then you can see exactly what the cover of your book will look like. While you're ordering you have the option of adding pages and a ribbon-tied card with your personal message. All the books are gift boxed and take about two weeks.

Site Usability:	★★★★★	Based:	UK
Product Range:	★★★	Express Delivery Option? (UK)	No
Price Range:	Medium	Gift Wrapping Option?	No
Delivery Area:	Worldwide	Returns Procedure:	Down to you

www.aquascutumgifts.com

Please be aware before visiting this website that although they call themselves 'Corporate Gifts', they offer everything in single quantities. The only really annoying thing is that you won't see the VAT-inclusive price until you pay. Having said that, there are some lovely (though expensive) gift ideas here, including crystal and sterling silver decanters, hallmarked wine coasters, Elizabethan dishes and bowls and photo frames in both silver and leather. Most items can be engraved and the prices include their high-quality gift wrapping.

Site Usability:	★★★★	Based:	UK
Product Range:	★★★	Express Delivery Option? (UK)	No
Price Range:	Luxury/Medium	Gift Wrapping Option?	Yes
Delivery Area:	Worldwide	Returns Procedure:	Down to you

www.arthurprice.com

There are some very traditional silver and silver-plate gift ideas here from a family business that was established in 1902. Move away from those for a moment and take a look at some of their other, more contemporary products, such as attractive cheese and steak knives, modern cutlery designs by Guy Degrenne, Llewelyn-Bowen and Clive Christian, and ham-

217

mered pewter flasks and tankards, all of which would make excellent gifts. You can order their silver-plated cutlery online, but if it's sterling silver you're after, you need to call them.

Site Usability:	★★★★★	Based:	UK
Product Range:	★★★★	Express Delivery Option? (UK)	No
Price Range:	Luxury/Medium	Gift Wrapping Option?	No
Delivery Area:	Worldwide	Returns Procedure:	Down to you

www.culinaryconcepts.co.uk

Going round the shops looking for a different wedding gift (when you don't want to buy into the wedding list) is sometimes very difficult because classic gifts may well clash with what's already been chosen. Here you'll find some new and clever design ideas, including unusual cheese knives and servers, hammered stainless steel bowls and plates, and table accessories such as unique sugar and olive bowls, wine buckets and vases.

Site Usability:	★★★★	Based:	UK
Product Range:	★★★★	Express Delivery Option? (UK)	No
Price Range:	Medium	Gift Wrapping Option?	No
Delivery Area:	Worldwide	Returns Procedure:	Down to you

www.harrods.com

Harrods is adding more and more products into its online store and most of them can be shipped worldwide. They include silver and glass, decorative accessories, food and drink and gorgeous bedlinen and although of course the range is nothing like as wide as in the Knightsbridge store, there are some excellent gift ideas here at a range of prices. Delivery takes up to two weeks, although you need to allow longer for overseas orders.

Site Usability:	★★★★	Based:	UK
Product Range:	★★★★★	Express Delivery Option? (UK)	No
Price Range:	Medium	Gift Wrapping Option?	No, but standard packaging is excellent
Delivery Area:	Worldwide	Returns Procedure:	Down to you

www.heals.co.uk

Heals is famous for its Tottenham Court Road store in London and the idiosyncratic modern/retro styling for all the products offered there.

Brides and grooms can set up their gift lists online or in store with the help of one of their personal shopping consultants. Once the list is set up, friends and family can just click through to where it's published online and make their selection. Alternatively, of course, you can select something independently from their wide range of ideas.

Site Usability:	★★★★★	Based:	UK
Product Range:	★★★★★	Express Delivery Option? (UK)	No
Price Range:	Medium	Gift Wrapping Option?	No
Delivery Area:	UK	Returns Procedure:	Down to you

www.jbsilverware.co.uk

There's a wide range of silver gifts here, from inexpensive silver plate to lovely sterling silver hallmarked pieces. Prices go from around £20 to £500, so you have a lot to choose from, including traditional sterling Armarda (their spelling) dishes and tumbler cups to contemporary glass and silver ice buckets, candlesticks and bowls. They offer an engraving service, express delivery (you need to call them for this) and they'll ship worldwide.

Site Usability:	★★★★	Based:	UK
Product Range:	★★★★★	Express Delivery Option? (UK)	Yes
Price Range:	Medium	Gift Wrapping Option?	No
Delivery Area:	Worldwide	Returns Procedure:	Down to you

www.johnlewisgiftlist.com

I'm sure you won't be surprised to learn that John Lewis has one of the most popular wedding list services in the country. With its huge range of products at different price levels and the excellent service it offers, this is a really good place to have a wedding list. Provided you know the list number and password, or the bride and groom's names and date of the wedding, you can access the list and choose your gift.

Site Usability:	★★★★★	Based:	UK
Product Range:	★★★★★	Express Delivery Option? (UK)	No
Price Range:	Medium	Gift Wrapping Option?	No
Delivery Area:	UK	Returns Procedure:	In store or they'll collect

www.juliannebalai.com

Julianne Balai originally specialised in jewellery and glass design and includes as her stockists Harvey Nichols, Liberty and Harrods. On her clear and simple website you can discover her unusual (and expensive) glass art, including handmade coloured glass decanters and unique vases, embossed leather photo frames and unusual coffee plungers, all of which would make excellent wedding gifts and that you would be unlikely to come across elsewhere. There's also her collection of beautiful and unusual jewellery.

Site Usability:	★★★★	Based:	UK
Product Range:	★★★★	Express Delivery Option? (UK)	No
Price Range:	Luxury/Medium	Gift Wrapping Option?	No
Delivery Area:	UK	Returns Procedure:	Down to you

www.mulberryhall.co.uk

Mulberry Hall offers you the opportunity of buying online some of the ranges that they hold in their York shop, including brands such as Baccarat, Herend, Lladro, Royal Copenhagen and Waterford. This would be a great place to find gifts for all sorts of occasions and particularly for weddings as there's a beautiful collection of traditional and modern items for the home and they offer a free gift wrapping service. If you're going to stray off the wedding list track, take a look at the stunning black John Rocha for Waterford glass and fun Alessi gifts and kitchen accessories.

Site Usability:	★★★★★	Based:	UK
Product Range:	★★★★★	Express Delivery Option? (UK)	No
Price Range:	Luxury/Medium	Gift Wrapping Option?	Yes
Delivery Area:	Worldwide	Returns Procedure:	Down to you

www.silvercompany.co.uk

You'll find some very traditional sterling silver gift ideas here plus some more unusual items, such as their Olympia silver and crystal candlesticks, glass and silver match strikers and churn wood and silver salt and pepper mills. Almost anything here would make a perfect wedding present, particularly as with some of the more unique ideas you're less likely to clash with the traditional wedding list. Many of the pieces can be engraved as well.

Site Usability:	★★★★	Based:	UK
Product Range:	★★★★	Express Delivery Option? (UK)	Yes
Price Range:	Medium	Gift Wrapping Option?	Yes
Delivery Area:	Worldwide	Returns Procedure:	Down to you

www.smallislandtrader.com

Small Island Trader is an excellent company offering not only china, glass and silver from a wide range of designers and manufacturers, including Waterford, Villeroy and Boch and Spode, but also kitchen equipment from juicers and steamers to copper and Le Creuset pots and pans, Sabatier knives, baking trays, and unusual kitchen products and homewares. You can order items separately or you may find that the couple you're buying for has selected to use the excellent Small Island Trader wedding list service and you can choose from that.

Site Usability:	★★★★★	Based:	UK
Product Range:	★★★★★	Express Delivery Option? (UK)	No
Price Range:	Luxury/Medium	Gift Wrapping Option?	No
Delivery Area:	Worldwide	Returns Procedure:	Down to you

www.theolivegrove.co.uk

The Olive Grove online was established in May 2000 and is home to an expanding range of beautiful interior and garden accessories from a number of independent designers alongside leading brands such as Mulberry Home. If you're looking for a slightly unusual wedding gift you would do well to have a look round here, where you can choose from iron candlesticks, glass ice buckets, slate cheeseboards and Mulberry's gorgeous cushions and willow baskets.

Site Usability:	★★★★	Based:	UK
Product Range:	★★★★★	Express Delivery Option? (UK)	Yes
Price Range:	Medium	Gift Wrapping Option?	Yes
Delivery Area:	Europe	Returns Procedure:	Down to you

Chapter 37

Silver Weddings

You instinctively think that you need to give something silver for a silver wedding celebration, at least I do. Having said that, surely after 25 years you would have just about all the silver you'd want or need?

Either way, if you're going to give silver it needs to be something really special, a beautiful stand-alone item that's also useful, as the last thing you want is for your gift to be stored away in a cupboard. Alternatively you could have a look through the websites below and find something unique – not necessarily silver – but a reminder of a special day that will be equally appreciated and perhaps more so for being just that little bit different.

Sites to Visit

www.abstractbottles.com

If you don't want to give silver but you do want to give something different and original, take a look at this website, where you can create and design your own bespoke bottle online, incorporating your personalised message. You first click on the type of celebration your bottle is for, then whether or not you want wine or champagne. Next you can choose the bottle and design colour and your wording and finally specify the exact wine and the gift packaging. Expect to wait 14 days for delivery.

Site Usability: ★★★★★		Based:	UK
Product Range: ★★★		Express Delivery Option? (UK)	No
Price Range: Luxury/Medium		Gift Wrapping Option?	Yes
Delivery Area: UK		Returns Procedure:	Only if faulty

www.antique-glass.co.uk

For a silver wedding gift for someone that you know loves beautiful glass, look here at this website tried and tested by my family several times and where you'll find unique alternatives to the traditional modern silver that many will give. If you're not sure what you're doing, give them a call (you cannot order directly online), particularly if you know that the recipient already collects antique glass, and they'll give you the best advice on what to buy for the amount you want to spend.

Site Usability: ★★★★		Based:	UK
Product Range: ★★★★		Express Delivery Option? (UK)	No
Price Range: Luxury/Medium		Gift Wrapping Option?	No
Delivery Area: Worldwide		Returns Procedure:	In agreement with them

www.gift-newspapers.co.uk

Here you can find another unusual celebration gift idea – genuine original newspapers (not copies) which have been preserved in a historic newspaper archive with papers dating back over 200 years. You first select a presentation folder or gift box, then the date and the newspaper of your choice, after which you can personalise the certificate of authenticity. You can then go on to add DVD and CD cards for the same year, but personally I think the newspaper is special on its own.

Site Usability: ★★★★★		Based:	UK
Product Range: ★★★★		Express Delivery Option? (UK)	Yes
Price Range: Medium		Gift Wrapping Option?	Presentation boxes and folders
Delivery Area: Worldwide		Returns Procedure:	Yes, but contact them first

www.halcyon-days.co.uk

The next time you want to buy a special present for someone to commemorate a particular event, such as a silver wedding or birthday or maybe just because you want to give something really unique, you should take a look at these exquisite ideas from Halcyon Days, where you'll find hand-painted enamel boxes with designs such as The Owl and The Pussycat, Jack Vettriano paintings, Andy Warhol, sayings and quotations and museum editions, plus musical boxes, jewelled boxes, clocks and other gift ideas.

Site Usability:	★★★★	Based:	UK
Product Range:	★★★★	Express Delivery Option? (UK)	Yes
Price Range:	Luxury/Medium	Gift Wrapping Option?	Yes
Delivery Area:	Worldwide	Returns Procedure:	Down to you

www.pomeroi.co.uk

I really like the fact that this online store, based at their shop in Tunbridge Wells, has taken the trouble to offer some different ideas, although be warned: some of these are expensive and maybe more than you would want to pay for a silver anniversary gift. Take a look at the silver watering can, for example, silver mussel eaters (for those who like their moules) and silver and blackwood pepper mills. All beautiful and well worth a look. Delivery is free.

Site Usability:	★★★★	Based:	UK
Product Range:	★★★★	Express Delivery Option? (UK)	Yes
Price Range:	Luxury/Medium	Gift Wrapping Option?	Yes
Delivery Area:	Worldwide	Returns Procedure:	Down to you

www.richardbramble.co.uk

OK, now for some quite unusual ideas for silver wedding gifts, but ones that I think would be very welcome as most people, by the time they reach their silver wedding, are not really collecting silver any more. Artist Richard Bramble has created a range of unique tableware, from wonderfully fishy plates and bowls to tablemats and clocks, plus his original paintings and prints, all of which you can buy online. As I would love to be given something by him (kids, are you listening?), I recommend you have a good look round.

Site Usability:	★ ★ ★ ★ ★	Based:	UK
Product Range:	★ ★ ★ ★	Express Delivery Option? (UK)	Yes for items in stock
Price Range:	Luxury/Medium	Gift Wrapping Option?	No
Delivery Area:	Worldwide	Returns Procedure:	Down to you

www.silversmiths.co.uk

Pruden and Smith makes beautiful, contemporary silver tableware that is spun, hand-raised or forged using traditional silversmith techniques, with sparing use of decoration in order to enhance its famous hammered finish. This really is modern silver at its best and there's a wide range to choose from. You can't buy directly through the website at the moment but need to email or call them with your enquiry – a small price to pay for such a special range.

Site Usability:	★ ★ ★ ★	Based:	UK
Product Range:	★ ★ ★ ★ ★	Express Delivery Option? (UK)	Yes for items in stock
Price Range:	Luxury/Medium	Gift Wrapping Option?	Ask them
Delivery Area:	Worldwide	Returns Procedure:	Down to you

www.simonbeer.co.uk

Simon Beer started as a silversmith in David Mellor's workshops in Sheffield and continues to supply his own cutlery designs as well as pieces of domestic silverware. You can order silver Marmite lids (supplied with Marmite), curved or straight swan-head spoons, silver goblets and silver teapots. This is a very small collection but one that is quite different from the run-of-the-mill silverware to be found on many silver websites.

Site Usability:	★ ★ ★ ★	Based:	UK
Product Range:	★ ★ ★	Express Delivery Option? (UK)	On most items
Price Range:	Luxury/Medium	Gift Wrapping Option?	No
Delivery Area:	Contact him for overseas orders	Returns Procedure:	Down to you

Also take a look at the following websites for silver wedding gifts:

Website address	You'll find it in
www.jbsilverware.co.uk	Chapter 36: Weddings
www.silvercompany.co.uk	Chapter 36: Weddings

Chapter 38

A Word About Christmas

This book is not about Christmas, so you won't find a special chapter here entitled 'Christmas Gifts'. It's about helping you with choosing gifts all the year round and for all sorts of occasions.

'But Christmas is when I have to choose most of my presents', do I hear you say? I'm well aware of that, which is why I've written this page, just to give you my thoughts about buying presents at Christmas - not, you understand, what to buy, but much more importantly how to buy and if I'm telling you what you already know I apologise in advance.

It's much too easy to have your Christmas present list to hand and then go for it. I personally think that far too little time is spent on thinking about the person concerned and trying to make each gift just that little bit more special. I also think it's completely useless (and I'm speaking from experience here) to give someone a gift that they're not going to love and use. Yes use, from the moment you give it to them.

Don't give someone a plant because *you* like plants. Never give *your* favourite fragrance - find out what theirs is and give that. Collect hints from family throughout the year and store them in a notebook so that you can really, really surprise them at Christmas. They'll think you've forgotten what they said - probably will have forgotten saying it at all - and think you're extremely clever.

People tell me that I'm impossible to buy for because I'm so selective - I like and use certain brands of cosmetics and fragrance and rarely move completely away from them. I love black and wear it far too much (in the daft hope that it really will make me look thinner) and I'm a collector of modern jewellery with semi-precious stones. I absolutely love white lilies and modern, hand-tied flower arrangements in white and green only.

So I should be easy to choose things for, shouldn't I? Apparently not - as my family constantly try to think 'outside the box' and find something different. Oh well, OK, I'm happy with diamonds, cashmere, silver and gold - but how often do those things come your way?

What I'm trying to say is, don't try to think 'outside the box'. Take the trouble to find out what someone likes and uses and stick to that theme. With that in mind I don't think you can ever fail.

Was this supposed to be about Christmas? I'll get right back to it. The reason why there isn't a chapter dedicated to Christmas is because now that you've bought this book you already have the ultimate Christmas gift guide. Every single retailer listed here offers you wonderful ideas for Christmas, for every member of the family, for all your friends and colleagues, for people who like to cook, garden and travel. There's a whole host of ideas here.

Go back to what I said originally - think of the person you're buying for, think about what they like, use and do, and then go shop. It really couldn't be simpler.

Chapter 39

General Gift Stores

ere you'll find the dedicated gift stores waiting to help you find something special and although I prefer (as I've said above) to use more specific places to buy gifts, you can often find some clever ideas – after all, that's what they specialise in.

Some of these retailers are very good indeed and have taken a great deal of time to solve your gift-giving problems, so the next time you're really not sure what to choose, or you're in a hurry, have a quick look and see if you can't find an instant solution.

Sites to Visit

www.coxandcox.co.uk

The Cox and Cox website is divided up into sections such as A Decorative Home, A Creative Diva, Any Excuse for a Party and Children's Corner. In each of the sections you'll find appropriate ideas, such as soft furnishings and pictures, linen ribbon and coloured tissue paper, outdoor table clips and tea light holders and gumball machines and butterfly garlands. They'll send this eclectic mix to you anywhere in the world and if you want something urgently you need to call them.

Site Usability: ★★★		Based:	UK
Product Range: ★★★		Express Delivery Option? (UK)	Yes
Price Range:	Medium	Gift Wrapping Option?	No
Delivery Area:	Worldwide	Returns Procedure:	Down to you

www.erinhousegifts.co.uk

This retailer offers a wide choice of gifts, including Halcyon Days Enamels, Churchill China (which uses images painted by Sir Winston Churchill), Franz porcelain and jewellery, delightful Winnie the Pooh classics, the extraordinary Yoro pen and pens by Swarovski. Then there are Country Artists, Lilliput Lane and Wild World figurines, plus fun Happy Cats tableware. They're happy to deliver all over the world.

Site Usability: ★★★★		Based:	UK
Product Range: ★★★★		Express Delivery Option? (UK)	No
Price Range:	Medium	Gift Wrapping Option?	Yes
Delivery Area:	Worldwide	Returns Procedure:	Down to you

www.giftinspiration.com

Based in Wiltshire, this website claims to be the UK's leading gift delivery service. They certainly have a good selection (think The Expresso Hamper, Hot Chocolate Cup and Saucer Gift Box, Hunter leather-covered flask and cups and silver Aspirin cufflinks) and if you need a gift in a hurry I would definitely have a look as they offer all the right services – gift wrapping, including your personal message and express delivery.

Site Usability: ★★★		Based:	UK
Product Range: ★★★★		Express Delivery Option? (UK)	Yes
Price Range:	Medium	Gift Wrapping Option?	Yes
Delivery Area:	UK	Returns Procedure:	Down to you

www.giftstore.co.uk

This is a good place for ideas for birthday and anniversary gifts, from flowers, chocolates and balloons to magic sets and greeting cards, which they'll personalise and send out for you. You'll also find teddygrams, personalised newspapers, Leonidas chocolates and a small selection of toys and games. Everything is well priced, so this would be an excellent retailer to visit if you have a last-minute panic.

Site Usability: ★★★★	Based:	UK
Product Range: ★★★★	Express Delivery Option? (UK)	Yes
Price Range: Medium/Very Good Value	Gift Wrapping Option?	Yes
Delivery Area: UK	Returns Procedure:	Down to you

www.luxeliving.com

The next time you want to give something luxurious, have a look round here, where you'll find gifts and accessories for the home, from cushions and mirrors to unusual ceramics and tableware, candles, notebooks and frames. It's not a huge range and it takes a while to get to the gifts (while you're listening to the music), but they offer all the right services – express delivery options, international delivery and gift wrapping – and the selection will almost certainly grow.

Site Usability: ★★★	Based:	UK
Product Range: ★★★	Express Delivery Option? (UK)	Yes
Price Range: Luxury/Medium	Gift Wrapping Option?	Yes
Delivery Area: Worldwide	Returns Procedure:	Down to you

www.nationaltrust-shop.co.uk

This is a real treasure trove of well-priced gifts and stocking fillers, such as pretty floral notecards, chocolate éclairs in pretty boxes, humorous t-shirts and giant crosswords. You can buy Christmas cards and good-value wrap and ribbon here too and take advantage of the free gift wrapping and personalisation service. Orders may take up to 21 days as deliveries come from the National Trust's various suppliers, so allow extra time.

Site Usability: ★★★★★	Based:	UK
Product Range: ★★★	Express Delivery Option? (UK)	No
Price Range: Medium/Very Good Value	Gift Wrapping Option?	Yes
Delivery Area: UKI	Returns Procedure:	Down to you

www.notonthehighstreet.com

There's almost an impossible amount of choice on this website acting as a marketplace for a group of small manufacturers and designers who'll supply you direct. Most of it is reasonably priced and most items are perfect for gifts. You'll find jewellery, scarves and shawls, pretty evening and day handbags, Cote Bastide and Willow bath and body products, unusual camisoles and t-shirts, albums and keepsake boxes, plus a selection of home accessories.

Site Usability:	★★★	Based:	UK
Product Range:	★★★★★	Express Delivery Option? (UK)	No
Price Range:	Medium/Very Good Value	Gift Wrapping Option?	No
Delivery Area:	UK	Returns Procedure:	Down to you

www.oliverbonas.co.uk

Voted Best Gift Retailer for 2006, this is a well-designed and easy-to-navigate website with a lovely range of products (just as you would expect). They offer some extremely attractive jewellery and accessories, gifts for the 'domestic goddess', ideas for the garden and leather albums, notebooks and address books. Delivery is free on orders over £50 and where items are in stock they'll despatch the same day. Contact them for overseas deliveries.

Site Usability:	★★★★	Based:	UK
Product Range:	★★★	Express Delivery Option? (UK)	Yes
Price Range:	Medium	Gift Wrapping Option?	No
Delivery Area:	Worldwide	Returns Procedure:	Down to you

www.sogifted.co.uk

So Gifted is a general gift website offering ideas for everyone, including christening gifts (pretty photo albums and a christening keepsake box), weddings, educational and general gifts for young children and unusual gifts for the home and garden. You'll also find the exquisite range of Rosana and Café Paris china of beautifully boxed expresso cups, dessert plates and Haute Shoes tea for two, which you'll probably want to keep for yourself.

Site Usability:	★★★	Based:	UK
Product Range:	★★★	Express Delivery Option? (UK)	Yes
Price Range:	Medium	Gift Wrapping Option?	No
Delivery Area:	Worldwide	Returns Procedure:	Down to you

www.tjklondon.com

TJK London offers a selection of classic and contemporary silver, wood and leather gifts, including jewellery, cufflinks, photo albums and frames designed in-house and sterling silver marmite and jam jar lids. (Also lovely glass match strikers/tea light holders with silver hallmarked collars.) A bonus here is that everything is automatically gift wrapped. For a small charge they will engrave items for you.

Site Usability:	★★★★	Based:	UK
Product Range:	★★★	Express Delivery Option? (UK)	Yes
Price Range:	Luxury/Medium	Gift Wrapping Option?	Luxury packaging is standard
Delivery Area:	Worldwide	Returns Procedure:	Down to you

Chapter 40

Luxury Gifts

To buy from these wonderful, luxury gift stores it isn't necessary to shell out the earth, although you can if you want. The point is that just about *anything* from the retailers below will be eclectic, beautiful and special. We all need a little luxury from time to time – at least I do (husband, children – is anyone there?) – and I'm sure that when you've had even a very short browse you'll agree.

Sites to Visit

www.alisonhenry.com

These are seriously gorgeous modern accessories, mainly in neutral colours, which would make superb gifts for weddings and other 'important' occasions, or when you feel in the need of adding something really special to your home. There's a cut-crystal fragrance bottle filled with Alison's signature bath oil, pure cashmere cushions and double-sided throws, plus other beautifully photographed objects.

Site Usability:	★★★★	Based:	UK
Product Range:	★★★	Express Delivery Option? (UK)	No
Price Range:	Luxury/Medium	Gift Wrapping Option?	No
Delivery Area:	UK	Returns Procedure:	Down to you

233

www.astleyclarke.com

Online designer jewellery retailer Astley Clarke has an attractive website, where you'll find the collections of New York- and London-based designers such as Coleman Douglas, Vinnie Day, Flora Astor and Catherine Prevost, some of which are exclusive to Astley Clarke. Prices for the precious and semi-precious jewels here start at around £100 and then go skywards. For gorgeous gifts or treats this is the perfect place, as everything arrives beautifully gift boxed and can be gift wrapped as well. There's also a collection for brides and bridesmaids.

Site Usability:	★★★★★	Based:	UK
Product Range:	★★★★★	Express Delivery Option? (UK)	Yes
Price Range:	Luxury/Medium	Gift Wrapping Option?	Yes
Delivery Area:	Worldwide	Returns Procedure:	Down to you

www.dior.com

At luxury brand Christian Dior's online boutique you can purchase from the range of beautiful, covetable handbags, shoes and boots, small leather accessories, scarves, watches and fine jewellery. Prices are steep, as you would expect, but if you want to be carrying the latest version of their instantly recognisable Gaucho or My Dior handbag on your arm this season, you'll no doubt be prepared. Dior has specific websites for overseas shipping, so you need to check whether they have one for your country.

Site Usability:	★★★★	Based:	UK
Product Range:	★★★★★	Express Delivery Option? (UK)	Yes
Price Range:	Luxury	Gift Wrapping Option?	No, but beautiful packaging is standard
Delivery Area:	UK, but US and other sites available	Returns Procedure:	Down to you and complicated

www.fortnumandmason.com

With its famous name and lovely packaging, anything from Fortnum and Mason is a pleasure to buy and receive. On this website you can order food and drink (think foie gras, smoked salmon, caviar and champagne), with lots of Christmas specialities in season and their marvellous teas, plus an eclectic range of gifts including hip flasks and albums for men and toiletries, jewellery and accessories for women. Most items can be delivered all over the world.

Site Usability:	★★★★	Based:	UK
Product Range:	★★★★	Express Delivery Option? (UK)	No
Price Range:	Luxury	Gift Wrapping Option?	No
Delivery Area:	Worldwide	Returns Procedure:	Down to you

www.gucci.com

Leading the way for 'superbrand' designers to come online, Gucci was one of the first to open up its website for online accessory orders. As you would expect, the site is very modern and beautiful (and heartstoppingly expensive) and the products irresistible. You can buy handbags, luggage, men's and women's shoes and gifts, such as key rings and lighters. Don't expect them to offer clothes, at least not for a while, as the fit would be very difficult and returns far too high.

Site Usability:	★★★★★	Express Delivery Option? (UK)	Yes
Product Range:	★★★★★	Gift Wrapping Option?	Yes/Automatic
Price Range:	Luxury	Returns Procedure:	Down to you
Delivery Area:	Worldwide most places		

www.harrods.com

Harrods is adding more and more products into its online store and most of them can be shipped worldwide. They include silver and glass, decorative accessories, food and drink, fashion and gorgeous bath and body products, and although of course the range is nothing like as wide as in the Knightsbridge store, there are some excellent gift ideas at a range of prices. Delivery takes up to two weeks, although you need to allow longer for overseas orders.

Site Usability:	★★★★★	Based:	UK
Product Range:	★★★★	Express Delivery Option? (UK)	No
Price Range:	Luxury/Medium	Gift Wrapping Option?	No
Delivery Area:	Worldwide	Returns Procedure:	Down to you

www.jimmychoo.com

Needless to say, the new Jimmy Choo website is beautifully and provocatively designed and makes you want to browse right through even though the prices are quite frightening in most cases, to say the least.

This is always a totally covetable collection, including diamante-encrusted sandals, killer-heel peep-toe slides, gorgeous boots and wonderful, right-on-trend handbags.

Site Usability:	★★★★★	Based:	UK
Product Range:	★★★★★	Express Delivery Option? (UK)	Yes
Price Range:	Luxury	Gift Wrapping Option?	Automatic
Delivery Area:	Worldwide	Returns Procedure:	Down to you

www.louisvuitton.com

Louis Vuitton's unmistakable (and luxuriously expensive) handbags are now available online directly through its quick and clear website. So you don't have to go into one of the stores any more and ask for help and information, you'll find everything you could possibly need to know here, such as interior details, care and sizing. Once you've selected your country you'll find which styles are available to you; simply choose the design you like and go shop.

Site Usability:	★★★★★	Based:	UK
Product Range:	★★★★★	Express Delivery Option? (UK)	Yes
Price Range:	Luxury	Gift Wrapping Option	Automatic
Delivery Area:	Worldwide	Returns Procedure:	Down to you

www.luluguinness.com

'Be a glamour girl, put on your lipstick' is the phrase welcoming you to this elegant website, from which exquisite handbags and accessories from famous British designer Lulu Guinness can now be shipped to you wherever you are. With unique styling, sometimes very quirky, sometimes just plain gorgeous, and a selection of cosmetic bags in stylish prints to take you anywhere, this is a website you should take a look at if you're in the mood for a treat or special gift.

Site Usability:	★★★★	Based:	UK
Product Range:	★★★	Express Delivery Option? (UK)	No
Price Range:	Luxury/Medium	Gift Wrapping Option?	No, but everything is beautifully packaged
Delivery Area:	Worldwide	Returns Procedure:	Down to you

www.mikimoto-store.co.uk

Mikimoto is a name synonymous with beautiful and luxurious pearls (they've been in business for over 100 years) and now you can buy a selection of their best selling jewellery online. Prices start at around £120 for a pair of timeless pearl studs and go up to around £2,000 for their Tahitian pearl and pink sapphire pendants and earrings. Everything is beautifully gift wrapped and you can have your order within 48 hours.

Site Usability:	★★★★★	Based:	UK
Product Range:	★★★	Express Delivery Option? (UK)	Yes
Price Range:	Luxury/Medium	Gift Wrapping Option?	Yes
Delivery Area:	Worldwide	Returns Procedure:	Down to you

www.net-a-porter.com

This is the uber fashionista's website where you'll find the most impressive range of designer clothes and accessories available online and a retailer that's becoming increasingly well known for its clever buying, excellent service and attractive packaging. So if you're looking for something special with a designer label, such as Marc Jacobs, Alexander McQueen, Burberry, Roland Mouret, Alberta Feretti, Marni, Jimmy Choo or Paul Smith (the list goes on and on), you should definitely have a look here.

Site Usability:	★★★★★	Based:	UK
Product Range:	★★★★★	Express Delivery Option? (UK)	Yes
Price Range:	Luxury	Gift Wrapping Option?	Yes
Delivery Area:	Worldwide	Returns Procedure:	Free using their DHL service

www.smythson.com

Smythson is famous as the Bond Street purveyor for over a century of absolutely top-quality personalised stationery and accessories, including diaries, leather journals, albums, frames and gold-edged place cards. They also have a luxurious, small collection of handbags, briefcases, wallets and small leather goods at totally frightening prices. You can use their online personalised stationery service or call to order. They'll send you a sample pack from which you can choose your paper and style. Just let them know your choice and you're away.

Site Usability:	★★★★★	Based:	UK
Product Range:	★★★★	Express Delivery Option? (UK)	No
Price Range:	Luxury	Gift Wrapping Option?	No
Delivery Area:	Worldwide	Returns Procedure:	Down to you

www.temperleylondon.com

There's no doubt that within a very short space of time Alice Temperley has become well known throughout the fashion world for her desirable dresses and separates, including her fabulous collection of evening dresses. Although you can view her clothing online only (and I don't expect this to change in the near future), you can buy her accessories, including handbags, gloves, belts and scarves. It's a small collection at present, but one that is bound to grow.

Site Usability:	★★★★★	Based:	UK
Product Range:	★★★	Express Delivery Option? (UK)	Yes
Price Range:	Luxury	Gift Wrapping Option?	No
Delivery Area:	Worldwide	Returns Procedure:	Down to you

www.theofennell.com

Theo Fennell is famous as the jewellery designer of stars such as Elton John. His modern, diamond-studded crosses and keys are recognised the world over, together with his solid-silver Marmite lids and Worcester sauce bottle holders. Nothing on this website is inexpensive, but you'll find some extremely beautiful and unique designs and if you buy anything you can be sure it will be exquisitely presented. Browse the site and see whether you're tempted.

Site Usability:	★★★	Based:	UK
Product Range:	★★★★	Express Delivery Option? (UK)	No
Price Range:	Luxury	Gift Wrapping Option?	Yes
Delivery Area:	Worldwide	Returns Procedure:	Down to you

www.tiffany.com

Exquisite and expensive: the two words that sum up one of the world's most luxurious jewellery emporiums. Anything in the signature Tiffany blue box is sure to make a perfect present, from the smallest piece of

Elsa Peretti or Paloma Picasso jewellery to wonderful classic diamonds and pearls. Beautiful Tiffany glass candlesticks, bowls and stemware, the new Tiffany fragrance in its lovely glass bottle or christening gifts for a new baby; it's all available online.

Site Usability:	★★★★★	Based:	UK
Product Range:	★★★★★	Express Delivery Option? (UK)	Yes
Price Range:	Luxury	Gift Wrapping Option?	Yes/Automatic
Delivery Area:	UK and USA	Returns Procedure:	Down to you

Section 7
Useful
Information

You may already be a seasoned online shopper or you may just be starting out, either way there are some things that can help you on your way, such as essential security information, help with price comparison shopping and what to do if something goes wrong.

I am frequently amazed to hear about what some people buy online; where they go to shop; how easily and far too quickly they're parted with their credit card details; and how little they know how to deal with problems. Do take the time to read the chapters that follow – in this ever-advancing world of online buying they're intended as signposts to help make sure that you don't take the wrong turning.

Finally, one word of warning: please be very careful before buying from an auction website. Any auction website. No matter how secure you feel on the auction site itself, you won't be buying from it but from an arm's length retailer. Some are wonderful and some are not. I'm not saying this because I've had a bad experience myself, and I've purchased through eBay several times successfully, but I have heard some strange tales. So please be careful.

Chapter 41

Top Tips for Safe Shopping Online

There are so many websites to choose from, for just about every product you can think of, not just fashion and beauty. Whether you're buying kitchen equipment, a new bed, cashmere knit or lipstick, the basic rules for buying online are the same. Here are the important things you need to know before you buy. Just keep them in mind before you start ordering and you should have no problems. Happy shopping.

- *Secure payment.* Make sure that when you go to put in your payment information, the padlock appears at the foot of the screen and the top line changes from http://to https://. This means that your information will be transferred in code. To make sure you're clear about this, just go to www.johnlewis.com, put something in your basket, then click on 'Go to Checkout'. You'll immediately see the changes and those are what you're looking for each time. If they don't happen, don't buy.
- *Who are they?* Don't buy from a retailer unless you can access their full contact details. Ideally these will be available from the 'Contact Us' button on the Home Page, but sometimes they are hidden in Terms and Conditions. You should be able to find their email address, plus location address and telephone number. This is so that you can

contact them in case of a problem. I get really annoyed by websites which hide behind their email addresses – they need to be out there saying to you, the prospective customer, 'This is who we are and this is where we are, get in touch if you need us'. Sometimes they don't.

Privacy policy. If it's the first time you're buying from this retailer you should check their privacy clause telling you what they'll be doing with your information. I suggest you never allow them to pass it on to anywhere/anyone else. It's not necessarily what *they* do with it that will cause you a problem.

Returns policy. What happens if you want to return something? Check the retailer's policy before you order so that you're completely informed about how long you have to return goods and what the procedure is. Some retailers want you to give them notice that you're going to be sending something back (usually for more valuable items), others make it quick and simple – they're definitely the best.

Keeping track. Keep a record, preferably printed, of everything you buy online, giving the contact details, product details and order reference so that if you need to you can quickly look them up. I also keep an email folder into which I drag any orders/order confirmations/payment details just in case I forget to print something. Then if you have a problem you can just click on the link to contact them and all the references are there.

Statements. Check your bank statements to make sure that all the transactions appear as you expect. Best of all keep a separate credit card just for online spending which will make it even easier to check.

Delivery charges. Check out the delivery charges. Again, some retailers are excellent and offer free delivery within certain areas while others charge a fortune. Make sure you're completely aware of the total cost before you buy. If you're buying from the US you will have to pay extra shipping and duty, which you'll either have to fork up for on delivery or on receipt of an invoice. My advice is to pay it immediately.

Credit card security. Take advantage of the new MasterCard Secure-Code and Verified by Visa schemes when they're offered to you. Basically they provide you with the extra facility of giving a password when you use your registered cards to buy online from signed-up retailers – a kind of online chip and pin. They're excellent and they're going to grow. For extra security, pay online with a credit rather than a debit or any other type of card as this gives you added security from the credit card companies on goods over £100 in value.

- *Shred the evidence.* Buy a shredder. You may think I'm daft, but most online and offline card fraud is due to someone having got hold of your details offline. So don't let anyone walk off with your card where you can't see it and don't chuck out papers with your information on where they can be easily accessed by someone else. You have been warned.

- *Payment don'ts.* Don't ever pay cash, don't pay by cheque (unless you've got the goods and you're happy with them), don't ever send your credit card details by email and don't give your pin number online to anyone *ever*. I'm amazed at the stories I hear.

- *PC security.* Make sure your computer is protected by the latest anti-virus software and an efficient firewall. Virus scan your system at least once a week so that you not only check for nasties but get rid of any spyware.

- *Auction websites.* Be very careful using an auction website. Make sure that you know absolutely what you're doing and who you're buying from. This is not to say that everyone who sells on auction websites is waiting to get you, but some of them definitely are.

- *Fakes and replicas.* Be wary of anyone selling you 'replica' products – don't go there. If you're tempted to buy from someone selling you something that looks too cheap to be true, it probably is. If you're buying expensive products, always check on the retailer's policy for warranties and guarantees.

- *Additional information.* Don't give any information that isn't necessary to the purchase. You're buying a book, for goodness' sake. Why do they need to know your age and how many children you have?

- *Take your time.* Don't buy in a hurry. Take the time to check the above before you click on 'Confirm Order'. If in any doubt at all, don't buy.

Have I managed to put you off yet? I assure you that's not my intention, but you really need to be aware of the above. Once you've carried out the checks just a few times you'll do them automatically. The internet is a marvellous place, but it's also a minefield of unscrupulous people waiting to catch you out. Don't let them.

Chapter 42

Deliveries and Returns – What to Look For and How to Make Them Easier

Deliveries

Deliveries from online retailers are getting increasingly better and more efficient. In many cases you can have your order tomorrow. Find a retailer you like who's stating the old 'within 28 days' policy and call them to find out if they're really that daft (being polite here). With most companies offering express delivery, who on earth is willing to wait for 28 days unless something is being specially made for them (in which case it may well take longer but at least you'll be aware before you order)?

Most companies offer the following:

- Standard delivery
- 24-hour delivery (for a small extra charge)
- Saturday delivery (very occasionally)
- EU delivery and sometimes EU Express
- Worldwide delivery and sometimes Worldwide Express.

The problem is that you very often don't find out about all these and the relevant charges until you've put something in your basket (note to online retailers: please make 'Delivery Information' a key button on your home page, it saves so much time). Yes, I have researched this information for you, but sometimes I had to practically place an order to discover a retailer's policies - ridiculous (are you listening out there)?

Returns

This is an area that often puts people off buying online (or from catalogues, for that matter). Well, don't be put off.

You will, of course, have read up on the company's returns policy before you bought, so you know how much time you have, but you might like to know the following:

- You are entitled to a 'cooling off' period (usually seven days), during which you can cancel your order without any reason and receive a full refund.
- You're also entitled to a full refund if the goods or services are not provided by the date you agreed. If you didn't agree a date, you are entitled to a refund if the goods or services are not provided within 28 days.

Having said that, and assuming that once you've started you're going to become a regular online shopper, the following will make your life easier:

- Buy a black marker pen, roll of packing tape and some different-sized jiffy bags (I use D1, H5 and K7, which are good for most things) just in case you want to return only part of an order and the original packing is damaged or too big.

- Keep these where the rest of the family can't get at them. (That tells you something about my family, doesn't it? Why doesn't anyone ever put things back?)

- Make sure that you keep the original packaging and any paperwork until you're sure that you're not sending stuff back and keep it somewhere easy to find.

- If you want to be really clever, go to www.vistaprint.co.uk and order some address labels. They're cheap and incredibly useful for returns, Recorded and Special Delivery postings and lots of other things.

- Don't be put off if a premium retailer wants you to call them if you're returning something valuable. It's essential that the item is insured in transit and this is something they usually arrange – for really expensive goods they may well use a courier service to collect from you.

- Rejoice when returns are free. Standard postage and packing is more and more frequently becoming free of charge from large online retailers. We'll be ordering far more when returns are free as well.

Chapter 43

Price Comparison Websites

There are, as I'm sure you've realised by now, hundreds of websites for every product, of which most of the best are listed here. If you're going to invest in something expensive like a high-tech buggy or car seat, you want to know that you're getting the best price (and it almost certainly won't be found on the first website you visit). So where do you go next?

My recommendation is that you first identify the make and model you want to buy and you can do that just by going on to one well-stocked online retailer. Read all the information you want, get an initial price, copy the item code and make (or just the make and model name) and paste it into the search box of one of the price comparison websites listed below. Be aware that on these websites you won't find absolutely every retailer, but there will be quite enough of a choice for you to see a wide range of prices.

Use these websites too for electrical equipment, appliances, computers, cameras and everything photographic. Just remember that you always need to know what you're looking for first.

There are lots of other price comparison websites. The ones here are the ones I always use and find the best, so rather than giving you a huge choice I've just selected a small number to make things easy.

www.uk.shopping.com

This is an excellent price comparison website. If you haven't given them an exact specification of the product you want (and as I've said, it's better if you can), you'll get a list of all the possible options and the relevant websites, plus website reviews. Make your choice and then you can compare prices on the exact item you want. You'll get all the information you need to decide based on price (of course), stock availability, delivery charge and site rating. You then simply click through to buy from the preferred retailer or wherever you choose.

www.kelkoo.co.uk

With Kelkoo you really do need to know the exact specification of what you're looking for to get the best results, as you don't get a defined product list offering you everything containing your initial search criteria but a mixture of relevant products. If you specify exactly what you want you'll get all those products at the top of the page, with prices, site ratings, descriptions and delivery costs.

Chapter 44

Help If Something Goes Wrong

If something goes wrong and you've paid by credit card, you may have a claim not only against the supplier of the goods but also against the credit card issuer. This applies to goods or services (and deposits) costing more than £100 but less than £30,000 and does not apply to debit or charge cards.

Contact the retailer with the problem initially by email and making sure you quote the order number and any other necessary details. If you don't get immediate assistance, ask to speak to the manager. Normally this will end your problem. However, if I tell you that I ordered some expensive goods from a luxury store recently which didn't arrive when I expected them to, was treated rudely by the call centre assistant and then unbelievably rudely by the manager, you'll get the message that this doesn't always work. OK, it's the company's fault for recruiting these people in the first place and not instilling in them the message that even if the customer isn't always right they should always be treated with the utmost care and politeness. What they're looking for is not your first order, believe me, it's turning you into a loyal repeat customer. This type of customer is the most valuable of all.

Again it's not things going wrong that cause most of the trouble, it's how the company sorts things out. Do it right, make you feel really important and do that little bit extra and they've got you hooked. Handle things badly and they've not only lost this order but any future orders. Not only that but they've lost your goodwill with regards to recommending them to others. Stupid, stupid, stupid – are you listening out there?

In my case, and probably because I'm pushier than most people and didn't stop at the manager, I got what I wanted. (Note: push hard. Contact the company's owner if you can or press office if need be and tell them what's going on.) And no, I'm not going to tell you who my problem was with, sorry.

If after all of this you do not get a satisfactory result to your complaint, you can contact www.consumerdirect.gov.uk (for the UK) or call on 08454 040506 for what to do next. If your problem is with a retailer based in Australia, Canada, Denmark, Finland, Hungary, Mexico, New Zealand, Norway, South Korea, Sweden, Switzerland or the US, you can click through for help to www.econsumer.gov, a joint project of consumer protection agencies from 20 nations.

If (horror) you find that someone has used your credit card information without your authorisation, contact your card issuer immediately. You can cancel the payment and your card company must arrange for your account to be re-credited in full.

Chapter 45

UK, European and US Clothing Size Conversions

Here's a general guide to the clothing size conversions between the US, Europe and the UK. If you need size conversions for other specific countries, or other types of conversions, go to www.online-conversion.com/clothing.htm where you'll find them all.

To be as sure as possible that you're ordering the right size, check the actual retailer's size chart against your own measurements and note that a UK 12 is sometimes a US 8 and sometimes a 10, so it really pays to make sure.

Women's shoe size conversions										
UK	3.5	4	4.5	5	5.5	6	6.5	7	7.5	8	8.5
EU	36.5	37	37.5	38	38.5	39	40	41	42	43	43.5
US	6	6.5	7	7.5	8	8.5	9	9.5	10	10.5	11

Men's shoe size conversions

UK	7	7.5	8	8.5	9	9.5	10	10.5	11	11.5	12
EU	40.5	41	42	42.5	43	44	44.5	45	46	46.5	47
US	7.5	8	8.5	9	9.5	10	10.5	11	11.5	12	12.5

Women's clothing size conversions

US	UK	France	Germany	Italy
6	8	36	34	40
8	10	38	36	42
10	12	40	38	44
12	14	42	40	46
14	16	44	42	48
16	18	46	44	50
18	20	50	46	52

Men's clothing size conversions

US	UK	EU
32	32	42
34	34	44
36	36	46
38	38	48
40	40	50
42	42	52
44	44	54
46	46	56
48	48	58

Children's Sizing

Babies' and children's sizing is based mostly on age and height and this applies wherever you are. Here are some basic guidelines to both clothing and shoe sizes for the UK, Europe and US. Measurements are never exact and will differ from brand to brand. When in doubt, take a size up.

Age	Height (cm)	Height (in)
6–12m	76	30
12–18m	83	33
18–24m	90	35.5
2–3y	98	38.5
3–4y	104	41
4–5y	110	43.5
5–6y	116	45.5
7–8y	128	50
9–10y	140	55
11–12y	152	60
13–14y	164	64.5

Children's shoe size conversions

UK	5.5	6	6.5	7	7.5	8	8.5	9	9.5	10
EU	23	23.5	24	24.5	25	25.5	26	26.5	27	27.5
US	6.5	7	7.5	8	8.5	9	9.5	10	10.5	11

UK	10.5	11	11.5	12	13	1	1.5	2	3
EU	28	28.5	29	30	31	32.5	33	33.5	34.5
US	11.5	12	12.5	13	1	2	2.5	3	4

Chapter 46

Top 20 Emergency Gift Retailers

www.aspinal.co.uk

Aspinal specialises in leather gifts and accessories, including jewellery boxes, photo albums, wedding albums, leather journals and books hand-made by skilled craftsmen using age-old traditional leather and bookbind-ing skills. This is also an extremely quick and cleverly designed website, where you can see a wealth of ideas with just a couple of clicks. There's a wide choice of colours for all the items and enchanting baby gift ideas as well.

Site Usability:	★★★★★	Based:	UK
Product Range:	★★★★★	Express Delivery Option? (UK)	Yes
Price Range:	Luxury/Medium	Gift Wrapping Option?	Yes
Delivery Area:	Worldwide	Returns Procedure:	Down to you

www.babiesbaskets.com

Babiesbaskets is a retailer offering (you guessed) 'basket' gift sets for new babies and they go right up to the luxury end of the spectrum, although prices start off quite reasonably. There's the 'Loveheart' baby basket, containing a babygro, cardigan, pram shoes, fleece and photo album, and the ultimate 'Fudge' baby basket, which offers as well a cableknit blanket, hand-embroidered towel and babygro, and handmade photo album. Everything is beautifully packaged.

Site Usability:	★★★★	Based:	UK
Product Range:	★★★★	Express Delivery Option? (UK)	Yes
Price Range:	Luxury/Medium	Gift Wrapping Option?	Yes
Delivery Area:	Worldwide	Returns Procedure:	Down to you

www.braybrook.com

If you're looking for a really special present then have a browse round this excellent website, offering hand-made fine silver designed by British master silversmiths and where you can expect to find an extremely personal service. Prices for gifts range upwards from £65, from beautifully coloured glass and silver bowls to gorgeous designs by leading silversmiths for over £1,000 and a wide selection at under £200. They offer worldwide delivery, gift wrapping and express delivery.

Site Usability:	★★★★	Based:	UK
Product Range:	★★★★★	Express Delivery Option? (UK)	Yes
Price Range:	Luxury/Medium	Gift Wrapping Option?	Yes
Delivery Area:	Worldwide	Returns Procedure:	Down to you

www.ctshirts.co.uk

You might not automatically think of visiting this website when looking for gifts for girls (or men), but think again, it's not just a shirt catalogue (maybe they should change their name). Not only do they have one of the easiest websites to navigate, but they also offer an attractive range of high-quality cashmere, both fine and luxury weight, Argyll patterned and with detailed stitching. There are some lovely stripy cashmere scarves here too. Oh yes, and lots of great shirts.

Site Usability:	★★★★★	Based:	UK
Product Range:	★★★★★	Express Delivery Option? (UK)	Yes
Price Range:	Medium	Gift Wrapping Option?	Yes
Delivery Area:	Worldwide	Returns Procedure:	Down to you

www.davidlinley.com

As you would expect, this is a beautiful website, offering you the opportunity to buy David Linley-designed accessories online, including frames, vases, lamps, candlesticks, home fragrance, jewellery boxes and cushions. Everything is beautifully photographed and there are some gorgeous gift ideas here – just receiving one of his dark blue boxes makes you feel special straight away. Prices start at about £55 for his key rings and head off upwards steeply.

Site Usability:	★★★★★	Based:	UK
Product Range:	★★★★	Express Delivery Option? (UK)	Yes
Price Range:	Luxury	Gift Wrapping Option?	No, but packaging is lovely
Delivery Area:	Worldwide	Returns Procedure:	Down to you

www.escentual.co.uk

Escentual offers one of the largest ranges of fragrance and bath and body products available in the UK, from classic brands such as Chanel, Dior, Bvlgari and Rochas to Calvin Klein, Gucci, Crabtree and Evelyn, Tisserand and I Coloniali. Delivery is free on orders over £30 and they also offer free gift wrapping if you register. The website is clean and clearly laid out, which makes it a pleasure to use. There are new products on offer all the time.

Site Usability:	★★★★★	Based:	UK
Product Range:	★★★★★	Express Delivery Option? (UK)	Yes
Price Range:	Luxury/Medium	Gift Wrapping Option?	Yes
Delivery Area:	Worldwide	Returns Procedure:	Down to you

www.h-s.co.uk

This is a name you may well never have heard of, but Harrison and Simmonds has been in business since 1928 offering pipes, cigar humidors and accessories and luxury gifts from companies such as Dalvey. There's also a wide range of Mont Blanc pens and accessories (you need to call them to order), plus chess sets, Hunter pocket watches and shooting sticks. They're happy to ship to you anywhere in the world and if you call them for advice you'll receive excellent service.

Site Usability:	★★★★	Based:	UK
Product Range:	★★★★	Express Delivery Option? (UK)	Yes
Price Range:	Luxury/Medium	Gift Wrapping Option?	No
Delivery Area:	Worldwide	Returns Procedure:	Down to you

www.imogenstone.co.uk

Imogen Stone is an exclusive online florist and luxury gift store, creating beautiful floral designs using the finest fresh flowers combined with scented herbs and interesting foliages. The flower and plant collection includes hand-tied bouquets, Fairtrade flowers, scented flowers and seasonal plants, plus special designs for Valentine's Day, Mother's Day, Easter and Christmas.

Site Usability:	★★★★★	Based:	UK
Product Range:	★★★★	Express Delivery Option? (UK)	Yes
Price Range:	Luxury/Medium		
Delivery Area:	Worldwide		

www.iwantoneofthose.com

This is an irresistible (and cleverly designed) gift and gadget shop with a huge choice and a well-designed website. Search by price or product type – you'll find there's a wide range of both. The excellent animation for most products makes it easy to choose from gadgets for garden, kitchen and office, plus the inevitable toys and games. They offer same-day delivery, free standard delivery on orders over £50, gift wrap services and are happy to ship to you anywhere in the world.

Site Usability:	★★★★★	Based:	UK
Product Range:	★★★★★	Express Delivery Option? (UK)	Yes
Price Range:	Medium	Gift Wrapping Option?	Yes
Delivery Area:	Worldwide	Returns Procedure:	Down to you

www.jomalone.co.uk

Most people when they think of Jo Malone think of her gorgeous and luxurious fragrance and bath and body products. Take a good look again at her attractively designed website and you'll also find beautifully scented cleansers, serums and moisturisers and her facial finishers:

finishing fluid and powder, lip gloss, blush and mascara. But beware: once you're on her site it's extremely hard to escape without buying. The service is excellent and everything is exquisitely packaged in her signature cream and black.

Site Usability:	★★★★★	Based:	UK
Product Range:	★★★★★	Express Delivery Option? (UK)	Yes
Price Range:	Luxury	Gift Wrapping Option?	Yes
Delivery Area:	Worldwide	Returns Procedure:	Down to you

www.kiarie.co.uk

This is one of the best ranges of scented candles, by brands such as Geodosis, Kenneth Turner, Manuel Canovas, Creation Mathias, Rigaud and Millefiori. There are literally hundreds to choose from at all price levels (this site is very fast, so don't panic) and you can also choose your range by make, fragrance, colour and season. Once you've made your selection you can ask them to gift wrap it for you and include a handwritten message. Then if you want you can use their express delivery service to make sure it arrives fast.

Site Usability:	★★★★★	Based:	UK
Product Range:	★★★★★	Express Delivery Option? (UK)	Yes
Price Range:	Medium	Gift Wrapping Option?	Yes
Delivery Area:	Worldwide	Returns Procedure:	Down to you

www.linksoflondon.com

Links of London is well known for an eclectic mix of jewellery in sterling silver and 18ct gold, charms and charm bracelets, cufflinks, gorgeous gifts and leather and silver accessories for your home. Inevitably each season they design a new collection of totally desirable pieces, such as the Sweetie Rolled Gold Bracelet or Annoushka gold and ruby charm. There are lots of lovely gift ideas here if you're looking for something special.

Site Usability:	★★★★★	Based:	UK
Product Range:	★★★★★	Express Delivery Option? (UK)	Yes
Price Range:	Luxury/Medium	Gift Wrapping Option?	Yes
Delivery Area:	Worldwide	Returns Procedure:	Down to you

www.lordswines.co.uk

There's a good selection of food and wine gifts here, from the clever stacking spirit bottles (if you haven't already seen them then take a look) to more traditional ideas such as port and stilton, well-priced food and drink gift boxes, wine and champagne selections and beautifully packaged hampers. Most gifts can be personalised, not just the card but the box as well, and they'll even produce a special wine or champagne bottle label for you.

Site Usability:	★★★★★	Based:	UK
Product Range:	★★★★	Express Delivery Option? (UK)	Yes
Price Range:	Luxury/Medium	Gift Wrapping Option?	Yes
Delivery Area:	UK	Returns Procedure:	Down to you

www.mankind.co.uk

This is definitely one of the top men's websites. It's modern, easy to use and has a great range of products on offer, showcasing the very best and most innovative shaving, skin and hair care brands made for men and offering them in a way that makes buying simple, fast and fun. There are shaving products, skin basics and problem skin solutions as well as gift ideas here.

Site Usability:	★★★★★	Based:	UK
Product Range:	★★★★★	Express Delivery Option? (UK)	Yes
Price Range:	Medium	Gift Wrapping Option?	Yes
Delivery Area:	Worldwide	Returns Procedure:	Down to you

www.moonpig.com

There are more than enough cards here for whenever you might need them and they'll personalise them for you and send them out within 24 hours. It's a very good site, quick and easy to navigate, with some excellent cards for birthdays where you can change the name and date to those of the recipient. They really are very funny (provided you want funny) and there's everything else as well. They also offer a good and reliable service.

Site Usability:	★★★★★	Based:	UK
Product Range:	★★★★★	Express Delivery Option? (UK)	Yes
Price Range:	Medium		
Delivery Area:	Worldwide		

www.net-a-porter.com

As the ultimate online fashion retailer you might not immediately think of net-a-porter for gifts. However, if you check through their accessories section you'll find lots of possibilities, from the latest fashion jewellery by Me & Ro, Kenneth Jay Lane and Erickson Beamon to scarves by Burberry, Pucci and Chloe and must-have small leather items. Couple all this with speedy service and lovely packaging and you have an excellent gift destination.

Site Usability:	★★★★★	Based:	UK
Product Range:	★★★★★	Express Delivery Option? (UK)	Yes
Price Range:	Luxury/Medium	Gift Wrapping Option?	Yes
Delivery Area:	Worldwide	Returns Procedure:	Down to you

www.objects-of-design.com

Here you'll find British designed and made gift and home accessory ideas, with everything either being made in small runs or specially for you. There's the Penguin (as in the book) collection of mugs, Emily Readett-Bayley bookends, wonderful Ferguson's Irish linen and Phil Atrill crystal stemware – and that's just a small selection to give you an idea. You can search by product type or by supplier and create a wish list as you go. You could spend a great deal of time here and you'll find gifts for everyone.

Site Usability:	★★★★	Based:	UK
Product Range:	★★★★★	Express Delivery Option? (UK)	Yes
Price Range:	Medium	Gift Wrapping Option?	No
Delivery Area:	Worldwide	Returns Procedure:	Down to you

www.sendit.com

The difference here, as this is yet another website offering games consoles, games, DVDs, computer peripherals and software, is the service.

They offer not only a courier service within the UK to make sure your order arrives when you need it, free UK delivery and speedy worldwide delivery, but also gift certificates and gift wrapping on most items with which they can include your personal message – and you can even choose your wrapping paper.

Site Usability:	★★★★★	Based:	Northern Ireland
Product Range:	★★★★★	Express Delivery Option? (UK)	Yes
Price Range:	Medium/Very Good Value	Gift Wrapping Option?	Yes
Delivery Area:	Worldwide	Returns Procedure:	Down to you

www.thankheavenforchocolate.co.uk

In the Chocolate Shop at thankheavenforchocolate.co.uk there are decorative chocolate hampers, selections of Belgian chocolates, gorgeous special chocs for Valentine's Day, handmade boxes of chocolate truffles and cute chocolate novelties such as Saddleback Piglets and Happy Ducks. This isn't a huge selection but a very well-thought-out range. Prices include free postage plus gift presentation and a card so that you can have your choice sent on your behalf to anywhere in the UK.

Site Usability:	★★★★★	Based:	UK
Product Range:	★★★★	Express Delivery Option? (UK)	Yes
Price Range:	Luxury/Medium	Gift Wrapping Option?	Yes
Delivery Area:	UK	Returns Procedure:	Down to you

www.theentertainer.com

This is one of the largest independent toy retailers in the UK, with a huge range and an excellent, easy-to-navigate website with 'More Toys, More Value and More Fun' as its motto. Here you can search by brand, type of toy, age group or price and you can choose from so many, including Baby Annabel, Dr Who, Hornby, Mattel, Nintendogs and Playmobil. Find something you like and you'll be offered lots more like it, helping you to narrow down your choice quickly.

Site Usability:	★★★★★	Based:	UK
Product Range:	★★★★★	Express Delivery Option? (UK)	Yes
Price Range:	Luxury/Medium	Gift Wrapping Option?	No
Delivery Area:	Worldwide	Returns Procedure:	Down to you

Index

118golf.co.uk 159

abebooks.co.uk 167
abstractbottles.com 222
accessorize.co.uk 134
adonisgrooming.com 99
agacookshop.co.uk 145
agentprovocateur.com 200
agold.co.uk 25
albertthurston.com 94
albumania.com 217
alisonhenry.com 233
amara.co.uk 212
amazon.co.uk 168
andreabrierley.com 195
antique-glass.co.uk 223
anusha.co.uk 58
aquascutumgifts.com 217
arenaflowers.com 124
artboxdirect.co.uk 183
arthurprice.com 217
aspenandbrown.co.uk 196
aspinal.co.uk 256
aspinaloflondon.com 196
astleyclarke.com 234
austique.co.uk 37

babas.uk.com 115
babeswithbabies.com 125
babiesbaskets.com 116
babiesbaskets.com 256
babybare.co.uk 116
babyblooms.co.uk 116
babycelebrate.co.uk 117
babydazzlers.com 130
babygiftbox.co.uk 117

babygiftgallery.co.uk 118
baby-toys.co.uk 130
baer-ingram.com 72
baileys-home-garden.co.uk 150
balloonsweb.co.uk 118
ballsbrothers.co.uk 19
bayley-sage.co.uk 26
bbr.com 197
belenechandia.com 59
belindarobertson.com 55
belladinotte.com 64
bellini-baby.com 118
best-book-price.co.uk 168
best-cd-price.co.uk 173
bettysbypost.com 212
beverlyhillsbakery.com 26
beyondtherainbow.co.uk 130
biju.co.uk 72
birstall.co.uk 151
black.co.uk 59
blacks.co.uk 158
blackwells.co.uk 168
blitzwatches.co.uk 103
bloom.uk.com 13
bloomsburystore.com 109
blueberrybarn.co.uk 119
bobijou.com 49
bodieandfou.com 72
bombayduck.com 73
bonsoirbypost.com 65
boodles.co.uk 201
bookbrain.co.uk 168
bookdepository.co.uk 169
bookgiant.com 169
bootik.co.uk 38

borders.co.uk 170
boutiqueenfant.com 119
boutiquetoyou.co.uk 38
bradleysthetannery.co.uk 151
braybrook.com 257
brissi.co.uk 73
brittique.com 59
brora.co.uk 56
brownes.co.uk 9
bunches.co.uk 14
butlerandwilson.co.uk 50
butlerswines.co.uk 19

cabane.co.uk 74
cambridgewine.com 19
cameraking.co.uk 179
cameras.co.uk 179
cameras2u.com 179
carluccios.com 146
carnmeal.co.uk 6
carterandbond.com 100
cartoonstock.com 162
cashmere.co.uk 104
caxtonlondon.com 60
cdwow.com 174
celtic-sheepskin.co.uk 60
champagnewarehouse.co.uk 20
chandlerystore.co.uk 164
chapmansjewellery.co.uk 50
charitycards.co.uk 4
chessbaron.co.uk 84
chezbec.com 51
chococo.co.uk 212
chocolatebuttons.co.uk 10
chocolatetradingco.com 10

chouchoute.co.uk 201
cityorg.co.uk 60
cku.com 65
claire-macdonald.com 26
clintoncards.co.uk 4
cntraveller.com 187
cocoaloco.co.uk 10
cocoribbon.com 38
coffeeandcream.co.uk 74
collinstreet.com 27
cologneandcotton.com 125
completeoutdoors.co.uk 158
compman.co.uk 170
contessa.org.uk 66
cooksknives.co.uk 146
cosyposy.co.uk 135
coxandcox.co.uk 228
crabtree-evelyn.co.uk 39
crewclothing.co.uk 165
cricketbits.co.uk 162
crocus.co.uk 151
crombie.co.uk 104
ctshirts.co.uk 95, 257
cucinadirect.co.uk 147
culinaryconcepts.co.uk 218
czechandspeake.com 100

dalvey.com 104
darksugars.co.uk 11
davidaustin.com 152
davidhampton.com 90
davidlinley.com 258
dawsonsonline.com 185
designerflowers.org.uk 14
designersguild.com 74
dianaforrester.co.uk 75
dibor.co.uk 75
digitalfirst.co.uk 180
digitalframesdirect.com 180
dillongreen.co.uk 131
diningstore.co.uk 147
dior.com 234
divertimenti.co.uk 147
dollshouse.com 135
dreambabyuk.co.uk 125
dunhill.com 105
dvdpricecheck.co.uk 174

echocs.com 201
efoodies.co.uk 27
elc.co.uk 131
elingerie.uk.net 66
ellis-brigham.com 165
emmabridgewater.co.uk 75
emmachapmanjewels.com 51
erinhousegifts.co.uk 229
escentual.co.uk 39, 258
essentials4travel.co.uk 188
eurostore.palm.com 83
everywine.co.uk 20

expansys.co.uk 181
expedia.co.uk 202

farleylane.co.uk 206
fastflowers.co.uk 202
figleaves.com 66
filofax.co.uk 91
florislondon.com 40
flowergram.co.uk 14
flowersdirect.co.uk 15
flowerworksoxford.co.uk 15
fly-fishing-tackle.co.uk 159
fortnumandmason.com 213, 234
forzieri.com 61
fotosense.co.uk 181
fototech.co.uk 181
franceshilary.com 152
frenchsoaps.co.uk 207
fruit-4u.com 28
fuzzybuzzys.co.uk 119

game.co.uk 175
gamleys.co.uk 131
garden.co.uk 40
gardengames.co.uk 157
gardentrading.co.uk 153
gievesandhawkes.com 95
giftinspiration.com 229
gift-newspapers.co.uk 223
gifts4fishing.co.uk 159
giftstore.co.uk 229
glamonweb.co.uk 67
glamorousamorous.com 203
gleneagles.com 160
gltc.co.uk 120
gogofruitbasket.com 28
goplanetgo.co.uk 188
gorgeous-food.co.uk 28
gorgeousthingsonline.com 126
grahamandgreen.co.uk 76
grandillusions.co.uk 153
greatexperiencedays.co.uk 84
groovychocolate.co.uk 213
grovelands.com 153
gucci.com 235

halcyon-days.co.uk 224
hamleys.co.uk 136
hamper.com 29
haroldcox.com 105
harrods.com 218, 235
harvieandhudson.com 96
hatchards.co.uk 170
hattiesmart.com 160
hawesandcurtis.com 96
hayesflorist.co.uk 15
heals.co.uk 218
heavenlybodice.com 67
helenbroadhead.co.uk 132

heroshop.co.uk 61
hi-baby.co.uk 126
hilditchandkey.co.uk 96
hippins.co.uk 132
hmv.co.uk 175
hotelchocolat.co.uk 11
hqhair.com 40
hqman.com 100
h-s.co.uk 110, 258
hush-uk.com 67

icecool.co.uk 51
imogenstone.co.uk 203, 259
in2decor.com 76
isla.uk.com 56
iwantoneofthose.co.uk 85
iwantoneofthose.com 259
izziwizzikids.co.uk 133

janconstantine.com 76
janepackerdelivered.com 126
janetreger.co.uk 68
jasonshankey.co.uk 101
jaycotts.co.uk 7
jbsilverware.co.uk 219
jeroboams.co.uk 20
jewel-garden.co.uk 52
jigsaw-puzzles-online.co.uk 136
jimmychoo.com 235
johnlewis.com 148
johnlewisgiftlist.com 219
jojomamanbebe.co.uk 120
jomalone.com 41, 259
jonkers.co.uk 171
josephturner.co.uk 97
juliannebalai.com 220
julieslaterandson.co.uk 62
justchampagne.co.uk 21
jwflowers.com 16

kabiri.co.uk 52
kelkoo.co.uk 250
kennethturner.co.uk 127
kiarie.co.uk 41, 260
kikijames.com 189
kirstengoss.com 203
kitbag.com 163
kjbeckett.com 97

laboutiquedelartisanparfumeur.com 41
ladybarbarella.com 68
laithwaites.co.uk 21
lakelandlimited.co.uk 29
laline.co.uk 127
lambertsflowercompany.co.uk 127
lambstoys.co.uk 136
laprovence.co.uk 204

lasenza.co.uk 68
launer.com 106
lawrence.co.uk 184
laywheeler.co.uk 21
leadingspasoftheworld.com 46
letterbox.co.uk 120
lewisandcooper.com 29
lilyandagathe.com 137
linksoflondon.com 52, 260
littlefolk.co.uk 137
littlepresentcompany.co.uk 197
loccitane.com 42
locketts.co.uk 77
longmire.co.uk 106
lordswines.co.uk 22, 261
louisvuitton.com 236
luluguinness.com 236
luxeliving.com 230

mad4ponies.com 161
maddiebrown.co.uk 207
mailorderexpress.com 137
manjoh.com 53
mankind.co.uk 101, 261
mariechantal.com 197
mastersgames.com 157
megrivers.com 214
meltons.co.uk 207
menkind.co.uk 110
microanvika.com 85
mikimoto-store.co.uk 237
millcrofttextiles.co.uk 7
minimarvellous.co.uk 133
mischiefkids.co.uk 138
mkn.co.uk/flower/ 204
modelhobbies.co.uk 138
moltonbrown.co.uk 189
montezumas.co.uk 11
moonpig.com 4, 204, 261
morelloliving.co.uk 121
mortimerandbennett.co.uk 30
moysesstevens.co.uk 16
mrpen.co.uk 91
mulberryhall.co.uk 220
murdocklondon.com 102
murrayforbes.co.uk 198
musicroom.co.uk 185
myfirstday.co.uk 128
myla.com 69

nationaltrust-shop.co.uk 7, 230
naturalmagicuk.com 42
net-a-porter.com 237, 262
nextday-champagne.co.uk 22
ninacampbell.com 77
nomadtravel.co.uk 189
notonthehighstreet.com 62, 230

nspccshop.co.uk 8
nurserywindow.co.uk 198

objects-of-design.com 78, 262
old.co.uk 91
oldeglory.co.uk 78
oliverbonas.co.uk 231
oliversweeney.com 106
oliviers-co.com 148
ollieandnic.com 62
optimacompany.com 30
oregonscientific.co.uk 85
ormondejayne.co.uk 43
otherlandtoys.co.uk 138
owzat-cricket.co.uk 163

pakeman.co.uk 97
paramountzone.com 86
parkscandles.com 208
parseme.com 208
pascal-jewellery.com 53
passionleaf.com 128
penandpaper.co.uk 92
penhaligons.co.uk 43
penshop.co.uk 92, 107
perilla.co.uk 98
peterdraper.co.uk 93
piajewellery.com 53
pickett.co.uk 107
pixmania.co.uk 182
plants4presents.co.uk 209
plantstuff.com 154
play.com 175
plumo.co.uk 63
polly-online.co.uk 78
pomeroi.co.uk 224
presentsformen.com 110
purecollection.com 56
pwp.com 166

queenshill.com 79

rachelriley.com 198
racquetlink.com 166
redhouse.co.uk 171
redletterdays.co.uk 86
reglisse.co.uk 54
rhs.org.uk 154
richardbramble.co.uk 224
richmondsilver.co.uk 199
rickstein.com 148
rigbyandpeller.com 69
rkalliston.com 154
roomersgifts.com 121
rose-apothecary.co.uk 43
rosesonly.co.uk 209
royalmail.com 5
rugbymegastore.com 163
rugbyrelics.com 164

sandstormbags.com 190
saralouisekakes.co.uk 31
sassyandrose.co.uk 70
savonneriesoap.com 44
sayitwithbears.co.uk 139
sciencemuseumstore.com 86
sendit.com 176, 262
sharpcards.com 5
shopping-emporium-uk.com 87, 139
signetmusic.com 185
silkstorm.com 205
silvercompany.co.uk 220
silvernutmeg.com 149
silversmiths.co.uk 225
simonbeer.co.uk 225
simplycigars.co.uk 89
skyhi.co.uk 5
smallislandtrader.com 221
smythson.com 237
snowandrock.com 165
sofresh.co.uk 214
sogifted.co.uk 231
sophieandgrace.co.uk 70
sophiec.co.uk 107
spabreak.co.uk 47
spacenk.co.uk 44
spafinder.com 47
steenbergs.co.uk 149
swaineadeney.co.uk 108
swarovski.com 54

tanners-wines.co.uk 23
tansen.co.uk 140
temperleylondon.com 238
thankheavenforchocolate.co.uk 12, 263
thanksdarling.com 47
thebaby.co.uk 121
thebookplace.com 171
thecandlecollection.co.uk 209
thecuttinggarden.com 155
thedrinkshop.com 31
theenglishshavingcompany.co.uk 102
theentertainer.com 140, 263
theequestrianstore.com 161
thefrenchhouse.net 79
thegadgetshop.com 87
thegiftgourmet.co.uk 31
thegluttonousgardener.co.uk 155
theheavenlyhampercompany.co.uk 32
theinsideman.com 111
thekidswindow.co.uk 122
thelittlepicturegallery.com 210
thelwell-horsey-gifts.com 161
themusiccellar.co.uk 186
theobroma-cacao.co.uk 214

theofennell.com 238
theolivegrove.co.uk 221
thesharperedge.co.uk 88
thesiteguide.com ii
thespasdirectory.com 48
thewatchhut.co.uk 108
thewhiskyexchange.com 23
thewoolcompany.co.uk 199
thewrappingco.com 8
thomaspink.co.uk 98
thorntons.co.uk 215
tiffany.com 238
timetin.com 122
timetospa.com 190
timothyhan.com 44
tinytotgifts.com 123
tjklondon.com 232
topcubans.com 90

toysbymailorder.co.uk 140
toysdirecttoyourdoor.co.uk
  141
toysrus.co.uk 141
trackday-gift-experiences.
  com 88
travelsmith.com 190
treesdirect.co.uk 155
truegrace.co.uk 45
trumpers.com 102

uk.gamestracker.com 176
uk.shopping.com 250

valentineandfrench.co.uk 63
valvonacrolla-online.co.uk 32
viamichelin.co.uk 205
viator.com 191

virginiahayward.com 32
virginmegastores.co.uk 176
vivelarose.com 16

waterstones.com 172
weegooseberry.com 123
whiskhampers.co.uk 33
whittard.co.uk 33
whsmith.co.uk 172
winedancer.com 23
wine-searcher.com 24
woodenwinebox.co.uk 24
woodwindandbrass.co.uk 186
worldofroses.com 17

yorkshireartstore.co.uk 184

zpm.com 191